Graduating from the Electoral College

Tomas J. McIntee

Copyright © Tomas J. McIntee
All rights reserved.

McIntee, Tomas J.
Graduating from the Electoral College / Tomas J. McIntee
Includes bibliographic references and index.
Library of Congress Control Number: 2022922853
ISBN 978-1-959266-00-6 (hardcover)
ISBN 978-1-959266-01-3 (paperback)
ISBN 978-1-959266-02-0 (electronic)
ISBN 978-1-959266-03-7 (alt. ed. hc.)
ISBN 978-1-959266-04-4 (alt. ed. pb.)

Published by Hurricane Lamp Press
PO Box 3715
Chapel Hill
North Carolina
27515

Cover design by Alexis Waters
Authored in RMarkdown

For the people of the United States of America

Contents

Preface	viii
1 Introduction	**1**
Common misunderstandings about the Electoral College	3
Major problems in early America	7
A chaotic cousin to a simple popular vote	11
2 The origin of the electoral colleges	**14**
The Constitutional Convention	15
The separate electoral colleges	20
The absent motives	24
A brief technical prelude on Electoral College geography	30
3 Hamilton's Electoral College (1788-1800)	**35**
The Washington elections	36
1796: The faithless elector problem	39
1800: A tied election	46

4 Jefferson's Electoral College (1804-1824) — 51
The 12th Amendment 51
A string of victories for the Jeffersonians 54
The end of the transitional Electoral College system 59

5 Jackson's Electoral College (1828-1852) — 66
Jackson's elections 68
The 1836-1840 elections and a regional strategy 70
1844-1848 and the first spoilers 76

6 Civil War, minority rule, and slavery (1856-1864) — 84
Three elections in brief 85
Minority rule resistant to spoiler effects 88
The impact of the Electoral College on slavery 92

7 Lincoln's Electoral College (1868-1916) — 98
The Reconstruction Era 98
1876: Uncertainty and fraud in the Electoral College 101
The era of the Empire State 106
Woodrow Wilson and the Condorcet problem 116

8 A coeducational Electoral College (1920-1956) — 124
A string of Republican landslides 124
The election of 1928 and the allocation problem 127
The Roosevelt elections 133
A Southern strategy 137
The Eisenhower elections 143

9 The system in transition (1960-1968) — 146
The uncertain election of 1960 147
The 1964 election and the Voting Rights Act 152
1968: The presidential election system reshaped 153

10 The modern system (1972-2020) — 160
Broad coalitions versus regional factions 167
Partisan advantage in the Electoral College 174
The Obama elections 180
The Trump elections 182
The challenges to the system 187

11 A Primer on Power in the Electoral College — 189
The mathematics of power in the Electoral College 190
Historical distribution of power in the Electoral College 193
Power in systems other than the Electoral College 198
The difference between small and large states' power 199

12 Problems and solutions — 201
The quirks of the Electoral College system 202
Minor reforms 206
Major reforms 209
Recommendations 213
A few final words 214

Bibliography — 216

About the author — 221

Preface

The purpose of this book is to more clearly illuminate the flaws in the Electoral College system. It is my hope that it will help clarify and solidify the public case against the Electoral College, and to build credibility for that case. Many of the flaws discussed in this book are already known by experts, but not widely understood. This book also offers rebuttals to many of the common arguments offered in favor of the Electoral College and seeks to debunk some of the myths about the Electoral College that have helped to preserve it.

What makes this book distinct from many others on the subject is that it comes from a mathematical perspective, informed by voting theory and systematic quantitative analysis of the historical record. It is intended to complement other books on the Electoral College coming from the perspectives of political science, history, and law - books like *Why the Electoral College Is Bad for America* (2019) by George Edwards, *Representation and the Electoral College* (2019) by Robert Alexander, and *Why Do We Still Have the Electoral College?* (2020) by Alexander Keyssar. For a fuller understanding of a topic, it helps to study it from many different perspectives.

While this book was written by a mathematician with a mathematical perspective, the reader does not need to have a background in advanced mathematics to follow its arguments. There are some aspects of the Electoral College that are mathematically complex to analyze, but I believe grasping the conclusions of that analysis does not present a mathematical challenge. It is also my hope that my different arguments with their similar conclusions might help bring around some of the skeptics who have not been convinced by the political scientists, historians, and lawyers who have written about the problems with the Electoral College.

This book starts with a brief overview of how the American presidential election system works, where it came from, and a little bit about what the system *is not*. An extensive mythology has grown up around the Electoral College, and not all of it is factual. This brief overview takes two chapters. The main body of the book is organized in chronological order, systematically examining the elections from 1788 to 2020. From Chapter 3 to Chapter 10, the various quirks of the Electoral College system are explored chronologically, with a brief discussion of every election. This builds up - slowly - to a systematic analysis of all elections.

About a third of the way through this pool of elections, we reach the year 1860, when something very important happened: Abraham Lincoln is elected. This in turn led to a civil war, which ended the South's "peculiar institution" of slavery. Chapter 6 provides a retrospective on the impact of the presidential elections of 1788-1860 on slavery, considering the argument that the Electoral College served to protect slavery or was designed to protect slavery.

Analysis of the whole body of presidential elections as a group takes place in Chapter 11, where I talk about how power has been distributed in the Electoral College over time - that is, in key battleground states, particularly *large* battleground states. Some readers may prefer to skip straight to Chapter 11 after the first two or three chapters and read the middle chapters afterward. The final chapter summarizes the problems of the Electoral College system and discusses briefly some of the many possible solutions to those problems.

Writing this book has been an education and an inspiration, and I feel obliged to thank a great many people who gave me significant insights into the subject at hand and the writing of the book. Particular thanks go to Rick LaRue, Robert Nemanich, Tom Cronin, Polly Baca, Michael Baca, David Paletz, Mike Flynn, David Armstrong, Rick Klima, Don Saari, and my family.

CHAPTER 1

Introduction

As of the time of the writing of this book, the United States elects its presidents in a most peculiar fashion: Every four years, several hundred people gather together in small groups scattered across the country to cast their ballots for president. These assemblies are collectively known as the Electoral College,[1] and they play a small but vital role in electing the president.

Unlike every other elected official, they are commonly elected without having their names appear on the ballots, and while their identities are a matter of public record, they remain obscure both before and after their term in office. The position of elector usually is won by reliable political loyalists rather than politicians, and the office that they serve is viewed as largely ceremonial – human cogs in a mechanical process.

The electors have the official power to decide the election. For example, after the 2016 election, in which Donald Trump won enough states to make him the putative winner of the election, many public calls were made for some Republican electors to break ranks.[2] This type of exercise of free will by the presidential electors would have been in line with some

---

[1] The use of a singular collective noun is a bit weird when you consider that each assembly convenes separately.

[2] C.f. the article in the *Atlantic* titled "Meet the 'Hamilton Electors' Hoping for an Electoral College Revolt" (2016) by Lilly O'Donnell.

of the Framers' intentions for the Electoral College,[3] but would likely also have led to a major political crisis. After all, no presidential election has ever been clearly decided by electors' discretion since 1796.

In 2020, the Supreme Court decided that states have the authority to dictate how electors vote, enforcing the pledges of electors.[4] For this reason, it is unlikely that electors' discretion will have a meaningful impact on many future presidential elections - with the notable exception of cases where a presidential candidate dies before the electors vote, as happened in 1872.

One of the various reasons that electors were asked to break their pledges of support for Donald Trump in 2016 was that he had, across the country as a whole, won fewer votes than Hillary Clinton. This feature of the Electoral College is one of the most peculiar features in a system dominated by the effects of popular votes; since electoral votes are awarded on a state-by-state basis, one candidate can win a majority of electoral votes while enjoying the support of fewer voters than another candidate. This has happened about half a dozen times.[5]

There are very few countries where a candidate can honestly win an election by getting fewer votes than their opponent. A common myth is that the Electoral College represents a unique and wise American institution, carefully designed by the Framers. In spite of the popularity of this positive myth, the Electoral College is still an immensely unpopular institution. From 1967 to 2011, Gallup conducted nine national polls on the Electoral College, showing 58% to 80% of the population in favor of amending the constitution to get rid of the Electoral College and only 12% to 37% opposed to reform.[6] Support for the Electoral College reached a historic high after 2016 due to a spike in support from Republicans, with 47% opposed to reform and 49% in favor of a constitutional amendment abolishing the Electoral College.

The partisan embrace of the Electoral College system by Republicans in the last few years is unique and interesting - and apparently based on the notion that the Electoral College system has a clear partisan bias that

---

[3] See in particular Federalist #68 for Hamilton's intentions; the picture *is* slightly murkier for other Framers, given that most of them would have preferred a different method even as they supported the compromise of the Electoral College system.

[4] *Chiafalo v. Washington* (2020).

[5] It is generally accepted that this has happened in 1824, 1876, 1888, 2000, and 2016. For various other reasons involving incomplete records, ordinary errors in counting ballots, fraud, divided tickets, and trying to count indirect voting for legislators who appointed electors, there are four other elections in which a popular mandate was doubtful: 1796, 1800, 1880, and 1960. There is even an argument that 1884 and 1892 belong on the list, due to widespread voter suppression and fraud in the South.

[6] This includes two polls each in 1968 and 2000; the wording of the question used changed in 1980, which may explain part of the rise in opposition to a constitutional amendment.

INTRODUCTION

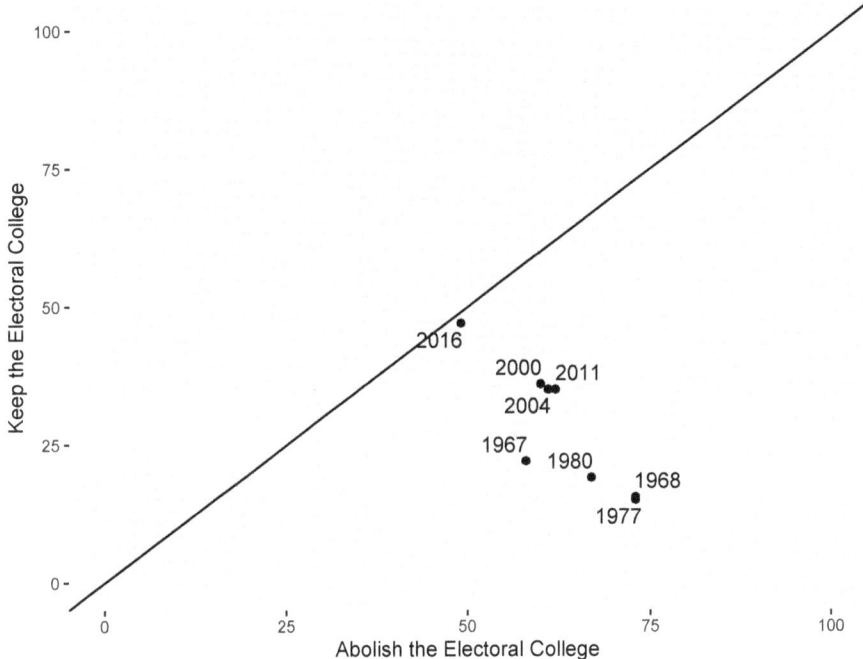

Figure 1: Gallup polling on the electoral college system by year

favors Republicans. While this is understandable given the results of the 2016 election, it is not well-founded, as discussed at length in Chapter 10. This is only one of a wide assortment of false myths about the Electoral College system, its behavior, and its origins.

Common misunderstandings about the Electoral College

There are many myths and misunderstandings about the Electoral College. Some are persistent; some are quite short-lived. For example, leading into the 2016 election, many political analysts believed that there was a "blue wall" of safely Democratic states that made it very difficult for a Republican to win, based on the last few electoral cycles.[7] The myth of the "blue wall" evaporated quite suddenly after the 2016 election. It's common for people to believe that one or the other political party has a

---

[7] For early mentions of the "blue wall" in print during this period, see Nicole Rae in "The Reaffirmation of the Post–Cold War Electoral Order: The Meaning of the 2012 Election" (2013) and Thomas Neale in "Electoral College Reform: Contemporary Issues for Congress" (2014).

real advantage in the Electoral College because the Electoral College is a chaotic system, and it's easy to misunderstand the behavior of a chaotic system.

One of the most popular and persistent myths is that the Electoral College protects small states. Contrary to assertions made by both defenders of the Electoral College and its critics, the Electoral College itself was neither designed to help small states nor has it had the effect of doing so. (See Chapters 2 and 11.) As a point of mathematical and historical fact, large states have held a disproportionate amount of power in the Electoral College thus far.

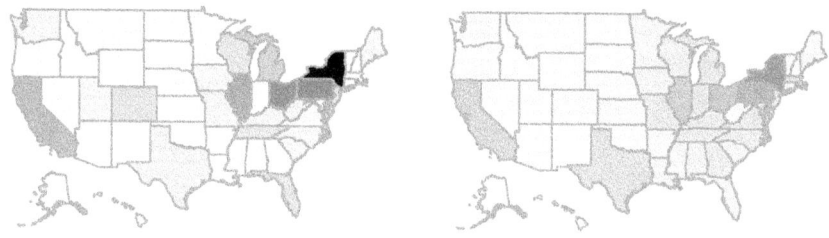

Figure 2: Share of electoral votes and electoral power by state in presidential elections 1828-2020.

The only part of the presidential election system that was designed to help small states was the House contingent election process, which has only been used twice. If small-state delegates like Roger Sherman had known this at the time of the Constitutional Convention, they may not have approved of the system.

A related claim is that the Electoral College helps rural voters, or was designed to help rural voters; and that without the Electoral College, only large cities would matter. This is similarly untrue. Machine politics in large cities has played a key role in presidential elections. For example, the election of 1888 (see Chapter 7) notably featured a multi-million dollar voter bribery scheme targeting voters in New York City. The election of 1888 was one of many elections decided by New York. More recently, machine politics in Chicago played a prominent role in the 1960 election.

Key battleground states tend to pivot as a result of shifts in their largest cities. For example, in the 2016 election, Hillary Clinton could have won Florida, Wisconsin, and Michigan by matching Obama's 2012 performance in Madison, Detroit, and the three counties of the Miami metro area. This would have shifted 54 electoral votes from Trump's column to Clinton's and given her the win.

INTRODUCTION

Another myth is that the Electoral College system prevents the election of populist demagogues. This might have been true of the version of the Electoral College envisioned by Alexander Hamilton, but the real Electoral College has functioned differently. There is nothing about the Electoral College system that prevents the election of demagogues or would-be dictators. While a few electors have tried to faithfully act in accordance with Hamilton's vision, such as the Hamilton electors of the 2016 election, they have never proven decisive.

The fact of the matter is that electors do not run under their own names or on their reputation as wise deciders, but are elected mostly anonymously based on their declared support for a named candidate. Pointedly, in any scenario where a violently anti-democratic candidate can command support from a significant minority of the voting population, it is not difficult for them to find loyal supporters to serve as electors.

The main difference between the evolved Electoral College system and a popular vote is simply that the Electoral College is *more chaotic*; which means that a divisive figure can manage to win a majority in the Electoral College with significantly less than a majority of the vote - in fact, it has been done with as little as 39.8% of the vote.[8] Contrary to the claims of those who defend the Electoral College,[9] regionally divisive candidates perform better in the Electoral College than candidates who appeal to a broad coalition across the country.

Many people suggest that the Electoral College is simply outdated.[10] While I would agree that it is outdated, the Electoral College was *never* the best solution to the problem of how to elect a president. It was an expedient political compromise, an exercise in hasty political sausage-making that was fatally flawed and crudely repaired with the 12th Amendment. At best, it avoided a set of political problems that no longer exist; those problems were permanently solved not by the Electoral College itself, but by continued democratic evolution, a civil war, and several constitutional amendments.

The role of slavery in the creation of the Electoral College system (discussed in Chapter 2) and the degree to which the Electoral College interacted with the institution of slavery (overviewed in Chapter 6) are frequently overstated.[11] While slavery may have helped fuel opposition

---

[8] Abraham Lincoln in 1860.

[9] Here we can include Judith Best in *The Case Against Direct Election of the President: A Defense of the Electoral College* (1975) as well as most later authors.

[10] This description of the Electoral College can be found even in Senate Judiciary Committee reports. See *The Electoral College and Direct Election: Hearings Before the Committee on the Judiciary, United States Senate, Ninety-Fifth Congress, First Session on ... S.j. Res. 1, 8, and 1* (1977) for an example.

[11] C.f. Akil Amar in *The Constitution Today: Timeless Lessons for the Issues of Our Era* (2016) and Paul Finkelman in "The Proslavery Origins of the Electoral College" (2001).

to a direct vote among Southern delegates, there was also significant opposition to a direct vote in New England - and significant opposition to the Electoral College from Southerners. The Framers never made a choice between the Electoral College and a direct vote, and most of the leading advocates for versions of the Electoral College wanted a popular vote.

The fact that the Electoral College was proposed mainly as an alternative to *election by Congress* (and backed by the Framers who preferred a direct popular vote) is often overlooked in the mythology of the Electoral College. This mythology seems retroactively constructed around the assumption that the Electoral College was proposed as an alternative to a direct popular vote. Instead, it was an alternative to election by Congress - something frequently referred to as a *parliamentary system*. This is well-known among those who have studied the origin of the system.[12]

The fact that the Electoral College *required* immediate alteration in the form of the 12th Amendment in order to become minimally functional is underemphasized. The Framers anticipated that each state's electors would make independent decisions, meaning that votes would be usually divided widely between many different candidates. They expected electors would usually use one of their two votes on a home state favorite.[13] Instead, a national two-party system developed, with each party trying to elect both a president and vice president. This resulted in the election of a president and vice president from different parties in 1796, and a political deadlock from a technically tied election in 1800.

Many – perhaps all – of the Founding Fathers disliked the Electoral College system once it was in operation.[14] This included James Madison, widely credited as the chief architect of the Constitution in general and of the Electoral College system in particular.[15] The Electoral College was a failure to begin with, in other words; and now it is not merely a failure, but an obsolete failure. We know much more about democracy now than we did 230 years ago. It is past time that we graduated from the Electoral College.

What the Electoral College should be replaced with is a question with a simple correct answer: *A direct vote by the people.* (A parliamentary system could also be a correct answer - but, thanks to gerrymandering,

---

[12] C.f. Chapter 3 of *Representation and the Electoral College* (2019) by Robert Alexander.

[13] Presidential electors are not allowed to cast both votes for candidates from their own home state.

[14] Alexander Hamilton may have been one notable exception, but his death at the hands of Vice President Aaron Burr was arguably *caused* by the presidential election system.

[15] See in particular his letters to George Hay, George McDuffie, and Thomas Jefferson endorsing significant further alterations to the system. More credit may be due to James Wilson, as Jesse Wegman points out in *Let the People Pick the President: The Case for Abolishing the Electoral College* (2020), but James Madison is more famous today.

not a simple one.) The details of what that answer should mean involve a few complexities. There are many different ways that people can - and do - vote. Many countries, as well as some American states, require a majority vote, which usually means providing for two rounds of voting. Ranked choice voting has recently gained traction in Maine. Most of the alternatives to the current Electoral College system are superior.

Major problems in early America

The reason why most of the Framers eventually came to prefer the Electoral College system to Congress electing the president was that it removed a potential conflict of interest. They *wanted* the executive to be able to effectively oppose Congress if necessary, one of many checks in a large system of checks and balances discussed at length in almost every basic textbook on American history. It wasn't introduced to address the problems that election by Congress already avoided; remember, election by Congress was the standard that every other method was measured against. There were serious obstacles to a direct vote.

The Electoral College shared in common with election by Congress one key feature: It finessed a serious disagreement among the various delegates coming from different states. The disagreement was over how to answer a simple and difficult question: *Who should be allowed to vote?* In other words, the United States was divided by deep and fundamental disagreements over the nature of democracy. The Electoral College was not the only possible method of finessing this problem, and the former deep disagreements over who should be allowed to vote have mostly been resolved.

In the early days of the United States, the different states had very different rules for who was permitted to participate in elections. Each state had independently arrived at its own set of rules, some of them strikingly different. For example, New Jersey allowed women with property to vote; Pennsylvania allowed any man to vote - even black men without property; while in Virginia, an adult white male householder who owned 24 acres of farmland did not have the right to vote.[16] In 1790, Virginia had a significantly smaller electorate than Pennsylvania in spite of having more free white residents.

These differences were not arbitrary, but the result of underlying disagreements over how democratic our society should be. Imposing

---

[16]Virginia required 25 acres of "improved" land or 50 acres of "unimproved" land. See "The Right to Vote and the Rise of Democracy, 1787—1828" (2013) by Donald Ratcliffe for a wonderfully comprehensive overview of voting rights at this point in history.

uniform voting standards was, at the time, a political and practical impossibility. Those who supported a popular vote tried to impose a uniform voting standard requiring land ownership for participation in federal elections but failed. Making presidential elections indirect allowed the Framers a way around this thorny issue.

The argument over which free citizens of the United States should be allowed to vote took a long time to resolve, but by now, it has happened. A significant number of constitutional amendments (notably the 14th, 15th, 19th, 24th, and 26th) have guaranteed the right to participate in elections to all adult Americans aged 18 or older regardless, with the notable exception of convicted criminals. Variation in turnout from state to state is affected by "swing state" status (in other words, by the Electoral College system itself) more than it is driven by the most aggressive exclusion of convicted felons from voter rolls.[17]

Even many informal obstacles to voting are no longer allowed. Poll taxes are forbidden. Literacy tests are forbidden. Any adult citizen *must* be allowed to vote unless they are a convicted criminal. The ability to vote in federal elections is determined mainly by federal law, not state law.

The slavery issue

The existence of slavery posed a difficult problem for *any* democratic institution on the federal level. This resulted in the Three Fifths Compromise, affecting delegation sizes in the House of Representatives. That is to say, for the purpose of allocating (sharing out) seats within the House of Representatives, slaves counted as three-fifths of a free person. Slaves could not vote, but their presence added weight to a state's delegation. The Electoral College is based on Congressional allocations, so it automatically inherited the distorting effects of the Three Fifths Compromise.

Slavery was legal in eight of thirteen states when the Constitution was ratified. In the census conducted in 1790, 55% of the adult white male population lived in slave states. However, once New York abolished slavery, a majority of the electoral votes were held by states where slavery was banned. Slavery was not, however, a unique factor; as noted above, the variation in *who was allowed to vote* was quite significant.

In spite of the Founding Fathers' best efforts to build a lasting political compromise that could keep the country together, disagreement over slavery eventually turned violent. Following a very bloody civil war

---

[17] As an example, Florida turned out almost 57% of the voting age population in 2016, slightly above the national average in spite of the combination of a significant non-citizen population and the greatest share of disenfranchised felons.

INTRODUCTION

and millions of deaths, slavery no longer exists in the United States, and the political calculus of the Three Fifths Compromise has become thoroughly obsolete. As slavery was banned by the 13th Amendment, slavery cannot be considered a relevant reason for keeping the Electoral College in the modern (post-Lincoln) era.

Future disagreements over who should be allowed to vote.

Originally, only white men who owned sufficient property could vote in Virginia. In Pennsylvania, any man could vote regardless of his wealth or race. In New Jersey, any property owner could vote – notably including unmarried women. The fraction of the population allowed to participate in the democratic process varied enormously from state to state.

This is no longer the case today. Various constitutional amendments require all states to allow all resident citizens 18 years or older to vote, regardless of race, sex, net worth, or land ownership. The only exception is that states are permitted to disenfranchise convicted felons. Some states allow convicted felons to vote; others do not. Overall, however, less than 10% of adults are convicted felons, so this creates only modest variations in the ratio of the population of a state to the number of voters in a state.

While constitutional amendments protect the rights of adult citizens to vote, they are silent on the issue of whether minors and non-citizens must be barred from voting. Federal election law[18] bars non-citizens from voting in federal elections, but this is a statutory regulation that could be repealed by a simple majority in Congress, rather than a congressional amendment. If the law barring non-citizens from voting was repealed and some states began to allow voting by non-citizen residents (who make up over 10% of the population of a few states) it could increase the influence of those states slightly in a national popular election. Similarly, lowering the minimum voting age (perhaps to 14 or 16) could increase the pool of votes available.[19]

The Electoral College, just like Congressional election of the president, does safeguard against variation in voter turnout created by states having different policies on who should be allowed to vote – but that variation no longer exists. Pragmatically, reformers seeking to replace the Electoral College may need to be willing to harden the existing limits on the voting franchise in order to succeed at implementing reforms to ease the worries of those who think that the voting franchise will once again vary significantly from state to state, *even if* the room for

---

[18] 18 U.S.C. 611
[19] Personally, I have always been in favor of lowering the voting age to 16.

variation in existing law is very small. The Electoral College does not help small states, help rural voters, or help ensure careful deliberation, but it does safeguard against states having looser or stricter requirements for someone to be allowed to vote.

Why uneven expansion of the franchise is not a concern

The argument that the Electoral College prevents key states from "flooding" the national election by adding unqualified voters is currently popular - and unlike almost every other argument offered in defense of the Electoral College, it has some basic theoretical justification behind it. There are three reasons to dismiss this argument: It is unlikely to happen, it would have a limited impact if it did happen, and the Electoral College is already distorted by non-voting populations.

First, it's *very unlikely* that states would allow non-citizens to vote in presidential elections. Federal law does not (and cannot) prevent states from allowing non-citizens to vote in state and local elections. Even in an era when one party enjoys a relative advantage among both youth and immigrants, *no state allows non-citizens or youth to vote in state elections* - even states where the state government is firmly under Democratic control. Only a small handful of municipalities permit youth or non-citizens to vote in local elections.

Extending presidential voting eligibility to non-citizens in some states would require *both* the repeal of existing federal election law *and* the passage of new state laws allowing non-citizens to vote. Youth voting in federal elections similarly would be subject to both state and federal regulation. State and local governments, as a general rule, are leery of increasing the franchise. If anything, state and local governments tend to try to suppress voter turnout in lower-level elections. Over time, the schedules of state and local elections have been shifting away from presidential election years, reducing overall participation in state-level elections.[20]

Second, even if such reforms were passed as the result of truly massive political shifts at both the state and federal level, naturalized immigrants and young voters vote at disproportionately low rates. Non-citizen immigrants would likely turn out at a lower rate than naturalized immigrants, and 16-17 year old youth voters would likely turn out at a lower rate than current 18-20 year old voters. The variation in voter turnout created by including youth or non-citizen voters would not likely be any larger than the existing variation created by felon disenfranchisement; given the current demographics of the various states

---

[20]C.f. the discussion by M. J. Streb in *Rethinking American Electoral Democracy* (2015).

and the low participation rates of immigrants and young voters, widening the voting franchise would have a small effect on presidential elections.

Third, *the Electoral College already gives states with high non-voting populations additional representation.* Congressional representation and representation within the Electoral College itself is based on total population, *not* total number of citizens or total number of eligible voters. Effectively speaking, citizens of states with high non-voting populations have (on average) slightly more influence than they would directly. This was particularly dramatic back in the days before the abolition of slavery (slaves being a very large population of non-citizens in the South), but the fact remains that states' representation in Congress, and by extension the Electoral College, is allocated based on a census of all residents – not simply on a count of eligible voters.

In other words, the Electoral College *already counts youth and noncitizens*. For this reason, it is very difficult to conceive of a plausible package of reforms that starts with some sort of national popular vote and ends up being more heavily influenced by the distribution of non-citizens than the Electoral College. Non-citizens aren't very interested in voting, there is little interest in changing the current legal *status quo* that bars non-citizens from voting, and the Electoral College already has a form of baked-in representation by proxy for non-citizens.

A chaotic cousin to a simple popular vote

The first thing to understand about the Electoral College is that in its modern state, it acts a lot like a popular vote. From 1892 to 1996, there were twenty-seven presidential elections in a row where the winner of the Electoral College was simply the person who had won the most votes.[21] The Electoral College is usually won by the candidate who won a plurality of the total vote.

It's hard to be sure that the candidate winning a plurality of the total vote enjoys more popular support overall because one thing the Electoral College does is discourage voters in "safe" states from voting at all. Presidential campaigns concentrate their efforts in a small number of "battleground" states, which have higher turnout rates as a result. However, since every state chooses electors by popular vote, the relationship between electoral vote and popular vote is fairly significant, particularly for elections with only two major candidates.

---

[21] That is, provided we count votes for Alabama's mixed slate in 1960 as being full votes. We'll talk about that later.

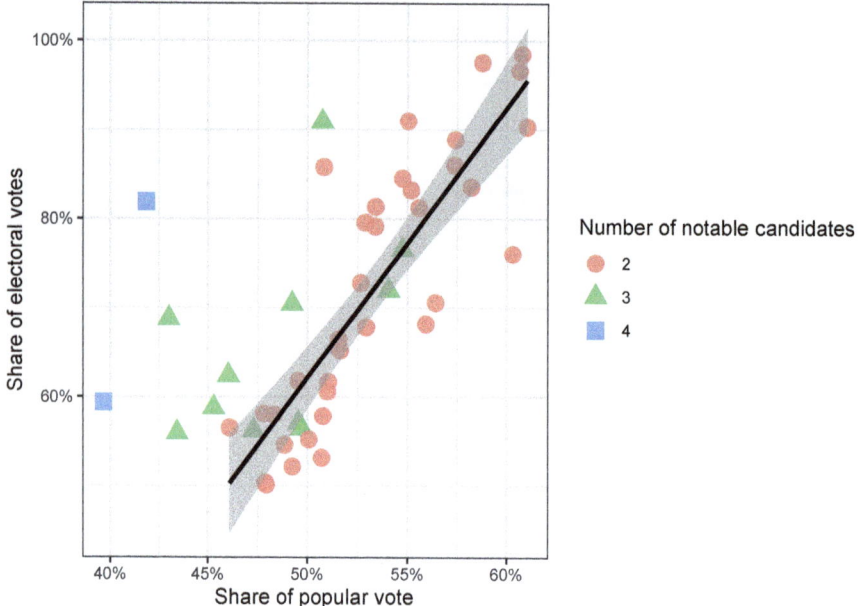

Figure 3: Comparison between share of popular and electoral vote for major candidates, 1828-2020. Line shows a regression of the relationship in elections with only two major candidates.

In the cases where the Electoral College gave a different result from a simple plurality vote, the margin of victory in key states – most dramatically in Florida in 2000 – has been razor-thin. These elections were close enough to be influenced by any small factor, such as weather in a particular region. The Electoral College is highly sensitive to small effects on battleground states, and for this reason, close Electoral College results can easily be decided by any number of small factors. A partial list of factors that usually have a very small effect on an election – but not so small that we can discard them from consideration in trying to determine the winner of a close battleground state:

- Weather patterns on Election Day.
- Hardware or software problems with voting machines.
- Which precincts are supplied with how many voting machines.
- Changes in precinct voting locations.
- Some qualified voters being incorrectly turned away.
- Some unqualified voters voting.
- Some voters voting in two different states (typically, one by absentee ballot).
- Losing track of some absentee ballots.
- How quickly absentee ballots are mailed out by the state.

INTRODUCTION 13

- Public transportation breakdowns.
- Fraud

The Electoral College functions like a noisy simulation of a simple plurality vote. I mean "noisy" in a mathematical sense: Close Electoral College results are very sensitive to small changes in a single state.[22] Close plurality vote results are less sensitive. Only once in American history have we ever seen a national popular vote margin that was closer than the effective popular margin in the Electoral College.[23] In a very real sense, this means the Electoral College system is less stable than a simple plurality vote system.

The instability of the Electoral College is an ironic feature. At least some of the Framers[24] thought that an indirect election would be *more* stable than a direct election, because electors chosen to be wise decision-makers would have more constant opinions than the general public. The Electoral College was intended to be a stabilizing institution, something less susceptible to the whims of the moment - and in particular less susceptible to foreign interference.

It's time to graduate from the Electoral College; while it was designed with good intentions, the evolved system of the Electoral College has few redeeming virtues. The main advantage of the Electoral College is that it is familiar, and can only be blamed for one civil war in the last two centuries.[25] That said, every problem that exists with a direct plurality vote has its simple counterpart in the Electoral College system, and the Electoral College has additional flaws on top of the flaws of a direct vote.

---

[22] The flip side of chaos is that sometimes very large shifts in non-battleground states have zero impact on the electoral vote.
[23] The election of 1880 is the only exception; in every other case, the effective popular margin was closer than the actual popular margin.
[24] Notably Hamilton. See again Federalist #68, but also his proposed elaboration of the Electoral College system.
[25] Based on the data of *Resort to War: 1816-2007* (2010) by Meredith Reid Sarkees and Frank Wayman, civil wars tend to be more frequent than one per 200 years per country, although the American Civil War was larger and deadlier than most of the civil wars in their data set.

CHAPTER 2

The origin of the electoral colleges

In each presidential election year, on a particular date that is the same across the entire country,[1] the electors of the Electoral College vote on who will become the President of the United States. Their votes are then sealed and sent to Congress, which tallies the votes and determines whether or not they are legitimate. The Vice President is the one who opens and announces the votes.

There are three relatively obscure and unique features of the presidential election system.

First, if no single candidate has an outright majority in the Electoral College, the responsibility of choosing the president falls on the House of Representatives. In a unique twist, this election uses the same "one state, one vote" rule used by the Continental Congress under the Articles of Confederation. This is the only case where the Framers retained this procedure.

Second, the electors meet in their home states, not the national capital. There is no national assembly of electors. In a real sense, there is no single "Electoral College." There are multiple electoral colleges of varying sizes, each meeting in its own state with its own rules and procedures.

---

[1]Currently, this is the first Monday after the second Wednesday in December, i.e., between the 13th and 19th of the month.

Third, and most importantly, the Constitution leaves most of the details of the Electoral College system indeterminate. The states have almost complete autonomy in determining how electors are chosen and the circumstances in which they meet.[2]

The Constitutional Convention

To understand the *intent* of the design of the Electoral College, or for that matter the intent of any feature of the Constitution, there are two types of sources. The first are records of what actually happened at the Constitutional Convention; the second are the explanations offered by the Framers and other early figures for why they did what they did. Because there's some scholarly contention over the completeness and accuracy of the records of what actually happened at the convention, it's worth noting a few things about sources.

My main source on what actually happened at the Constitutional Convention is Max Farrand's *The Records of the Federal Convention of 1787* (1911), a massive scholarly effort to compile all available primary source documents on what happened at the Constitutional Convention. Of the sources included by Farrand, the most comprehensive are James Madison's exhaustive notes on the proceedings of the Constitutional Convention, which were mostly[3] written at the time of the convention and provide a relatively complete record. From Madison's notes, we know what alternatives to the Electoral College system were considered, what the strengths and weaknesses of those approaches were, and much of what the people involved with writing the Constitution thought about various methods of electing a president.

Another key group of sources for the intentions of the Framers of the Constitution are the Federalist Papers and other documents that cover the public and private debates on ratifying the Constitution. While only three of the Framers contributed to writing the Federalist Papers, they represent very well the winning side of the argument over whether or not America should adopt the newly-written Constitution. Since Madison was also one of the authors of the Federalist Papers, his perspective is overrepresented in the record.

Under the Articles of Confederation, there had been effectively no federal executive branch of government - a strong reaction against the

---

[2]*If* states hold public elections to choose electors, then they are subject to the restrictions placed on elections by the 14th, 15th, 19th, 24th, and 26th Amendments; however, they are not required to hold elections at all.

[3]To what degree is a matter of some scholarly contention. See in particular Mary Sarah Bilder's *Madison's Hand* (2015).

excesses the Founders perceived in the actions of the British executive branch (i.e., the monarchy). There was a person holding an office called *president*, but their duties consisted of presiding over legislative proceedings[4] and they had no powers outside of this procedural role *within* the legislature.

At the Constitutional Convention, a consensus quickly arose that there was a need for some sort of executive branch of government, but there was heated contention over whether or not that executive should be a single person, or a committee.[5] In some cases, Founding Fathers' support or opposition to a singular president, as opposed to an executive committee of some kind, was tied to the power of the president.[6] The nature and scope of the presidency were matters of very heated debate, and the ultimate version of the presidency that emerged - a singular president with a limited veto power - was itself a political compromise.

The method of selection of the president was no less contentious of a topic. During the Constitutional Convention, a variety of methods were proposed. Fundamentally, there were three completely different groups that could be responsible for selecting the president: The states, the people, or the federal government itself. Various proposals were made for the president to be elected by:

- State legislatures.
- State governors.
- The public at large.
- A specialized body of electors selected by one of the above groups.
- The federal Congress.
- The newly-designed Senate.
- A randomly-selected smaller group of members of Congress, chosen by lottery.

The details of these methods varied. Some proposals gave different states different numbers of votes or electors; others gave each state, small or large, an equal say in selecting the president. Additional methods may have been discussed but not brought to a vote on the convention floor. It is clear enough from the record of Madison's notes that different delegates had sharply different opinions on how the president ought to be elected.

---

[4] Much like the modern role the Vice President performs in the Senate.

[5] Edmund Randolph, who was at the time the governor of Virginia as well as one of Virginia's delegates to the Constitutional Convention, suggested a committee of three men - this can be recognized as the Roman model of the *triumvirate* - while Elbridge Gerry of Massachusetts suggested an executive checked by an executive council.

[6] E.g., Benjamin Franklin thought that veto power was too much to put in the hands of a single executive.

THE ORIGIN OF THE ELECTORAL COLLEGES

Many of the Founding Fathers considered the ideal term length of a president to be tied closely to the method of election. The most common term lengths that came up in discussion were three and seven-year terms; some members of the convention suggested life-long terms for the executive, or a term limited only by the possibility that the executive might be impeached for misbehavior.

Direct election by the people faced several objections. When James Wilson first proposed direct election of the president, his motion wasn't even seconded. Most critics of direct voting charged that the people would be too ignorant to make good decisions, and would be biased in favor of candidates from their own states. Roger Sherman of Connecticut claimed that this would tend to mean that the president would never be elected with majority support. Charles Pinckney of South Carolina suggested that the voters of the largest states would collude with one another to win the election.

As James Madison readily admitted in a speech supporting direct election, his home state was at a disadvantage as well, as they had a significant population that was unable to vote.[7] Delegates from slave states, small states, and states with more restrictive requirements for voting all could recognize how a popular vote was not in the interests of their state compared to alternative methods. While Madison supported direct election, he was outnumbered within his own delegation, and only Pennsylvania's delegation consistently voted in favor of direct election.

Election by governors was a fairly novel suggestion. This idea came from Elbridge Gerry of Massachusetts; it was seconded by Rufus King, also of Massachusetts.[8] Gerry's proposal weighted the governors' votes in proportion to the size of their states.

Edmund Randolph of Virginia, himself the governor of a large state, shot down this proposal, noting that it would disadvantage small states, questioning that election by governors would be any different from election directly by state legislatures, and finally adding that governors might not feel inclined to support a president who would, by virtue of being a federal executive, take executive power out of their own hands. Not a single state delegation voted in favor of Gerry's motion.[9]

Election by the Senate alone was considered as a method of producing a president who was as detached as possible from the pressures of popular opinion. It was disliked both by populists (who naturally

---

[7]To vote in Virginia required owning at least 25 acres of land - 50 acres if it was undeveloped land. See Donald Ratcliffe's article "The Right to Vote and the Rise of Democracy, 1787—1828" (2013).

[8]Elbridge Gerry is perhaps more famous for the salamander-shaped congressional district he drew when governor of the state, leading to the term "gerrymander."

[9]Delaware's delegation tied, so the vote against was 9-0 rather than 10-0.

preferred to have a president more directly accountable to the people) and by representatives of large states, who were keenly aware that this would place disproportionate power in the hands of small states.

Election by state legislatures was the most natural continuation of the way that the federal government had been run under the Articles of Confederation. This was attractive to those who wanted to see relatively modest changes to the United States under the new Constitution; however, most of those attending the convention thought that more than modest changes were required. Most were inclined towards federalism as a solution to the problems with the Articles of Confederation.

Election by electors came up in several different forms, the first version being a proposal from James Wilson near the beginning of the convention. Common criticisms included accusations of unnecessary complexity, concerns over the quality and integrity of the men who might serve as electors, and the number of electors that might be assigned to each state. However, while many attendees liked the idea of a separate body of electors, they disagreed fiercely on the question of who would choose those electors (the people or state governments). These disagreements left the motion to use electors dead in the water after several days of vigorous debate.

From the moment that James Madison drafted the Virginia Plan through the first complete draft of the Constitution written into the record on August 6th, and nearly through the end of the convention, the leading method was **election by Congress**, for a fixed (but non-renewable) term of seven years. Both the long term and the ineligibility for re-election were intended to help the president to check the power of Congress, and mitigate the degree to which the president would be a "creature of" Congress - that is, the degree to which the president would just do what Congress wanted. In modern terms, this would be classified as a parliamentary system.

On September 4th, less than two weeks before the end of the Constitutional Convention, a committee of eleven people returned from private deliberations with a revised draft of the Constitution that changed the method of electing the president (and the term for which the president would serve) putting it in the hands of electors. This version of the Electoral College was slightly different from the final version: If no candidate had a majority, the Senate would decide. The Vice President would then be the person with the largest number of electoral votes aside from the President (with the Senate again breaking any ties). This new proposal read as follows:

> Each state shall appoint, in such manner as its legislature may direct, a number of electors equal to the whole number of

THE ORIGIN OF THE ELECTORAL COLLEGES

senators and members of the House of Representatives to which the state may be entitled in the legislature. The electors shall meet in their respective states, and vote by ballot for two persons, of whom one at least shall not be an inhabitant of the same state with themselves; and they shall make a list of all the persons voted for, and of the number of votes for each, which list they shall sign: and certify, and transmit, sealed, to the seat of the general government, directed to the president of the Senate. The president of the Senate shall, in that house, open all the certificates, and the votes shall be then and there counted. The person having the greatest number of votes shall be the President, if such number be a majority of that of the electors; and if there be more than one who have such a majority, and have an equal number of votes, then the Senate shall immediately choose, by ballot, one of them for President; but if no person have a majority, then, from the five highest on the list, the Senate shall choose, by ballot, the President; and in every case, after the choice of the President, the person having the greatest number of votes shall be Vice-President; but if there should remain two or more who have equal votes, the Senate shall choose from them the Vice-President. The legislature may determine the time of choosing and assembling the electors, and the manner of certifying and transmitting their votes.

Unlike previous proposals involving electors, this proposal sidestepped the question of who would choose electors by leaving it up to state legislatures to decide how electors would be chosen. This was a very clever political compromise. Leaving the method of selection of electors up to state governments satisfied those who wanted to leave power in the hands of state legislatures; but it left open the possibility of popular elections or even gubernatorial appointment for those who thought that state legislatures would be ill-suited to making those choices.

Many attendees of the convention thought that the Senate would frequently be in the position of resolving the election, thinking that one person would rarely command majority support. George Mason went as far as to venture a guess that the Senate would decide "nineteen times in twenty," and suggested that the majority requirement be struck out entirely. James Madison, after expressing similar concerns that the Electoral College would serve mostly as a nominating body, suggested that the threshold to win should be lowered to one-third of the vote, rather than a majority.

Madison's notes on the convention make it clear that many[10] of the

---

[10]Though not all - Gouverneur Morris being one notable exception.

Framers, whether they were in support of the Electoral College or not, believed that this version of it would frequently leave elections to be resolved by the Senate. This led to a contentious debate over whether the Senate was the most appropriate body to elect the president (as opposed to the House of Representatives, a joint meeting of both houses of Congress, or a smaller committee of members of Congress), and how many of the top candidates from the Electoral College should be considered, with proposals ranging from automatically electing the top candidate (removing the role of Congress entirely) to considering the top thirteen candidates (a number intended to ensure that small states would be able to have candidates considered by the Senate).

After contentious debate, the Senate's role in this process was transferred to the House of Representatives, with a "one vote per state" rule used to preserve small states' level of influence over that step of the process. Voting by delegation (with one vote per state, cast in the same direction as the majority of the delegates from that state) may seem like a strange rule today, but this was the same manner as votes were held in the Continental Congress, or in the Constitutional Convention itself. While there was heated disagreement over the five-candidate rule and majority requirement, none of the motions to change either requirement passed. The majority threshold still exists today, although the five-candidate rule was changed to a three-candidate rule by the 12th Amendment.

The more contentious modern questions surrounding the Electoral College today - namely, the use of "winner-take-all" slates, and the question of how many electors to assign to which states - were not debated in September of 1787 when the Constitutional Convention voted to adopt the Electoral College. The re-use of the compromises over Congressional representation was good enough to stave off debate, and the question of the relative power of small and large states hinged on the balance between the Electoral College itself (where large states were expected to dominate) and the contingent election process (where the rule of voting by state delegations would allow small states to dominate).

The separate electoral colleges

Unlike most democratic decision-making bodies, the Electoral College does not meet as a single assembly. The very name "Electoral College" is something of a misnomer. It would be more accurate to say that there are many separate electoral colleges: One for each state.[11] Each of the fifty-one assemblies of today's Electoral College meets separately

---

[11] In presidential elections taking place after 1960, this includes one additional assembly for the District of Columbia, courtesy of the 23rd Amendment.

THE ORIGIN OF THE ELECTORAL COLLEGES

– on the same day, but in fifty-one separate assemblies with fifty-one separate sets of rules. So far, the largest college of electors has consisted of fifty-five members (California in 2012-2020) while the smallest has only had two electors (Nevada in 1864).

This separation of the states' electoral colleges is deliberate, and the comments recorded at the Constitutional Convention on the topic show that there were two major reasons for having thirteen separate electoral colleges instead of a single national assembly. First, the geographic separation was intended to serve as a safeguard against foreign interference in American elections; even if foreign powers were able to subvert one assembly of electors by bribery or force, it would be very difficult for a foreign power to compromise multiple assemblies scattered across the country.

Even with the limited powers that the Framers intended to allow the president, a president whose true loyalties lay with a foreign power could do significant harm to the country's interests. The power of the presidency has grown significantly over time, and the Framers' concern is as topical today as it was in 1787 during the Constitutional Convention. A president who acts on behalf of another country's interests could do immense damage.[12]

This was not simply an exercise in paranoia. To understand why the Founding Fathers chose to have thirteen (now fifty-one) separate electoral colleges rather than a single Electoral College meeting jointly in the federal capital, it helps to look at the history of Poland and Germany and their elective monarchies.

While the United States' particular form of government was new and experimental in many ways, there were both contemporary 18th-century examples of elected monarchs as well as historical examples dating back to classical Greece and Rome. Contemporary examples included the king of the Polish-Lithuanian Commonwealth (Poland) and the emperor of the Holy Roman Empire (Germany). At the Constitutional Convention on July 25th, 1787, James Madison had this to say:

> Germany & Poland are witnesses of this danger. In the former, the election of the Head of the Empire, till it became in a manner hereditary, interested all Europe, and was much influenced by foreign interference — In the latter, altho' the elective Magistrate has very little real power, his election has at all times produced the most eager interference of forign [sic] princes, and has in fact at length slid entirely into foreign hands.

---

[12]This concern is a perennial one - e.g., see discussion of John F. Kennedy and the Pope during the 1960 election, or Donald Trump and Putin during the 2016 election.

James Madison was not the only one of the Framers to draw comparisons to those two elective monarchies. Most of the Framers were likely familiar with at least the rough outline of recent events in the Polish-Lithuanian Commonwealth and the Holy Roman Empire.

The elective monarchy of the Holy Roman Empire

James Madison and the other Framers at the Constitutional Convention had an indirect stake in the politics of the Holy Roman Empire. They had quite recently been through a war, which we know today as the American Revolutionary War. In that war, their forces, commanded by George Washington, fought against the army of the Duke of Brunswick-Luneberg, Archtreasurer and Prince-Elector of the Holy Roman Empire.

This German duke was better known as King George III of Great Britain.

In 1787, the Holy Roman Empire was a relatively loose confederation of German principalities, with most decisions related to governance being made at the level of principalities - much like the early United States under the Articles of Confederation. It was not, however, an equal confederation. The title of Emperor had been generally held by the Austrian branch of the Habsburg dynasty, making Austria the preeminent state within the Holy Roman Empire.

The prince-electors of the Holy Roman Empire were a small and select group of secular and religious authorities, each the ruler of one of the major principalities making up the empire.[13] They had political interests of their own. Within the previous century, eight foreign monarchs (two Polish kings, three Prussian kings, and three British kings) had been electors of the Holy Roman Empire. Other electors had personal ties to foreign monarchs.

When Madison noted that the Imperial inheritance had "interested all Europe" and "was much influenced by foreign interference," he was referring to conflicts that plunged Europe into war and threatened to tear the Holy Roman Empire apart entirely. The issue of Imperial inheritance and the power struggles between the prince-electors was linked to several major European wars, some of which had spilled over into the American colonies.

To the American colonists, the North American theaters of these wars were known as the French and Indian Wars. George Washington and

---

[13] Historically, the number of electors was typically seven, but at the time of the Constitutional Convention, that number had been expanded to nine.

THE ORIGIN OF THE ELECTORAL COLLEGES

most of the other experienced American military officers were veterans of those wars.

It is worth noting that one of the Framers proposed adopting a system very similar to the electoral college of the Holy Roman Empire: Elbridge Gerry. He proposed that the president should be elected by the state governors, with the democratic modification that each governor's vote should be weighted based on the size of their state. This would have been as close to the system used by the Holy Roman Empire as practical within the American political system.

The Polish elective monarchy

The Polish-Lithuanian Commonwealth had a very different form of elective monarchy, one in which every Polish noble capable of traveling to the site of the election could cast a vote – over a thousand times as many electors, in other words. While assembled all in one place, these electors could be bribed or coerced. Uncooperative electors could be killed or driven away. The electoral assembly itself, with knights and attendant soldiers, was a significant concentration of military force, and the elective nature of the Polish monarchy proved a major vulnerability.

In 1787, the current (and final) king of Poland was Stanislaw II Augustus. He had been elected in 1764 by an assembly of about five thousand Polish nobles under the close supervision of an invading Russian army. While Poland would not be completely divided up between Prussia, Austria, and Russia until 1795, the process had already begun. James Madison and the other Founding Fathers could see the writing on the wall – Poland was done for.

Considering the large size of the Polish electorate, as well as the stringent property requirements some American states required of voters at the time, the Polish electoral system was not very far removed from a direct popular vote. The example of Poland was brought up on some occasions when debating the merits of direct election of the president, and it is clear the Framers carefully considered the specific liabilities of the Polish electoral system.[14]

The exact procedures used to govern each state's Electoral College are not fixed by the Constitution.

Electors might vote secretly and anonymously, or their votes might be identified publicly. Most (though not all) states have laws that try to compel electors to vote in a particular way, based on the outcome of the

---

[14]E.g., by James Wilson on July 17th of the convention. See *The Records of the Federal Convention of 1787* (1911) by Max Farrand.

popular vote in that state. Most of these laws either call for the removal and replacement of disobedient electors or punish them for voting for a candidate other than the candidate the state wants them to vote for.[15]

Without the presence of those laws, it is entirely possible that we would have faced a surprise (and a constitutional crisis) on December 19th, 2016; a record number of electors violated their pre-election pledges, and from what I have been told by presidential electors in interviews, there were significantly more electors interested in doing so in order to prevent Donald Trump from taking office.

The absent motives

There are three common myths about the motives behind the creation of the Electoral College. First, that the Electoral College was created in order to protect small states. Second, that it was created in order to protect slavery. Third, that it was created because the Framers were uncomfortable with having too much democracy. To address these claims properly, we will refer to a timeline of key votes at the Constitutional Convention. While these factors played a role in creating opposition to a popular vote and shaped the development of a presidential election system, they were not the reasons that the Electoral College itself was introduced.

On May 29th, what is widely known as the Virginia Plan was proposed by Governor Edmund Randolph of Virginia, arguably the ranking member of the convention as the sitting governor of the largest and most powerful of the thirteen states. This plan was mostly written up by one of the most junior members of the Virginia delegation and one of the earliest to arrive from out of state, James Madison. This plan specified that the "executive" would be selected by the "national legislature." The convention then proceeded to work from this plan, although several alternates were proposed.[16]

On June 1st, James Wilson, a delegate from Pennsylvania - which had just abolished slavery - said that the president should be elected by popular vote. This idea was met with immediate and widespread opposition and not brought to a vote; neither the Southern delegates nor the New England delegates were interested in the idea. On June 2nd, Wilson

---

[15] The constitutionality of these laws has been affirmed in *Chiafalo v. Washington* (2020) but was uncertain until then.

[16] One was known as the "New Jersey Plan." The other two were the personal brainchildren of Charles Cotesworth Pinckney (the younger of the two Charles Pinckneys in attendance and the one who we will later discuss as a nominee for vice president and president) and Alexander Hamilton, and are known as the Pinckney and Hamilton plans.

THE ORIGIN OF THE ELECTORAL COLLEGES

returned with a proposal that he felt could possibly gain wider support than a popular vote: Having a set of electors, each of which was chosen by popular vote in his district. This was voted down 8-2, with only his own delegation of Pennsylvania and the delegation of neighboring Maryland voting in favor.

Table 1: Brief timeline of the Constitutional Convention

Date	Event
May 29th	Virginia plan proposed.
May 31st	Vote to have popular election of representatives.
June 1st	Wilson proposes popular vote for president.
June 2nd	Wilson proposes electoral college chosen by popular vote by district.
June 6th	Second vote on popular election for representatives.
June 7th	Vote against popular election of senators.
June 18th	Hamilton proposes his plan, including variant electoral college system.
June 21st	Third vote on popular election for representatives.
June 25th	Second vote against popular election of senators.
June 25th	Wilson again proposes district-based electoral college.
July 17th	Morris proposes popular vote for president.
July 17th	Martin proposes electoral college chosen by state legislators
July 19th	Vote to have electoral college of some kind.
July 19th	Vote that if having electors, have them chosen by state legislatures.
July 23rd	Vote to reconsider using an electoral college.
July 24th	Vote to have Congress elect president.
August 7th	Morris proposes only freeholders vote for representatives.
August 24th	Carroll proposes popular vote for president.
August 24th	Vote to have Congress use a joint session for electing the president.
August 24th	One state, one vote rule for Congressional election of president.
August 24th	Morris proposes district-based electoral college.
August 24th	Vote against having electoral college of some kind.
August 31st	Vote against selection by Congress
September 6th	Final vote on having an electoral college.

The proposal caught the fancy of Alexander Hamilton, generally accounted an opponent of slavery,[17] who included a slightly more complex version in the plan he proposed on June 18th. Hamilton would later write fairly effusively about the merits of the Electoral College system in the Federalist Papers, particularly #68, in which he described the system as better than a simple popular vote.

The Pennsylvanian delegation was probably the most radically democratic. The Pennsylvania delegation favored electing senators, representatives, and the president by popular vote; its two most vocal members, James Wilson and Gouverneur Morris, were outspoken advocates for having more direct democracy. Both of them favored a popular vote but were willing to back a system involving intermediate electors as the closest they could get to a popular vote.

There was one limit to Morris's degree of support for greater democracy, however; Gouverneur Morris thought that for federal elections, the electorate should be all freeholders, i.e., landowners. He said this when he proposed that the president be elected by popular vote on July 17th; and he suggested it again on August 7th, moving that voters should all have the same qualifications for electing representatives across the entire country. Benjamin Franklin - an elder statesman and fellow Pennsylvanian - made one of his rare speeches in opposition to Morris's motion, and it was voted down.

The issue of who should be allowed to vote, and the dream of an electorate with uniform qualifications across the entire country, was therefore fresh in Madison's mind when he voiced support for a district-based Electoral College system on July 19th. This speech is fairly widely-cited, so I will quote Madison's notes on what he said:

> The people at large was in his opinion the fittest in itself. It would be as likely as any that could be devised to produce an Executive Magistrate of distinguished Character. The people generally could only know & vote for some Citizen whose merits had rendered him an object of general attention & esteem. There was one difficulty however of a serious nature attending an immediate choice by the people. The right of suffrage was much more diffusive in the Northern than the Southern States; and the latter could have no influence in the election on the score of the Negroes. The substitution of electors obviated this difficulty and seemed on the whole to be liable to the fewest objections.

This is an interesting quote that is often taken as a reason why we have the Electoral College rather than a popular vote. However, there

---

[17] E.g., by Ron Chernow in *Alexander Hamilton* (2004).

THE ORIGIN OF THE ELECTORAL COLLEGES

are a few points worth considering carefully. First and foremost, the draft Constitution called for the president to be elected by Congress. A national popular vote was proposed three times, but at no point during the convention was there a choice between a system involving electors and a system involving a direct vote by the people; both methods were introduced *as alternatives to election by Congress.*

Second, Madison directly said that he thought that a popular vote would be the best system. He wasn't arguing against its adoption as much as acknowledging that he could not even get his own home state delegation to support it.

Third, when Madison referred to suffrage being "more diffusive" in northern states and then said Southern states would not have extra votes "on the score of the Negroes," he was providing two distinct reasons. Virginia and other Southern states commonly had more stringent requirements attached to voting rights; Virginia itself had among the most restrictive rules in the entire country, requiring ownership of 25 acres of "improved" land or 50 acres of "unimproved" land. Madison supported Morris's motion on August 7th, speaking out in favor of restricting the federal franchise to landowners.

The next set of key debates and votes on the subject of the Electoral College occurred on August 24th. Daniel Carroll of Maryland proposed that the president should be elected by popular vote. It's worth noting that Maryland had the third-largest population of slaves (slightly less than South Carolina) and required that voters had a net worth of at least 30 pounds.[18] In this light, it is not surprising Carroll failed to convince a majority of his own delegation to lend support to the measure, but unusually, the Delaware delegation joined the Pennsyvania delegation in voting in favor of direct democracy at that point.

Morris then proposed a district-based electoral college again, and the motion came close to passing with the support of five states. At this point in time, the three states south of Virginia (Georgia, North Carolina, and South Carolina) had consistently voted against an electoral college of any kind at every opportunity, and New England delegates had been vocally skeptical of a national popular vote each time it was proposed.

The committee of eleven

At this point, it seemed inevitable that the president would be elected by Congress. While a clear majority of delegates were dissatisfied with

---

[18] According to Donald Ratcliffe in "The Right to Vote and the Rise of Democracy, 1787–1828" (2013), this meant about two-thirds of the adult white male population was qualified to vote.

Congress, there was no consensus on an alternative method. Different delegates wanted to place power in the hands of the people, state legislatures, or even state governors.

A committee of eleven - one member from each state represented at the convention - to deal with leftover business was selected on August 31st. The committee included Daniel Carroll, James Madison, and Gouverneur Morris - three key supporters of a direct popular vote, who had all advanced an electoral college of some kind as the closest approximation they could get to a popular vote. In their own meetings, the committee resurrected the idea of a separate body of electors, coming up with two key compromises. First, they delegated the method of appointment to the states, allowing them to gain the support of delegates who preferred that state legislatures be in charge of choosing the president.

Second, they hybridized the system with the system of election by Congress by adding a contingent election process: If no candidate got an outright majority in the electoral college, a contingent election would resolve the results in the Senate - a feature necessary to gain the support of delegates from smaller states, who expected that large states would dominate such a system. As Roger Sherman was on the committee and a notable supporter of small states, this element of the system may owe its existence to him.

On September 4th, the committee reported these changes to the convention at large. Madison's notes say that "Mr. Randolph & Mr. Pinkney [sic] wished for a particular explanation & discussion of the reasons for changing the mode of electing the Executive." I suspect these wishes were expressed quite loudly and with a sense of affront; the idea of having a dedicated body of electors had been brought up and killed by the convention at large several times. Randolph and Pinckney probably thought this was a bad idea that had already been buried. Instead, it was brought to debate. The hybrid nature of the newly-proposed system played a key role in the debate immediately, and the issue of small state power was brought up fairly quickly by Roger Sherman:

> Mr Sherman reminded the opponents of the new mode proposed that if the Small States had the advantage in the Senate's deciding among the five highest candidates, the Large States would have in fact the nomination of these candidates.

It's important to note that while the *system* was designed in part to appease small state delegates, the part of it so designed was *not* the Electoral College itself, but rather the contingent election process. George Mason of Virginia as a large state delegate was one of the few delegates opposed to the proposal as a whole, saying that "nineteen times in twenty the President would be chosen by the Senate, an improper body for the purpose." Gouverneur Morris disagreed; he felt that the key rule requiring electors to vote for at least one candidate from outside of their own state would help build a majority.

Mason's objection was dealt with by moving the contingent election to the House, keeping the "one state, one vote" rule that had bought the support of key small state delegates. Madison was concerned enough by the possibility that contingent elections would be common that he suggested lowering the threshold for victory in the Electoral College itself to one-third. However, aside from moving the contingent election from the Senate to the House, the committee's clever compromise remained intact through two days of debate. On September 6th, the vote in favor of the new system was 9-2.

The two dissenting state delegations were North Carolina and South Carolina, whose delegations had been opposed to every method of election that involved a popular vote for president or an intermediate body of electors. The original idea of an electoral college had originated with delegates from states without slavery. The leading advocates for a popular vote and the leading advocates for a college of electors were almost the same groups of Framers; the lone likely exception, Alexander Hamilton, was opposed to slavery, and delegates from slave states were the most persistently skeptical of the system. Slavery did not motivate the construction - or adoption - of the Electoral College. It was simply the closest to a national popular vote that supporters of a direct vote, such as Wilson, Morris, Carroll, and Madison, could get.

The original expectations for the Electoral College

George Washington was an obvious first president to those at the Constitutional Convention,[19] but most Framers thought he was an exceptional case. In considering election methods, they were trying to consider who might eventually follow Washington. It may be worth noting that John Adams and Thomas Jefferson - the men who became the second and third presidents after Washington - were not at the Constitutional Convention. The debate might have gone differently with either or both of them in the room.

As noted above, there was significant disagreement in how the Framers expected the system to work. Roger Sherman's expectations were likely typical among the Framers. The large states would nominate; the small states would decide.

---

[19] C.f. Edward Larson's *The Return of George Washington: Uniting the States, 1783-1789* (2015).

Since each assembly of electors would meet separately from the other states' electors and deliberate at their assemblies, it was natural to assume they would not coordinate with other states' electors.[20] Thus, while Virginia's electors might decide to cast most of their second votes for a Pennsylvanian, it might not be the same person that the Pennsylvanian electors chose in their own discussions. After a process like this, the top five candidates would therefore usually consist of the home state favorites of each of the largest five states.[21]

Whichever one of those candidates was most popular among small state representatives in the House would then probably become president through the contingent election process. Of the other four candidates, the one with the largest number of votes in the Electoral College would become vice president. This is not how things turned out, but the Framers did not anticipate the rise of national political parties that would take over the process of nominating candidates for consideration by electors.

A brief technical prelude on Electoral College geography

In the next part of the book, we'll be taking a guided tour through every American presidential election from 1788 to 2020. For each election, we'll briefly identify the electoral vote totals, the House contingent vote totals (if there was a House contingent election), the *pivotal state*, any *critical states*, and a set of what we will call *crucial states*. While the two-party system predominates, minor candidates are a frequent part of the scenery; however, I have decided to omit mentioning most minor candidates except as necessary to explain the action.

For 1828 to 2020, I have mostly drawn my data from David Leip's *Atlas of US Elections*; for data on earlier elections, I have mostly relied on Phillip Lampi's *A New Nation Votes*.[22] Other sources may have slightly different data for the returns, or count the vote totals differently; however, most of these differences are minor. Important exceptions arise in trying to count popular votes when electoral votes in a slate of electors are divided (e.g., New York's losing fusion slate in 1860 or Alabama's mixed winning slate in 1960).

---

[20] Very few state capitals were close enough together to pass messages back and forth within the same day.

[21] At the time, Virginia, Pennsylvania, Massachusetts, New York, and North Carolina.

[22] Online versions of these two data sets are available at https://uselectionatlas.org and https://elections.lib.tufts.edu/ as of the writing of this book.

THE ORIGIN OF THE ELECTORAL COLLEGES

Definitions and vocabulary

There are a few pieces of key vocabulary I'll be using to discuss elections throughout the course of the book. The book also includes a number of standardized illustrations of elections, such as the map below that shows the results of the 2016 Electoral College. The maps are colored based on the number of electoral votes - in the below example, red for Donald Trump and blue for Hillary Clinton. Following with recent popular convention, I've assigned blue to the main branch of Democrats, which can be traced back to the Jacksonian offshoot of the Democratic-Republicans and therefore has also been assigned to the main line of Democratic-Republicans preceding Jackson.

Similarly, I've assigned red to the main branch of the Republican Party, and then also the various other national parties that were in opposition to the party colored with blue. This means that red is used for Republicans, the Whigs, a variety of Federalists, and two candidates who ran under multiple party labels.[23]

States are shaded by number of electoral votes as well as party of electoral votes. This means that states that cast more electoral votes (such as California) are darker. States that cast electoral votes for multiple candidates will show up in blended colors; the small maps below the main map will help clarify what combination of votes was present in a particular state, and provide an alternate view on the geography of that candidate's electoral votes.

The *pivotal state*, also known as the *tipping point state*, is the single state that served as the fulcrum of the Electoral College. If we take the candidate who earned the most votes in the Electoral College and put the states in order based on how closely they were won, adding the electoral votes from the easiest states to win first, the pivotal state is the one whose electoral votes reach a majority. For the most part, I have chosen to identify the tipping point based on the percentage margin of victory, which is relatively non-controversial. The pivotal state is marked on the election maps using a large white star. In 2016, Pennsylvania was the pivotal state. In elections from 1788-1824, it is difficult to identify a pivotal state because the modern "winner-take-all" rule had not yet come to dominate the Electoral College; in these cases, I have marked likely pivotal states.

If we look at all the states without worrying about how easily they were won or lost, *critical states* are ones that could have changed the result of the election if their electoral votes had been cast for a different candidate. This includes states that were won by a large margin as well as states

---

[23]John Quincy Adams and Abraham Lincoln.

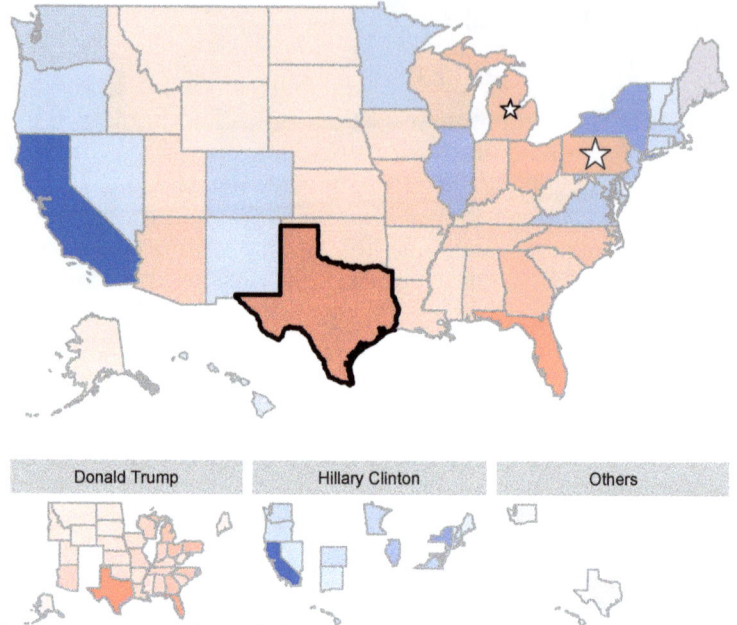

Figure 4: The 2016 presidential election. Texas has a bold outline because it was critical; Pennsylvania is marked with a larger white star because it was pivotal; and Michigan is marked with a smaller white star as a crucial but not pivotal state.

that were won narrowly. Critical states are marked with a heavy black outline. In 2016, Texas was critical, because without Texas's electoral votes, Trump would not have won a majority.

For elections after 1824,[24] I've also identified a collection of *crucial states*, which combines the ideas behind critical and pivotal status: It is a certain minimal collection of states that could alter the result of the election. If there are multiple crucial states, they are marked with smaller white stars. If one state is both pivotal and critical, that state will be the unique crucial state in addition to being pivotal and critical, and will have both a dark outline and a large white star.

In particular, this collection of crucial states is built by taking the states with the narrowest percentage margins and removing them from the winner's column until the result of the election changes; and then going back through the list to remove any states whose electoral votes could be safely added back to the former winner's column without turning them back into the winner of the election. These states are crucial, in that if

---

[24]It's true that not *all* electors were directly elected after 1824. However, while South Carolina continued to use legislative appointment in the 1828 through 1860 presidential elections, it seems clear that South Carolina was not a battleground state during this period. The other notable outlier after 1824 is Colorado in 1876, its debut presidential election.

THE ORIGIN OF THE ELECTORAL COLLEGES

the winner had lost all of these states as a group, the result of the election would have changed; and that changing the result of the election with any smaller collection of states would have required flipping states with larger percentage margins. In 2016, Michigan and Pennsylvania were crucial.[25]

The idea of what it means for a state to be pivotal or critical has major implications for how power is distributed within the Electoral College. Mathematically, we will see that over the course of American history, power has been concentrated quite disproportionately in certain key large states. New York in particular has been disproportionately important in presidential elections, while New England and the deep South have only rarely been political battlegrounds.

Third party candidates (and more)

Most presidential elections have included multiple minor candidates who earned a small fraction of the popular vote or electoral vote. History has forgotten most of these candidates, and I have as well - even after reading about many of them! In some cases, scattered electoral votes for multiple candidates will be lumped together in a single category for improved clarity. Most minor candidates who did not earn any electoral votes will not be mentioned in the description of the election.

While I can mostly ignore minor candidates who earned no electoral votes, there are a number of elections featuring three or four major candidates. In terms of the mathematical analyses based on the above definitions, things get potentially complicated once we consider a third major candidate. In elections where there are three or more candidates who each won at least one state, I calculate pivotal, critical, and crucial states from the perspective of the leading candidate and what it would take to *potentially* change the outcome.

For example, in 1968, if Hubert Humphrey had won New York instead of Richard Nixon, this would have denied Nixon a majority in the Electoral College, so I consider New York a critical state in that election - even if it is entirely possible that Nixon would have won the resulting House contingent election.[26] For one thing, we can't be certain of the outcome of that hypothetical scenario; for another, it's entirely possible that the political negotiations surrounding the contingent election would have had very significant historical consequences. A Nixon who owed his presidency to political negotiation with George Wallace might have governed quite differently.

---

[25] If all of Texas's electors had voted for Donald Trump, as anticipated based on their pledges, the list of crucial states in 2016 would also include Wisconsin.
[26] Southern Democrats were not fond of Humphrey, to put it mildly.

Caveats about early elections

For presidential elections prior to 1828, it's difficult to talk about popular vote margins meaningfully, which makes it hard to determine a pivotal state or a set of crucial states. There are two reasons for this. The first is that before 1828, many states did not allow their citizens to vote for presidential electors. The second is that many early election records are incomplete; good data analysis is very difficult in the absence of good data.

In one particularly interesting early case in 1812, a couple of towns in New Jersey held elections for presidential electors after the Federalist state legislature had decided to cancel the state's presidential elections. Per the records in "A New Nation Votes: American Election Returns 1787-1825" (2007), the result was a 1671-1 vote landslide rebuke of the Federalists. In a certain sense, New Jersey had a popular vote total for the 1812 presidential election; however, it is not very meaningful.

I've marked the most probable 1-2 pivotal states on the maps for some early elections, but systematic analysis of the earliest elections is particularly difficult due to the evolving nature of the system. Each of the first four presidential elections was a completely unique affair, as we will discuss in the next chapter. In the first four presidential elections, electors mattered as individual agents; as some might put it, more as trustees than as delegates.[27] This is in accord with Alexander Hamilton's vision for the institution, and also involved significant activity by Alexander Hamilton behind the scenes, so I tend to think of this first version of the Electoral College as being Hamilton's Electoral College.

---

[27] For further discussion of this distinction and the tension between these two roles for electors, see *Representation and the Electoral College* (2019) by Robert Alexander.

CHAPTER 3

Hamilton's Electoral College (1788-1800)

Out of all of the Framers, Alexander Hamilton may have been the only one who thought the Electoral College system was the best possible option, rather than a pragmatically better second choice. Those who were the most prominent advocates of the system - Wilson, Morris, and Madison - all preferred a direct popular vote. Others were on the record preferring that state governments select the president, and those on the losing side of the final vote on the Electoral College preferred to have Congress elect the president.

Hamilton effusively praised the Electoral College system in the *Federalist Papers*; and his own proposed draft Constitution featured a two-layer system of electoral colleges. Hamilton was clearly in favor of electors exercising their own political discretion.[1] He practiced what he preached, meeting with electors and writing letters to them in order to try to influence their votes; Hamilton attempted to influence the results of presidential elections until his death and the passage of the 12th Amendment.

---
[1] See Federalist #68.

The Washington elections

George Washington presided over the Constitutional Convention. The fact that the Framers expected the president of the Constitutional Convention to become the first President of the United States influenced what powers they were willing to give the president. In terms of their top-ticket results, the first two elections went as anticipated by the Framers, resulting in the election of George Washington as the first president. However, there was still contention over second place.

1788: A minority for Adams

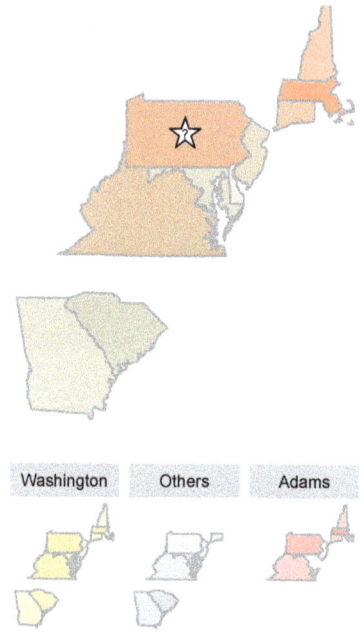

Electoral vote: 69-34-9-6-6-4-3-2-2-1-1-1
Pivotal state: Unclear; possibly Pennsylvania
Critical states: None
Crucial states: Unclear

The first presidential election was highly irregular in nature. Three out of thirteen states had not yet ratified the Constitution - North Carolina, New York, and Rhode Island. The electoral votes assigned to each state were based on loose estimates of relative population totals, rather than an organized census. There was also no political competition. George Washington was the choice of every major political faction in each participating state.

George Washington was elected by the unanimous consent of all electors. Anti-Federalists did not organize themselves to put forward an alternative to John Adams for vice president; Adams won with a minority of the vote, with other candidates receiving scattered votes. Alexander Hamilton did actively campaign to reduce John Adams's electoral total, which was embarrassingly low; only three vice presidents have ever taken office with less than majority support.[2]

Due to the sparsity of popular voting as a method of selecting electors, combined with the fact that this election featured no major rivals to either Washington or Adams, it is very difficult to estimate what state should be identified as pivotal. From 1792-1820, based on the results in closer elections, it's most likely Pennsylvania was a politically pivotal state at this time.

---

[2] The next was Thomas Jefferson, who was trying to run for president. The third was Richard M. Johnson in 1836, who had to face a contingent election in the Senate. Adams did not have to face a contingent election, because the Senate contingent election was introduced with the 12th Amendment.

1792: A two-party election

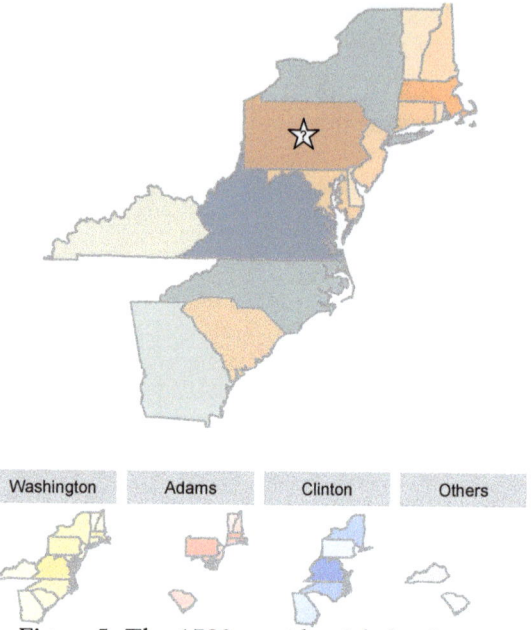

Figure 5: The 1792 presidential election.

Electoral vote: 132-77-50-4-1
Pivotal state: Probably Pennsylvania
Critical states: Pennsylvania, Massachusetts
Crucial state: Pennsylvania

George Washington was re-elected unanimously in the first regular presidential election. The presidential election of George Washington was not contested; every elector was expected to vote for George Washington and did so. However, this race featured the first competitive race for vice president, between Democratic-Republican George Clinton and Federalist John Adams.

If we consider the vice presidential election as the main executive contest between the two emerging political parties, the pivotal state in this election was most likely Pennsylvania, which elected 14 pro-Adams electors and one pro-Clinton elector; had George Clinton won all of Pennsylvania's electors, instead of just one, he would have become vice president by a narrow 64-63 margin.

1796: The faithless elector problem

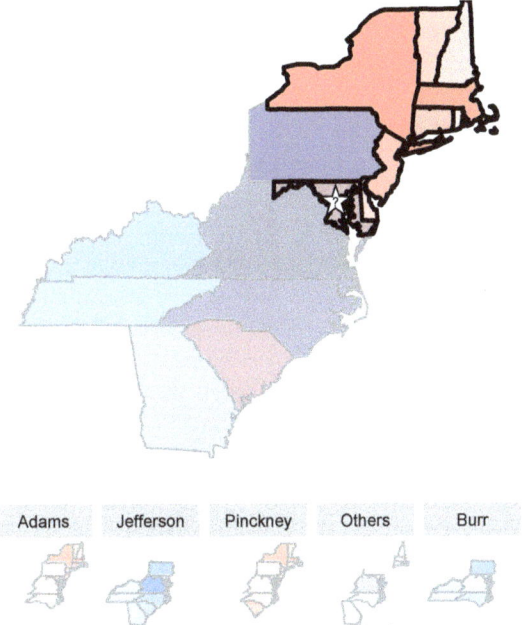

Figure 6: The 1796 presidential election.

Electoral vote: 71-68-59-30-15-11-7-5-3-2-2-2-1
Pivotal state: Likely Maryland
Critical states: All states won by Adams
Crucial state: Likely Maryland

The election of 1796 was closely contested between John Adams and Thomas Jefferson. The margin was close enough that every state won by Adams was critical. Maryland is the most likely candidate for a pivotal state, as seven of its ten electors voted for Adams and four voted for Jefferson,[3] although the other central states voting for Adams are also possibilities for the pivotal state (NY, NJ, and DE). This was the first election to show a clear regional division between North and South.

It is worth noting that since Adams won nine states and Jefferson won seven, this is one of only three elections to be decided by the bonus "Senate" electors. It was also arguably the first election featuring so-called faithless electors. This is a major potential complication for the Electoral College system.

---
[3] This includes one elector who voted for both.

The faithless electors of 1796

Many sources cite Samuel Miles of Pennsylvania as the first faithless elector,[4] mostly thanks to an angry letter to the editor published in the *United States Gazette* in 1796:

> Do I chuse Samuel Miles to determine for me whether John Adams or Thomas Jefferson shall be President? No! I chuse him to act, not to think!

One of the difficulties of the Electoral College system is that while presidential electors are chosen based on who they will vote for, they can, and sometimes do, vote for someone else entirely. These electors are known colloquially as faithless electors, referring to a breach of an implied (in some cases explicit) promise to vote a particular way. While Samuel Miles is often cited as the first faithless presidential elector, it's difficult to make the case that he deserves this unique distinction.

In 1796, the first contested presidential election, the hotly contested battleground state of Pennsylvania held a state-wide popular vote to choose presidential electors. The Federalists and Democratic-Republicans each nominated a slate of fifteen electors, for a total of thirty candidates. While neither party had anything so formal as a party convention, party leaders had come together and agreed on who should be president and vice president. For the Federalists, John Adams of Massachusetts and Thomas Pinckney of South Carolina; for the Democratic-Republicans, Thomas Jefferson and Aaron Burr.

Pennsylvania's election was exceptionally narrow.[5] The first-place elector, Thomas MacKean, a Democratic-Republican, earned 12,306 votes; the thirtieth-place elector, Thomas Stokley, a Federalist, earned 12,071 votes, just 235 fewer. The two most popular Federalist electors, Robert Coleman and Samuel Miles, placed 13th and 14th. If Samuel Miles had received 14 fewer votes, he would have been replaced by a Democratic-Republican elector, Jonas Hartzell, rather than another Federalist elector.

Samuel Miles cast his two votes for Thomas Jefferson and Thomas Pinckney, splitting the difference between the Democratic-Republican ticket (Jefferson-Burr) and the Federalist ticket (Adams-Pinckney). There are three reasons we should be skeptical of crowning him as the *first faithless elector*, however.

---

[4] E.g., *Why the Electoral College Is Bad for America* (2019) by George Edwards and *Representation and the Electoral College* (2019) by Robert Alexander.

[5] All 1796 vote totals referred to here are taken from "A New Nation Votes: American Election Returns 1787-1825" (2007) by Phillip Lampi, which I recommend highly as a resource for looking at very early elections.

Table 2: Official presidential election results for Pennsylvania in 1796

Candidate	Party	Votes	Place
Thomas MacKean	Democratic-Republican	12306	1
James Boyd	Democratic-Republican	12294	2
William Brown	Democratic-Republican	12282	3
John Whitehill	Democratic-Republican	12280	4
Peter Muhlenberg	Democratic-Republican	12274	5
Abraham Smith	Democratic-Republican	12271	6
Jacob Morgan	Democratic-Republican	12269	7
James Hanna	Democratic-Republican	12267	8
John Smilie	Democratic-Republican	12266	9
Joseph Heister	Democratic-Republican	12260	10
John Piper	Democratic-Republican	12260	11
William Irvine	Democratic-Republican	12237	12
Robert Coleman	Federalist	12217	13
Samuel Miles	Federalist	12214	14
William MacClay	Democratic-Republican	12208	15
Jonas Hartzell	Democratic-Republican	12201	16
Samuel Postlethwaite	Federalist	12197	17
William Wilson	Federalist	12190	18
Israel Whelen	Federalist	12185	19
John Carson	Federalist	12175	20
James Edgar	Democratic-Republican	12173	21
Henry Wynkoop	Federalist	12164	22
Thomas Bull	Federalist	12158	23
Jacob Hay	Federalist	12145	24
Benjamin Elliott	Federalist	12137	25
John Woods	Federalist	12136	26
Valentine Eckhart	Federalist	12134	27
Ephraim Douglas	Federalist	12132	28
John Arndt	Federalist	12096	29
Thomas Stokely	Federalist	12071	30

First, Samuel Miles was simply doing what he felt was his duty. There had never been a competitive presidential election before, and no established norm of electors following the dictates of a political party. He felt that it was his duty to make his own decision, and felt that as president, Adams would lead the country into war with France.[6] His view of the duties of a presidential elector were not unprecedented, and were exactly as advertised by prominent Federalists; in Federalist Paper #68, Hamilton described the office as one of "deliberation" and "discernment":

> It was equally desirable, that the immediate election should be made by men most capable of analyzing the qualities adapted to the station, and acting under circumstances favorable to deliberation, and to a judicious combination of all the reasons and inducements which were proper to govern their choice. A small number of persons, selected by their fellow-citizens from the general mass, will be most likely to possess the information and discernment requisite to such complicated investigations.

The title of "faithless elector" is a questionable one to begin with, given that Samuel Miles and many other faithless electors since[7] have tried their hardest to exercise their duty faithfully *as they saw it.* In the case of Samuel Miles and other 1796 electors, it's very hard to charge them with violating an unwritten norm of how electors are supposed to act, because *those norms hadn't yet been set by previous electors.* George Washington's election in 1788 and 1792 had been supported by electors from across the political spectrum.

Second, while the angry letter to the editor shows that some Federalist voters were angry with his choice, it is not evident that Samuel Miles had ever *promised* to vote for John Adams. His autobiography paints a very interesting picture of a man whose peers put him forward to office, sometimes over his own objections. When re-elected as mayor of Philadelphia, he refused the office. This would be unusual for a politician today, but in the era of George Washington, the visibly reluctant public servant was in fashion. It is plausible that the Federalists had simply decided to put Samuel Miles on the ballot, trusting that as a well-known member of their party, he would vote like a typical Federalist.

Third, Samuel Miles was not the only elector who cast his votes across or against party lines in that same election. While records of the 1796 election are incomplete, my best guess is that a total of 59 out of 138

---

[6] This is according to his own notes on the subject, dated to February 4th, 1802. See "Auto-Biographical Sketch of Samuel Miles" (1873).

[7] I would certainly include the Hamilton electors of the 2016 election that I interviewed.

electors voted across or against party lines, including one who voted for both Adams and Jefferson.[8] This count includes:

- One elector who voted for Adams and Jefferson.
- Five electors who voted for Adams and did not cast a second vote at all.
- Ten electors who voted for Jefferson and Pinckney, including Samuel Miles.
- Sixteen electors who voted for Adams and someone not on either party ticket.
- Twenty-seven electors who voted for Jefferson and someone not on either party ticket; fifteen of Virginia's electors voted as a group for Samuel Adams.

Samuel Miles can be credited as *among* the first faithless presidential electors, but if we call him that, we should acknowledge he was only one among dozens who broke with their party's official ticket in 1796. There's even a tenuous argument for dating the first unfaithful presidential electors to 1788.

Hamilton's plot

The biggest story of the 1796 election was about Alexander Hamilton, not Samuel Miles. Allegedly, Alexander Hamilton had plotted to elect Thomas Pinckney in place of John Adams; the news about Samuel Miles's vote was a local footnote for a handful of disappointed Pennsylvanian Federalists. While Hamilton denied the accusations, the expected results of his alleged efforts materialized: South Carolina's Federalist electors, appointed by the state legislature, voted as a unified slate for Thomas Jefferson and native son Thomas Pinckney.[9] Historians place Hamilton at the center of similar plots against Adams in 1788 (trying to ensure that Washington had a clear and large margin of victory) and 1800 (in favor of vice presidential candidate Charles Pinckney, Thomas Pinckney's brother).[10] Arguably, any Federalist swayed by Hamilton in 1788 could

---

[8]There was no record kept of which elector cast which votes in Virginia. There were twenty votes for Jefferson, one vote for Adams, one vote for Thomas Pinckney, and one vote for George Washington. Washington and Jefferson were both Virginian, so a Jefferson / Washington vote would have been illegal. Leven Powell, the lone Federalist elector, can be counted a friend of George Washington, as evidenced by their correspondence; his casting an Adams / Washington vote with another elector casting a Jefferson / Pinckney vote seems the most likely scenario to me. See in particular "A New Nation Votes: American Election Returns 1787-1825" (2007) by Phillip Lampi.

[9]See in particular "To Alexander Hamilton" (1796) by Stephen Higginson – whether or not the allegations are true is an interesting question.

[10]See *Alexander Hamilton* (2004) by Ron Chernow.

be counted as "faithless," which would set the date of the first faithless electors at 1788, rather than 1796.

Given that John Adams was particularly unpopular in the South, while Thomas Jefferson was admired by numerous key South Carolina politicians, it's entirely possible that South Carolina's electors would have made the same decision without any Hamiltonian influence.[11] However, since their votes were *anticipated*, northerners could, and did, vote differently. In response to rumors that some votes would be cast for Jefferson and Pinckney in southern and western states, other Federalist electors, particularly in New England, decided to vote against Thomas Pinckney. A total of twenty-two Federalist electors cast votes for Adams but not Pinckney.

The consequences were that John Adams became president – but Thomas Jefferson became vice president. Having the president's strongest political rival as vice president has some unfortunate consequences. First, the vice president, as part of the administration, has access to information and resources at the highest level and is in a position to sabotage the administration from within. Second, if the president dies in office, control of the White House disruptively shifts to a rival party, which provides a motive for assassination.[12]

It's worth noting that if Thomas Jefferson had won the presidential election, he would have had a Federalist vice president. Numerous Democratic-Republican electors declined to support Aaron Burr, who placed a distant fourth. In fifth place was Samuel Adams, courtesy of Virginia's electors. Had neither Adams nor Jefferson gotten a majority, all five of these candidates would have competed in a contingent election run by the House of Representatives.[13]

The election of 1796 was one where the results were only partially under the control of the intentional democratic process. Plots and counterplots controlled the day. With wild rumors flying, many electors unsure of how best to vote, questions over the legitimacy of Vermont's slate of electors, and narrow margins of victory, this election could have easily gone differently.

If rumors of forthcoming Pinckney / Jefferson votes in South Carolina hadn't spread so quickly, for example, Thomas Pinckney could very easily have been elected president in place of Adams or vice president in place of Jefferson. It is easy to construct plausible scenarios where any

---

[11] This argument can be found in "The South Carolina Federalists, II" (1909) by Ulrich Phillips, and echoed via citation in later sources.

[12] Given that eight presidents have died in office, four from assassination, this is not a trivial concern.

[13] The 12th Amendment later reduced the number of candidates in the contingent election process to three for president and two for vice president.

HAMILTON'S ELECTORAL COLLEGE (1788-1800)

one of the three leading candidates became president, and either of the other two became vice president. The course of the election depended largely on the decisions made by electors – not on the will of the voters or the state legislatures.

Another wrinkle in the process came from John Adams's role as the person in charge of counting the ballots. Public questions had been raised about the legitimacy of Vermont's electoral votes.[14]

Faithless electors today

Over time, political parties have become more effective at making sure that electors vote as directed. However, until quite recently, it was not clear that there is any legal way to prevent electors from voting however they wish to vote, even via state law. While no election since 1796 has been decided by faithless electors, the threat that it might happen again has been present in every closely contested presidential election.

Surveys of recent presidential electors conducted by political scientist Robert Alexander show that a surprisingly large number of electors have seriously considered voting unexpectedly. Moreover, when electors either consider breaking ranks or actually break ranks, they frequently do so in groups. The election of 1796 was not the only time that multiple electors from the same state coordinated their decisions together.[15]

More than half of all states have laws on the books which require that state's electors vote as pledged, penalizing electors either with a fine or by summarily removing them from office and retroactively erasing their vote. The constitutionality of these laws has been recently upheld,[16] and it is likely that no presidential election will be decided by electors' discretion until and unless a winning candidate dies at an inconvenient time.[17] Previously, courts decided[18] that states can force electors to make a pledge to vote for a particular candidate as a pre-condition for serving in office.

The problem posed by electors making independent decisions should pose a real dilemma for anyone supporting the Electoral College system. If states compel electors' votes in addition to controlling their methods of appointment, all of the reasons Hamilton and others gave for supporting

---

[14] See "Thomas Jefferson Counts Himself into the Presidency" (2004) by Brian Ackerman and David Fontana.
[15] In particular, see the elections of 1836, 1872, and 2016.
[16] *Chiafalo v. Washington*, 2020
[17] After electors are chosen, but before electors vote.
[18] *Ray v. Blair* (1952).

an indirect form of election are null and void. There is no need for deliberation or discernment for an elector who votes only as directed.

If states do not compel electors, then we run a constant risk of having an election decided by intrigue. Even among those scholars who support the existing Electoral College system, there has been strong support for reforming the Electoral College system in order to make electoral votes automatic.[19]

1800: A tied election

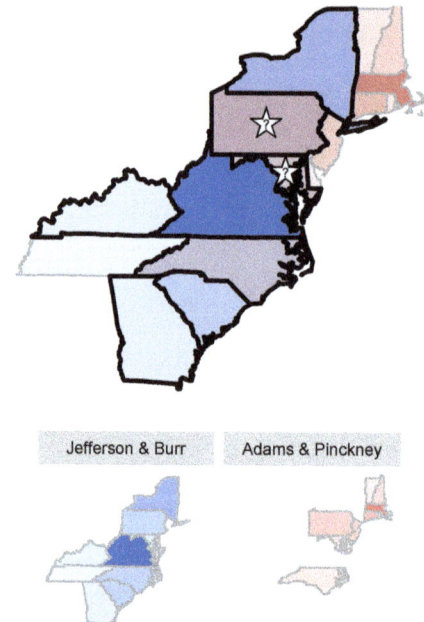

Figure 7: The 1800 presidential election.

Electoral vote: 73-73-65-64-1
Pivotal state: Pennsylvania or Maryland
Critical states: All Jefferson / Burr states except Tennessee
Crucial state: Pennsylvania or Maryland

---

[19] C.f. Judith Best in *The Case Against Direct Election of the President: A Defense of the Electoral College* (1975) and *The Choice of the People?: Debating the Electoral College* (1996). Not that this is universal; Tara Ross in "The Indispensable Electoral College" (2017) stakes out a position opposed to even that reform, expressing trust that electors will only violate their pledges for good unusual reasons such as the sudden death of a candidate, rather than bad unusual reasons.

HAMILTON'S ELECTORAL COLLEGE (1788-1800)

The 1800 rematch between John Adams and Thomas Jefferson was a close election, much like their first contest in 1796. It is worth noting that without the extra electors from the slave populations of the states supporting Jefferson, Adams would have won. This was also the peak of state legislature power; ten out of sixteen state legislatures appointed electors directly. John Adams won by popular vote in only one state: Rhode Island.

The result in the Electoral College was an exact tie, with 73 electoral votes cast for each of Thomas Jefferson and Aaron Burr; every Democratic-Republican elector cast a vote for both their presidential and vice presidential candidate.

The deadlocked house

Because both Jefferson and his running mate Aaron Burr received 73 electoral votes, the House of Representatives had to break the tie between them, which took 36 ballots. This was the last election before the 12th Amendment was passed.

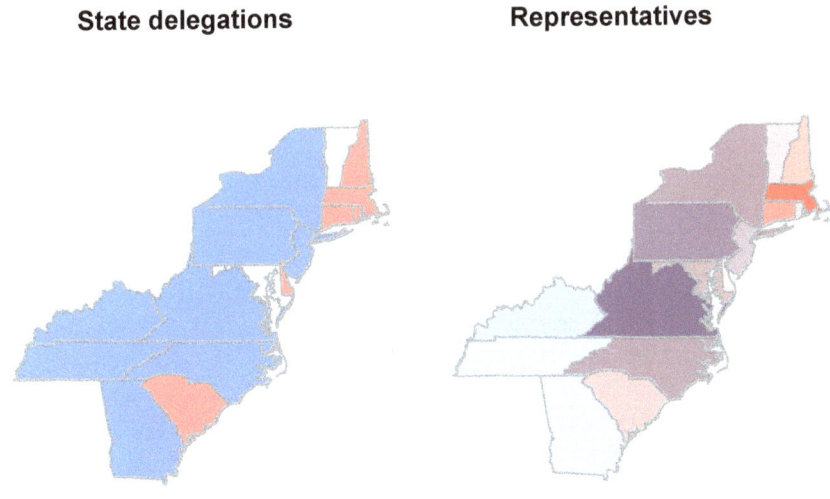

Figure 8: The 1800 House contingent election. Votes backing Burr came mainly from Federalists, marked in red; votes for Jefferson are marked in blue. The two pivotal states that initially deadlocked and later voted for Jefferson are marked in white.

The presidential election of 1800 was not simply a close election, but also one of the most frustrating presidential elections that ever occurred – for reasons other than the closeness of the contest. After the votes were tallied, it was clear that Thomas Jefferson's Democratic-Republican Party had won a narrow majority.

Unlike in the election of 1796, however, in which many presidential electors voted against one or both of their party's nominees, only one presidential elector cast a distinct vote,[20] and it was not one of the Democratic-Republican electors. Thus, all of the electors who had voted for Thomas Jefferson also voted for Aaron Burr; this meant that both Jefferson and Burr were tied with 73 votes each.

This meant that the 1800 election had to be resolved by a contingent election in the House of Representatives in 1801. While Democratic-Republicans had just won a clear majority of seats in the House in the Congressional elections that took place around the same time, the 8th Congress with its newly minted Democratic-Republican majority would not convene until March. The ballots of the Electoral College were officially unsealed and counted on February 11th, which meant that the election was carried out by the outgoing House – Federalists held 60 out of 106 seats.

The nature of the contingent election depended on another small technical wrinkle. If no candidate had a majority of the vote, the House would choose between the top five candidates; if two or three candidates were tied with majority support, the House would choose between those two or three candidates. Although Jefferson had been widely reported as the winner of Georgia's electoral votes, the actual documentation of Georgia's electoral votes was irregular.[21]

If those votes were discounted as irregular, with Georgia's electors having therefore effectively abstained by casting invalid ballots, Jefferson would have only had confirmed votes from 69 out of 138 electors, just shy of a majority; in that case, the procedure would arguably have been for the Federalist House of Representatives to choose between the top five candidates – Thomas Jefferson, Aaron Burr, John Adams, Charles C. Pinckney, and John Jay. It is not clear who would have eventually won a contingent election in this case. As a Federalist from the South with the backing of Alexander Hamilton, Pinckney was well-positioned to emerge as a compromise candidate. The first ballot would likely have been deadlocked, with eight states voting for a Federalist, seven voting for a Democratic-Republican, and Vermont

---

[20]This was not a faithless vote. The Federalists had planned this in order to avoid having their presidential and vice presidential candidates tied.

[21]See "Thomas Jefferson Counts Himself into the Presidency" (2004) by Brian Ackerman and David Fontana for details.

abstaining as its two representatives deadlocked 1-1.[22] As the outgoing vice president, Thomas Jefferson was in charge of reading out the results of the Electoral College; he chose to treat Georgia's votes as valid in spite of the documentary irregularity, a decision that went unchallenged.

A tie between two majority Democratic-Republican candidates meant that Federalists in the House were in the unpalatable position of deciding between two candidates from their opposition. Most, though not all, decided to vote against Jefferson. The House promptly deadlocked for 35 straight ballots, finally selecting Jefferson on the 36th ballot. Alexander Hamilton is frequently credited with resolving the deadlock.[23]

A tied vote between the top two candidates may seem like an unlikely possibility, but under the rules of the House contingent election, a deadlocked ballot is not unusual. The contingent election is carried out under the old "one state delegation, one vote" rule that had been used in the Continental Congress under the Articles of Confederation, and the winner must have the support of a majority of state delegations. So, if a state has two representatives, and those two representatives vote for different candidates, the state is treated as having abstained.

The Democratic-Republicans controlled majorities in seven state delegations; adding in the vote from the lone representative present from Georgia, Jefferson led by eight states to six states on the first thirty-five ballots. He also had the support of fifty-five representatives on the first ballot, a majority of the members of the House. However, while eight out of fourteen states would be a majority, there were sixteen states in total. Vermont, with two representatives, was tied 1-1; Maryland, with eight representatives, was tied 4-4. On the thirty-sixth ballot, the Federalist representatives who had voted for Burr in those two states personally abstained, which allowed the Democratic-Republican representatives to cast those two states' votes for Jefferson.

This contingent election had three very alarming features. First, under the rules of the process, it was very easy for the House to deadlock. Second, it placed the power to resolve the election in the hands of the losing party. Third, it could easily put the presidency in the hands of someone who was the chosen candidate of neither major party – a risk that worried both the Federalists and the Democratic-Republicans.

---

[22] Brian Ackerman and David Fontana in "Thomas Jefferson Counts Himself into the Presidency" (2004) more or less arrive at the same conclusion.
[23] Not coincidentally, Hamilton was killed in a duel with Burr three years later, in 1804.

The Hamiltonian problem

Considering that Federalist legislators ultimately decided the election, why would the close results of the 1800 race worry the Federalists? I believe that the short answer to that question is *because of Alexander Hamilton*.

Earlier in the election process, Alexander Hamilton had once again tried to undermine John Adams, incumbent Federalist president and the choice of the majority of the party, supporting vice presidential Charles C. Pinckney instead. We discussed the previous two episodes earlier in this chapter; this was the third time that Hamilton tried to undermine Adams, twice in favor of a Pinckney.[24] If Hamilton had either convinced two Democratic-Republican electors to vote for Pinckney or two Federalist electors to refrain from voting for John Adams, the Federalist vice-presidential candidate would have had more electoral votes than their presidential candidate.

This was only the second contested election for president, and in three out of four cases, a major party's intended vice presidential candidate had threatened to get more votes than their presidential candidate. The election of 1800 also revealed how painfully difficult a House contingency election could be with a two-party system: Unless one party had an overwhelming majority, a deadlocked House would be likely, leaving the government unable to function. And what would happen if the House never chose a president?

Something had to be done to prevent the newly-developed two-party system from causing a constitutional crisis, and that something was the 12th Amendment.

---

[24] Charles Pinckney was the older brother of Thomas Pinckney.

CHAPTER 4

Jefferson's Electoral College (1804-1824)

In the first four presidential elections from 1788 to 1800, the rules used to choose electors varied wildly and there was no difference between presidential candidates and vice presidential candidates. This proved an issue with significant consequences in both 1796 and 1800 as the Federalists and Democratic-Republicans grappled with trying to control who would become president. The system was clearly broken, and needed fixing.

The 12th Amendment

The presidential election procedure changed dramatically with the passage of the 12th Amendment, the longest and arguably most complex amendment to the Constitution. This created a permanent structural change of four features of the presidential election system.

First, it separated the election of the president and the vice president. This addressed the concern raised by Hamilton's attempts to undermine Adams; in the original version of the Electoral College, a small handful of electors could reverse a party's ticket, as could have easily happened in both 1796 and 1800.

Second, it gave a deadline for the House contingent election process. If the House could not elect a president before March 4th, then the vice president would serve as president. This put a deadline on the House contingent election process, limiting the possibilities for a major constitutional crisis caused by a deadlock.

Third, it reduced the number of candidates who were eligible for election to the presidency by the House of Representatives – from five to three. The impact and importance of this change are easily underrated by modern readers living in a time with a strong and stable two-party system; it would be of critical importance in the election of 1824.

Fourth, it increased the role the Senate was expected to play. Previously, the vice president had been chosen automatically; after determining the president, the remaining candidate with the most electoral votes automatically became vice president. The Senate's responsibility was limited to the rare case of breaking exact ties between a second and third-place candidate. The separate election for vice president included a contingent election process in the Senate, with each senator having a vote. However, unlike the House, the Senate would only be allowed to consider the top two candidates.

The third change may have been the most controversial. As we discussed earlier, small state delegates, particularly Roger Sherman of Connecticut, only agreed to the Electoral College because they expected the Electoral College to serve as a nominating body, with most elections decided in the House of Representatives. If the House could only decide between the top three candidates, this would make it much more difficult for a small-state candidate to become president, and limit the power of the House in the presidential election process.

The topic of how many candidates the House should be allowed to consider was a heated debate at the Constitutional Convention. Five was the lowest number that small state delegates were willing to accept; three was unacceptable to Roger Sherman, as it would ensure that the Electoral College would only nominate candidates from the largest states. Opposition to the 12th Amendment was concentrated among Federalists and in small states, and the amendment barely reached the required two-thirds majority in the Senate.[1] Three states rejected the 12th Amendment in 1804 during the original ratification process – Delaware, Connecticut, and Massachusetts.

Not coincidentally, the Connecticut and Delaware delegations to the Constitutional Convention had included the most vocal supporters of small states; it is easy to see the incentive for both states to block changes that reduced the power of small states. Massachusetts, however, was a larger state, and its favorite presidential candidate John Adams had

---

[1] For a more detailed account, see *Why Do We Still Have the Electoral College?* (2020) by Alexander Keyssar.

placed second or third in the Electoral College in every election thus far. In what way was rejecting the 12th Amendment in the interests of the state of Massachusetts?

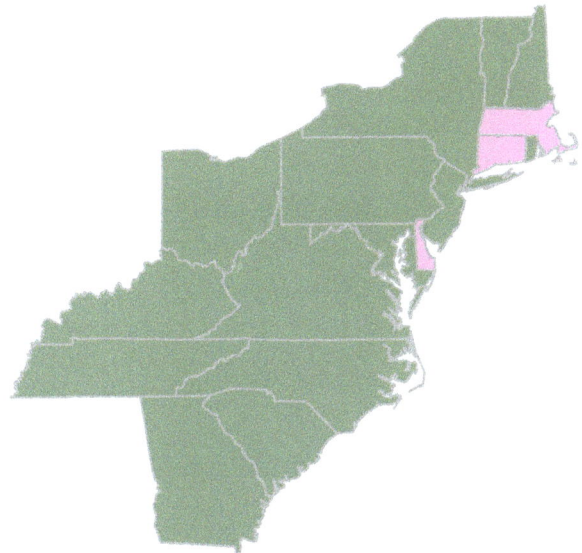

Figure 9: 12th Amendment ratification vote by state in 1804. States voting against are marked in magenta.

In the original Constitutional allocation of electoral votes prior to the first census, Massachusetts was one of the three large states given ten electoral votes. Massachusetts both had a large population, and a significant quantity of frontier territory in which to expand its population further.[2] New York had experienced much more rapid population growth, and now the three most populous states were Virginia, Pennsylvania, and New York. If each state fielded its own candidate and the largest three states' candidates were nominated, Massachusetts could expect to be shut out in the future – and the entire region of New England, with multiple small states and closely aligned interests, had less power in the Electoral College than in a House contingent election.

If two other New England states had rejected the 12th Amendment on similar grounds, it would not have been ratified, even though it addressed several clear problems with the system. Some New Englanders would later offer objections to adding states west of the Mississippi on the grounds that it would dilute the political power of the older states.[3] New

---

[2] Massachusetts's northern territory of Maine became an independent state in 1820.
[3] Among other places, this is documented in *Mr. Buchanan's Administration on the Eve of the Rebellion* (1866) by James Buchanan as part of an argument in defense of Southern

England had a set of common cultural and economic interests that were not shared by either the South or the new Western states.

After the passage of the 12th Amendment, there was significant support for mandating that states use the same methods for selecting electors, particularly a district-based system. Proposed amendments on the topic failed narrowly numerous times from 1813-1822, with significant opposition from representatives from large states.[4]

A string of victories for the Jeffersonians

Following the passage of the 12th Amendment, the potential for devious electoral plots was significantly reduced, since it was no longer possible for a vice presidential candidate to be elected as president. Alexander Hamilton's death may have also been a factor.

From 1804 to 1824, many states' electoral colleges were selected by rules that changed significantly from election to election; Federalists and Democratic-Republicans both routinely changed the laws in their own favor. The Democratic-Republicans remained the dominant political force throughout this period, with the Federalists in the minority. Jefferson won re-election easily, and his next two chosen successors won four more terms. Only one of these elections was close - the election of 1812.

Both the first party system and the second version of the Electoral College would come to a halt due to the realignments associated with the election of 1824.

---

secession.

[4]See in particular Chapter 2 of *Why Do We Still Have the Electoral College?* (2020) by Alexander Keyssar for an extensive account of this.

JEFFERSON'S ELECTORAL COLLEGE (1804-1824)

The 1804 election

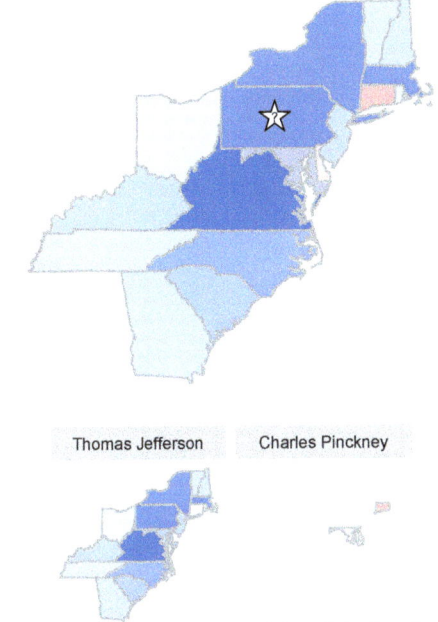

Figure 10: The 1804 presidential election.

Electoral vote: 162-14
Pivotal state: Unclear
Critical states: None

In 1804, the Federalists fielded Charles Pinckney against Thomas Jefferson, a popular incumbent president. There was also a shift towards the use of a popular vote: Unlike the previous four presidential elections, a clear majority of states chose electors by popular vote, either by district or across the whole state. The result was a landslide election in Jefferson's favor.

While Pennsylvania is the most likely pivotal state throughout this period, it is very difficult to be sure due to three key facts. First, as with many other elections in this period, the use of a popular vote was far from universal. Second, unlike John Adams before him or DeWitt Clinton afterward, Pinckney was from South Carolina and in favor of slavery. Since neither of Charles Pinckney's bids for the presidency came close to succeeding and the geography of his support was very different from the closer Adams-Jefferson contests, it is difficult to identify which states were closest to the national median.

The 1808 election

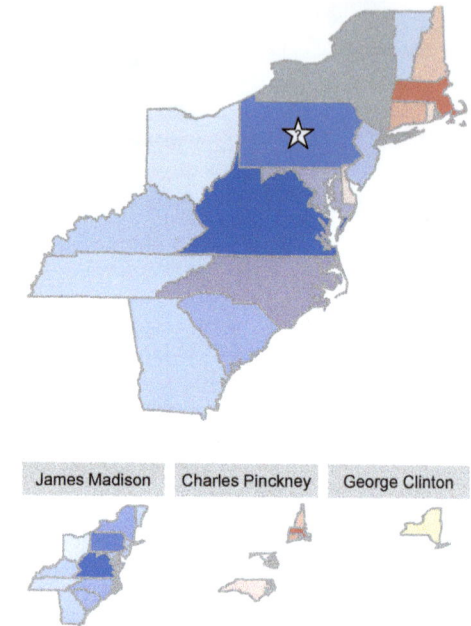

Figure 11: The 1808 presidential election.

Electoral vote: 122-47-6
Pivotal state: Unclear
Critical states: None

Federalists renominated Charles Pinckney; Democratic-Republicans nominated Thomas Jefferson's chosen successor and fellow Virginian, James Madison. This was closer than the 1804 election, but still not particularly close. George Clinton also earned six electoral votes in his home state of New York, which did not hold a popular vote. As in 1804, it is difficult to identify a pivotal state in this election, because the closer Federalist elections involved candidates from the northern part of the country.

The 1812 election

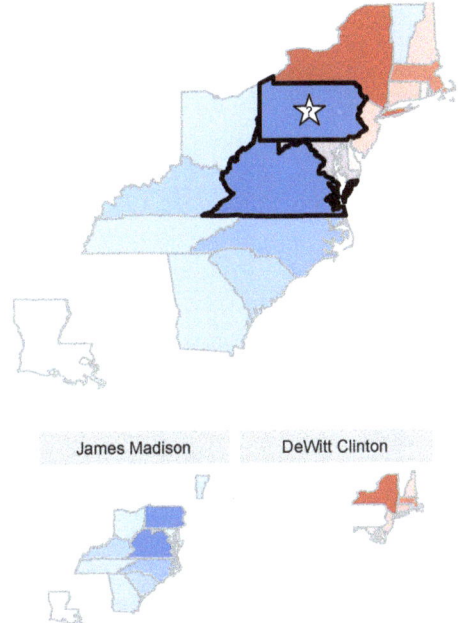

Figure 12: The 1812 presidential election.

Electoral vote: 128-89
Pivotal state: Likely Pennsylvania
Critical states: Pennsylvania, Virginia

This election pitted incumbent James Madison against DeWitt Clinton. It seems reasonable to identify Pennsylvania as the pivotal state in this election even though the popular vote in Pennsylvania was not particularly close by modern standards; Pennsylvania was also a critical state in this election. Other possibilities include Maryland, Vermont, and New Jersey.

An interesting feature of this election is that Clinton was not a Federalist; he was a Democratic-Republican who many Federalists endorsed as a challenger to the incumbent Democratic-Republican president. This makes the political structure of this race particularly complex.

The 1816 election

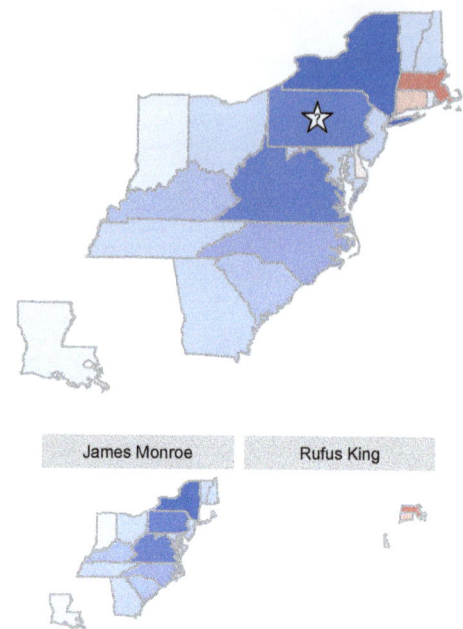

Figure 13: The 1816 presidential election.

Electoral vote: 183-34
Pivotal state: Likely Pennsylvania
Critical states: None

This election was the final attempt of the Federalist Party to run a presidential candidate. With the support of both Thomas Jefferson and James Madison, James Monroe was nominated as the Democratic-Republican candidate. James Monroe won in a landslide over Federalist Rufus King, who even lost his home state of New York (though carrying his birth state of Massachusetts). It is difficult to identify a pivotal state in this election; considering the geography of Rufus King's limited support, the Adams elections, and the central role of Pennsylvania in this era, it could easily have been Pennsylvania.

The 1820 election

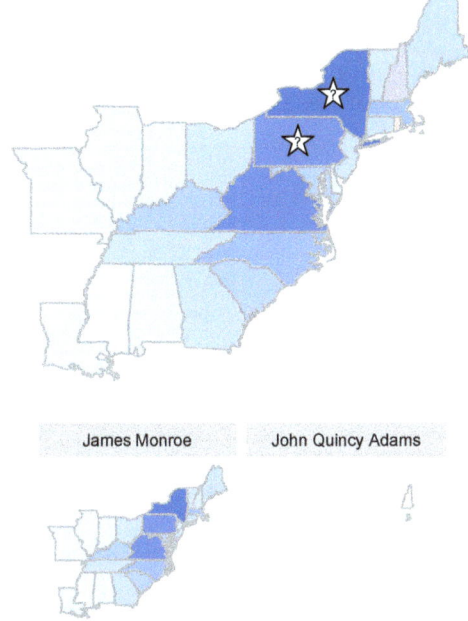

Figure 14: The 1820 presidential election.

Electoral vote: 238-1
Pivotal state: Unclear
Critical states: None

Democratic-Republican James Monroe ran essentially unopposed for re-election. It's worth noting that some Federalist electors were elected to the Electoral College, but almost all of them voted for James Monroe anyway. One lone elector chose to vote for John Quincy Adams; fourteen voted for various Federalist candidates for vice president. As a nearly unanimous election, it is difficult to identify a pivotal state, but it's likely that either Pennsylvania or New York was at the national political median.

The end of the transitional Electoral College system

The election of 1824 was arguably the most unusual presidential election in all of American history. In spite of the fact that the 12th Amendment had radically changed the operation of the Electoral College system, the election of 1824 was also the single election closest to the original vision the Framers had in mind when they designed the presidential election system.

One of the parallels to the Framers' original vision: Existing political parties weren't a factor. Every candidate ran as a Democratic-Republican, which made the label completely meaningless. A new party system would, however, form in the wake of the election – Adams's faction became briefly known as the National Republicans. Following Jackson's eventual 1828 victory, his faction would become known as the Democrats, and the anti-Jacksonian opposition coalition became the Whig Party.

Another feature of the election anticipated in the Framers' original vision: After all, as George Mason had expected to happen "nineteen out of twenty" times,[5] no single candidate received a majority in the Electoral College, which left the result up to the House of Representatives. The Electoral College functioned as a nominating body, with the House of Representatives choosing the ultimate winner.

As many Framers expected, while the Electoral College result depended on large states, the House contingent election process went according to the desires of small-state representatives. In spite of numerous other close calls,[6] the actual frequency of this type of election has been one out of fifty-nine, nowhere close to nineteen out of twenty. The election of 1824 has - so far - been the only occasion where no candidate received a majority in the Electoral College.

---

[5]Tuesday, September 4th. See *The Records of the Federal Convention of 1787* (1911).

[6]Notably, the election of 1800, with a tiebreaker contingency election between two majority winners, as well as the close elections of 1796, 1860, 1876, 1948, 1960, 1968, and 2000.

JEFFERSON'S ELECTORAL COLLEGE (1804-1824)

The election of 1824

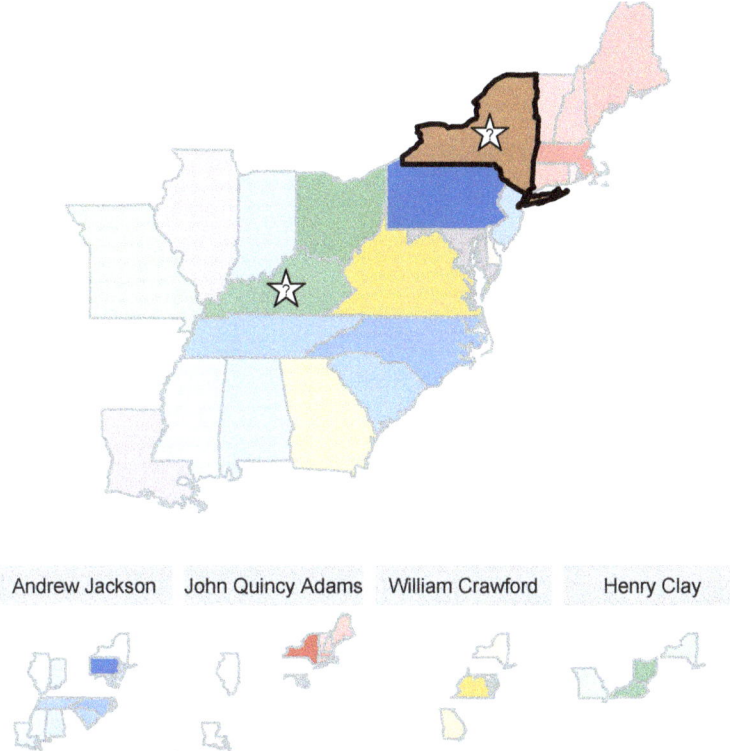

Figure 15: The 1824 presidential election.

Electoral vote: 99-84-41-37
Popular vote: 41%-31%-11%-13%
Pivotal state: Kentucky or New York
Critical state: New York

There were initially five major presidential candidates, all of which ran under the banner of the Democratic-Republican Party: Andrew Jackson, John Quincy Adams, Henry Clay, William Crawford, and John C. Calhoun. Calhoun dropped out to run for vice president. He successfully positioned himself as the running mate of both Adams and Jackson, handily winning a majority in the Electoral College.

Under the old rules, this would have been a successful enough vice presidential candidacy to win him the presidency. Two of the remaining four major presidential candidates – Henry Clay and Andrew Jackson – received scattered vice presidential votes, in spite of the fact that the 12th Amendment had separated the votes for president and vice president.

New York was critical; Jackson could have won a majority in the Electoral College if he had won New York's electoral votes. Determining whether or not New York was also pivotal is unclear, because New York's state legislature appointed the state's electors. In terms of the popular vote, another possible route for Jacksonian victory was through the states of Kentucky, Ohio, and Maryland, with Kentucky occupying an apparent pivotal position between Jacksonian and anti-Jacksonian factions.

The rapid changes of 1824

The election of 1824 marked a transition point in the party system, a transition point in how the Electoral College was conducted, and a remarkably difficult election. It was also the second-to-last election in which the results depended on states using rules other than a winner-take-all plurality. While the constitutional rules governing the mechanics of the Electoral College have not changed since 1804, the state-level reforms carried out in the wake of the 1824 election created the modern version of the Electoral College system.

While the election of 1824 was closer to the Framers' original vision of how the Electoral College was supposed to operate, the reforms caused by the 12th Amendment played a very important role in 1824, for two reasons. First, the separation of votes for president and vice president was critical. Calhoun's performance as a vice presidential candidate would have earned him the presidency under the old rules. Second, the reduction of the scope of the House contingent election from the top five candidates to the top three candidates eliminated a key major candidate: Henry Clay.

At the time, Henry Clay was the Speaker of the House, positioning him uniquely well to influence negotiations during a House contingent election. However, Clay narrowly placed fourth in the Electoral College, with 37 votes to Crawford's 41. Clay could (and did) exercise a decisive role in the subsequent political negotiations, but he could not negotiate himself into the presidency.

I can give three reasons why Clay was the most natural compromise candidate in political terms: First, Clay earned 13% of the popular vote to Crawford's 11%; his support was broader than Crawford's. Crawford earned more electoral votes because his support was more narrowly concentrated.[7] Second, Clay was a slave-owner in favor of eventually ending slavery who came from a border state (Kentucky), placing him in an unusual centrist position on the geographically divisive issue of

---

[7]This may not seem intuitive, but we'll see more examples of broad support being worse than narrow support in Chapters 6 through 10.

slavery. Third, his subsequent political career showed a lot of effective coalition-building.

Unable to rally support for himself in the contingent election, Clay eventually backed Adams. The degree to which Clay's support was essential to Adams's victory in the contingent election is open to some debate. However, given that Adams won by an exceptionally narrow margin, it seems very unlikely that Adams would have been able to easily put together a majority without Clay's support, and there is documentary evidence in Adams's memoirs suggesting that the two of them communicated some about the matter.[8]

With Clay's support, Adams won in the first round of voting by an exceptionally narrow majority. He won thirteen out of twenty-four delegations, five of them by the margin of a single representative's vote (including four small states and New York). This added up to a total of only 87 out of 212 representatives, with 24 of those representatives being individually critical to Adams's victory.

There is an interesting story about one of those critical representatives. According to Martin Van Buren's autobiography,[9] New York representative Stephen Van Rensselaer originally intended to vote for Crawford. Henry Clay and Daniel Webster had worked hard to convince him, and as a deeply religious man, he felt the need to pray for guidance to be sure his vote for Crawford was the correct choice. While doing so, he spotted a piece of paper with John Quincy Adams's name written on it. He took this as divine guidance, picked up the piece of paper, and slipped it into the ballot box as his vote. Adams won the support of the New York delegation by the narrowest possible margin, with 18 out of 34 votes.

There were 23 other representatives who, if they had individually voted against Adams, would have prevented his victory on the first ballot. It's not clear if any of them voted for reasons as unusual as Van Rensselaer's, but Adams's victory in the contingent election was by an extremely narrow margin with minority support. The structure of support for Adams was very similar to what would have happened in the Electoral College by combining Clay's support with Adams's support.

Adams then appointed Clay to the position of Secretary of State, the highest appointed office within the executive branch. Jackson and his supporters were incensed about the quid pro quo, calling it a "corrupt bargain." This was a critical point in the development of the

---

[8]See quite specifically p. 368-369 of *The Life of Andrew Jackson* (1911) by John Basset. For the opposing view arguing that Adams's victory was independent of Clay's support, see "The Spatial Theory of Voting and the Presidential Election of 1824" (1998) by Jeffrey Jenkins.

[9]This is discussed in *The Life of Andrew Jackson* (1911) by John Basset.

JEFFERSON'S ELECTORAL COLLEGE (1804-1824)

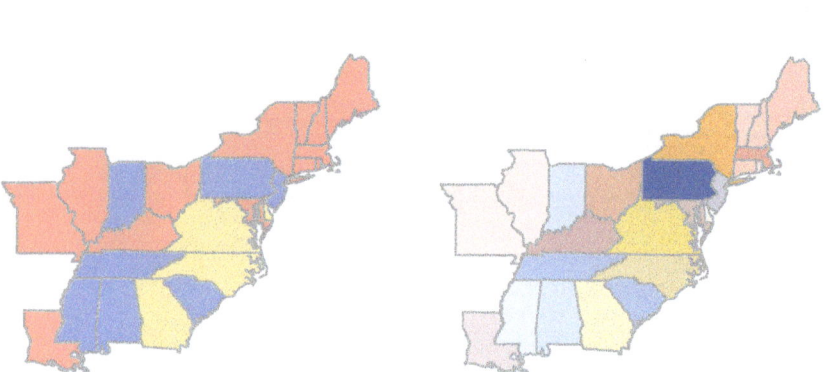

Figure 16: The 1824 House contingent election. Blue marks support for Jackson, red marks support for Adams, gold marks support for Calhoun.

Electoral College; if the 1824 election had unfolded differently, the Electoral College system would have likely changed differently. After his subsequent victory, Jackson pushed for reforms of the presidential election system in order to limit the ability of members of Congress to engage in *quid pro quo* trades of contingent election support in exchange for Cabinet appointments. He also pushed for the abolition of the Electoral College system and for presidential term limits.[10]

Alternate possibilities

The election of 1824 was a highly chaotic one because of the split of the Democratic-Republicans, and the Electoral College system made it even more chaotic. In a national plurality vote, the results would have been predictable: Jackson would have become president. Under the Electoral College system, small changes in the process of the election could have resulted in dramatically different consequences. Any of the five major candidates could have become president – including Calhoun, who had dropped out of the race for president in order to run for vice president!

---

[10]See in particular Jackson's 1831 annual address to Congress, recorded in "Register of Debates in Congress" (1832). Unusually, Jackson proposed limiting presidents to a single term in office.

To begin with, if New York had changed over to a winner-take-all vote in 1824 instead of 1832, or if one of the losing candidates had dropped out, Jackson could have won an outright majority in the Electoral College.

If Clay had been in third place in the electoral vote rather than a narrow fourth place, he might have been able to emerge from the contingent election victorious as a compromise candidate. He was the Speaker of the House and very well-respected by his colleagues in the House. For similar reasons, if Clay had decided to back Jackson or Crawford in the contingent election instead of Adams, he might have been able to deliver the presidency to either one of them.

If Adams had not won narrowly on the first ballot, almost anything could have happened on subsequent ballots, depending on how political negotiations between the different factions played out, up to and including a victory by Crawford. Even an Adams victory following multiple ballots and substantial open political negotiations between the different factions in the House might have had different consequences.

With more forewarning, the result might not have been as much of a shock, and it might not have galvanized reform efforts in the same way. If Adams hadn't subsequently appointed Clay to the position of secretary of state, Jackson might have accepted the result with more complacency and less animosity; it was the perception of a *quid pro quo* exchange that led to claims that Adams and Clay had made a "corrupt bargain."

Even Calhoun could have become president. While the 12th Amendment separated the election of the president and vice president, it also put a deadline on the House contingent election process. If the House deadlocked with no candidate reaching the required thirteen-state majority, Calhoun would have automatically become president on March 4th by default. Calhoun was an outspoken pro-slavery radical, with very distinct political views; it's unclear what sort of impact he would have had as president.

The election of Adams by the House was the sort of result envisioned by the Framers when they designed the House contingent election. The contingent election was where small states were expected to exercise disproportionate influence, and it was small state delegations that formed the spine of Adams's support in the House. However, this was no longer a nation where the democratic process was novel and experimental; the people wanted a say in how the president was elected. This provided the impetus for a major change in how the Electoral College worked.

CHAPTER 5

Jackson's Electoral College (1828-1852)

Jackson wanted to eliminate the Electoral College system entirely, but failed to do so. However, the Jacksonian era saw reforms at the state level that amounted to a complete redesign of the presidential election system. Under pressure from Jacksonian reformers, states shifted from using a variety of methods to the evolved system of a winner-take-all popular vote - a system known as the *unit rule*. In 1824, only twelve out of twenty-four states used a winner-take-all vote.

Four years later, there were only two states where electors were chosen directly by the state legislature, and eighteen out of twenty-four states used a winner-take-all vote. Jackson won handily. In 1832, when Jackson ran for re-election, only Maryland still used a district system, and only South Carolina's state legislature still reserved the power of appointing presidential electors to itself. From 1836 to 1860, South Carolina was the only state that did not use the unit rule.

The Jacksonian shift in the democratic process also involved steadily eliminating property requirements; the last state to eliminate property requirements was North Carolina in 1856. The result of these two sets of reforms was a dramatic increase in how many people had a say in presidential elections. In 1820, before Andrew Jackson launched his political career, barely over 1% of the population voted in presidential elections; by the time of Jackson's death in 1845, nearly 15% of the population voted in presidential elections. The sheer magnitude of this shift is difficult to overemphasize.

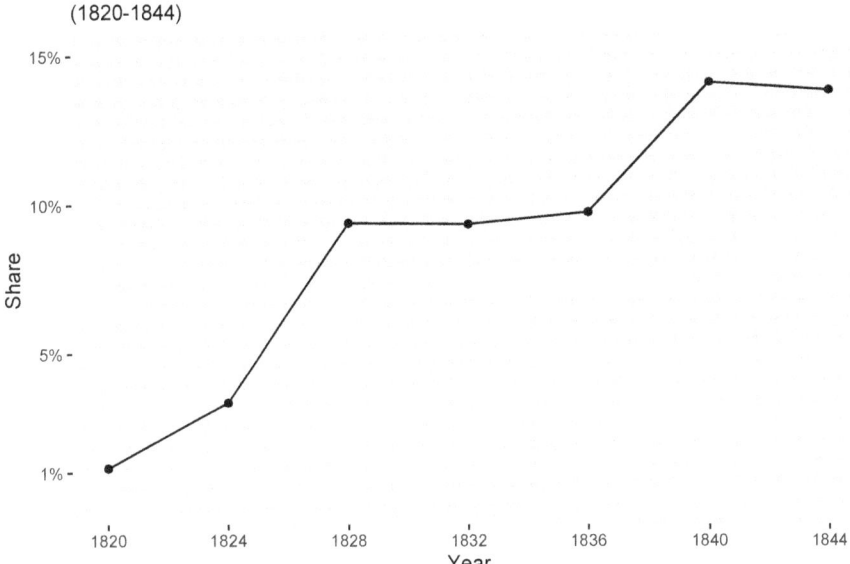

Figure 17: Share of the United States population voting in presidential elections 1820-1844.

From 1828 to today, there has only been one presidential election, that of 1876, in which electors chosen by state legislatures were potentially critical; and no presidential elections in which states dividing their electoral votes by district has changed the winner. State legislatures used to routinely change the method of choosing electors based on perceived partisan advantages in the next presidential election; they no longer do so. From 1828 to the present, the unit rule has dominated the Electoral College system. The Jacksonian branch of the Democratic-Republican Party became known simply as the Democrats.

This marked the beginning, in other words, of something recognizable as the evolved presidential election system, one in which the rules of the game have been fixed by tradition rather than constitutional law. However, the modern system is fragile: While tradition and game-theoretic incentives present strong obstacles to any change, there are no legal or constitutional obstacles that prevent state legislatures from taking power back. We could at any time return to the older style of the Electoral College where state legislatures routinely change how the presidential election system works based on short-term partisan advantage.

This is not to say that the evolved system functions *well*. It functions particularly poorly with three or more candidates, which was not unusual in this period. The Democrats faced a more fragmented opposition until 1860 when it became the Democratic Party's turn to fracture. In 1828, 1840, and 1852, the election was effectively a two-candidate election; however, in every other election from 1828 to 1860, there was at least one other candidate who either earned electoral votes or acted as a likely spoiler. The modern Electoral College system is not well-designed to handle multi-candidate elections. Electoral difficulties reached an acute peak in 1860 with four major candidates - the result of the 1860 election being, infamously, a civil war.

Jackson's elections

Under a presidential election system heavily impacted by Jacksonian reforms, Andrew Jackson was easily able to win two terms in office. He did not have enough political capital to completely eliminate the Electoral College.

The 1828 election

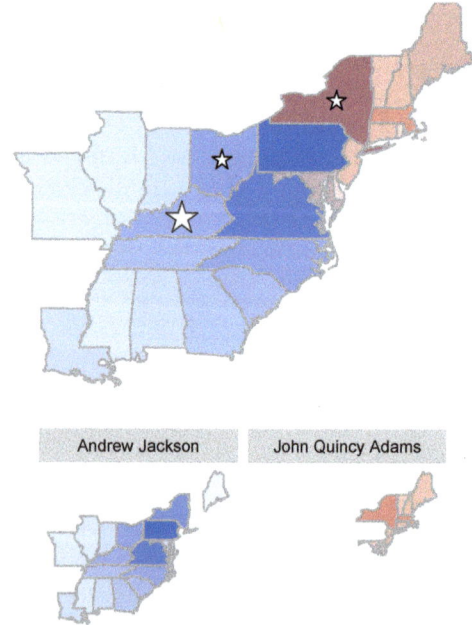

Figure 18: The 1828 presidential election.

Electoral vote: 178-83
Popular vote: 56%-44%

JACKSON'S ELECTORAL COLLEGE (1828-1852)

Pivotal state: Kentucky
Critical states: None
Crucial states: Kentucky, Ohio, New York

The 1828 election was a rematch between incumbent John Quincy Adams and Andrew Jackson, the candidate who had won the most votes in the previous election. Adams had placed second in both the popular vote and Electoral College in 1824, changes in the rules for how electors were chosen favored Jackson, and there were no other candidates in play. Jackson won by a large margin.

A few states still used alternate methods of selecting electors, notably New York; however, this would be the last election in which methods other than the unit rule played a significant role.

The 1832 election

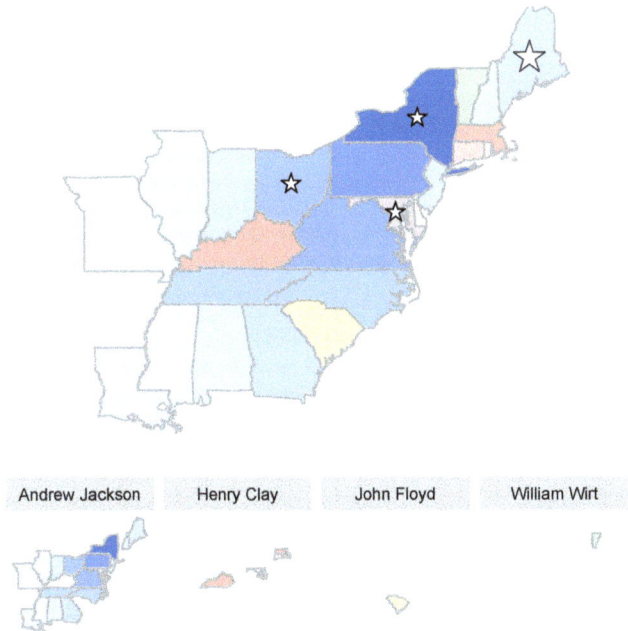

Figure 19: The 1832 presidential election.

Electoral vote: 288-49-11-7
Popular vote: 55%-37%-8%
Pivotal state: Maine
Critical states: None
Crucial states: Maine, New York, Ohio, New Jersey

Incumbent Democrat Andrew Jackson faced off against one of his other 1824 opponents, National Republican Henry Clay, with two minor-party candidates winning one state each. The electors appointed by South Carolina's state legislature backed Nullifier John Floyd as part of a major political crisis involving threats of secession.[1] Anti-Masonic William Wirt, who was on the ballot in nine states, won a narrow 41% plurality in Vermont. Notably, he also won 42% of the vote in Pennsylvania, where Henry Clay was not on the ballot. The clear regional patterns of 1828 were not as clear in 1832, likely because Clay was a slave owner from Kentucky, while John Quincy Adams had been an abolitionist from Massachusetts. Clay's more moderate position on slavery left the issue muddy.

The pivotal state in this election was Maine; in order to block Jackson from winning a majority in the Electoral College, Clay would have needed to win not only Maine, but also New York, Ohio, and New Jersey. Clay had almost no support in the deep South, winning five votes in Alabama in a remarkable 99.97%-0.03% loss - one of the most lopsided victories on record involving a non-zero number of dissenting ballots.

The 1836-1840 elections and a regional strategy

The short-lived National Republican Party disintegrated after 1832. The main anti-Jacksonian faction became known as the *Whigs*. The first two presidential elections with Whig candidates featured a number of key similarities: Both featured Martin Van Buren (Jackson's designated successor) and William Henry Harrison. The first two Whig elections showed a test of a very interesting strategy, even if it was likely the result of their low level of organization as a group rather than a planned strategy: During the first election, other Whigs ran for president alongside William Henry Harrison.

For various reasons, the Whigs ultimately would prove a short-lived political party, lasting only for five presidential election cycles. In theory, multiple regional candidates might get more votes than a single national candidate; but what the elections of 1836 and 1840 suggest is that if they all run under the same banner, instead of running against each other, the voters are unlikely to see them as truly distinct.

---

[1] South Carolina had decided to nullify a tariff passed by the federal government. The governor put together a volunteer army consisting of 25,000 infantry and 2,000 cavalry in preparation for possible civil war.

JACKSON'S ELECTORAL COLLEGE (1828-1852)

1836 election in summary

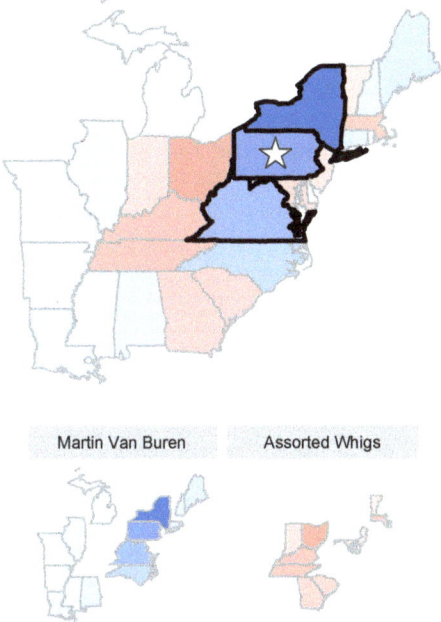

Figure 20: The 1836 presidential election.

Electoral vote: 170-124[2]
Popular vote: 51%-49%
Pivotal state: Pennsylvania
Critical states: Pennsylvania, New York, Virginia
Crucial state: Pennsylvania

Andrew Jackson's designated successor, Democrat Martin Van Buren, ran against a combination of four different Whig[3] candidates (different Whig candidates ran in different regions), the most popular of which was William Henry Harrison.

The totals above are for all Whig electors combined, though not all Whig electors had pledged to support the same candidate. The primary Whig candidate was William Henry Harrison, who competed in fifteen states with a total of 182 electoral votes. Hugh L. White competed in another nine states, including Missouri and eight future Confederate states - a total of 87 electoral votes.

---

[2] Counting all Whig candidates together.
[3] The Whigs took their name from an earlier British political party that was intended to limit the power of the monarch. It was founded in opposition to the man they called "King Jackson," and had the stated mission of wanting to limit the power of the president. Like the Federalists, they were clearly a major party but did not last for long as such.

Two other candidates competed in only one state each. Daniel Webster ran for president in Massachusetts, and South Carolina's appointed electors chose Willie Mangum.

The use of multiple candidates is sometimes described as a deliberate strategy by the Whig Party, but the Whigs were fragmented - arguably not yet a national party as much as an anti-Jacksonian movement that had adopted a common name - and there is little evidence that this was anything other than the result of the Whigs being disorganized in their first presidential election.[4] Nevertheless, while not a deliberate strategy, it came very close to forcing a House contingent election.

The Senate contingent election

Both Whigs and Democrats divided their vice presidential votes in the Electoral College. The Whigs divided regionally, with Francis Granger earning more votes in northern states and John Tyler earning more votes in southern states. Nationally, Democrats had agreed on Richard M. Johnson, for vice president. However, he had a *de facto* common-law marriage with a slave woman who was an octaroon, i.e., one-eighth African descent; and he acknowledged their children together. The Democratic electors of Virginia decided *en masse* to vote for William Smith instead.

New York, Virginia, and Pennsylvania were all critical to the Democratic majority - so without Virginia's electors, the Democratic vice presidential ticket fell short of a majority, leading to a Senate contingent election. Only the top two candidates are eligible to compete, and Richard M. Johnson won out over Francis Granger with little fanfare.

What if there had been a House contingent election?

William Henry Harrison lost the vote in Pennsylvania by a narrow margin. If he had won instead, no candidate would have received a majority of the votes in the Electoral College. Resolving the election would have fallen to the House, as it had in 1824 and 1800. The Democrats (Jacksonians) controlled a majority in thirteen out of twenty-six delegations in the outgoing House of Representatives and held half of two more state delegations.

The result of a House contingent election would have been uncertain. Van Buren would have needed votes from the opposition in order to

---

[4]For details, see "Was There a "Whig Strategy" in 1836?" (1984) by Richard McCormick.

gain a majority; the Whigs would have needed to win over votes from Van Buren's party in order to gain a majority. In the event that the vote deadlocked, the winner of the Senate contingent election would have become president by default.

Strategically, if the Whigs had planned on running multiple regional candidates in order to deny a majority to Van Buren, running one candidate in a majority of the states and two single-state candidates would have been a bad choice. To qualify for a contingent election, Martin Van Buren needed to only place third in the Electoral College. Since Daniel Webster and Willie Mangum only competed in a single state each, placing third only required winning fifteen electoral votes. To force a national candidate out of the House contingent election process requires that at least three regional candidates do better than a national candidate.

A national strategic decision to run multiple regional candidates would probably have resulted in running Willie Mangum in his home state of North Carolina as well as neighboring Virginia; similarly, Daniel Webster would logically have been the rational choice of candidate to run in all of New England as well as possibly serving as the challenger to Van Buren in his home state of New York.[5]

Any party trying to adopt a multi-candidate strategy in order to force a House contingent election also has to face a curious problem: Why should potential swing voters disregard the likelihood that voting for a candidate from their own region would lead to the election of a different regional candidate from the same political party?

On paper, running multiple regional candidates may seem appealing, but in practice, there are a number of potential complications. It's difficult to evaluate whether or not the supposed "Whig strategy" of 1836 was a good strategy or not - but one way to evaluate it is to look at the election of 1840. One simple question: Did the other regional Whig candidates do better, relative to the national environment, than William Henry Harrison did in their states four years later?

---

[5] Note that Webster had a claim to home state advantages in both New Hampshire and Massachusetts, having represented both states in Congress; he also had ties to New York through his wife.

The 1840 election and the test of a united Whig Party

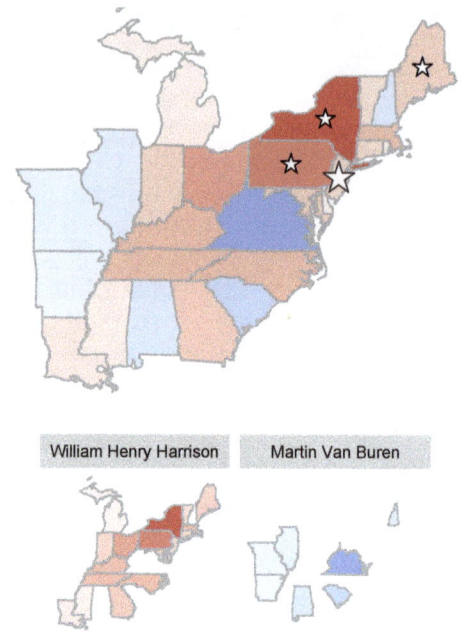

Figure 21: The 1840 presidential election.

Electoral vote: 234-60
Popular vote: 53%-47%
Pivotal state: New Jersey
Critical states: None
Crucial states: New Jersey, New York, Maine, Pennsylvania

The Whig Party organized; as might be expected from the balance of electoral power between the northern and southern states, the northern Whigs pushed forward their choice of nominee, William Henry Harrison. The southern Whigs were mostly appeased by the nomination of their previous choice for vice president, John Tyler. In the rematch between William Henry Harrison and incumbent Democratic president Martin Van Buren, William Henry Harrison won with broad geographic support, earning votes from both northern and southern states.

In pointed contrast to the Whigs' newly united front, Democrats had difficulty agreeing on anything at all. While Martin Van Buren was able to secure a nomination for a second term, he was left without a vice presidential candidate - an oversight that could have left him coping with a Whig vice president if he had won.

New Jersey was the pivotal state in this election. The contest was quite close; Harrison's large Electoral College Margin was based on a combination of extremely narrow victories in key battleground states. Van Buren only needed seventeen thousand more votes distributed between New Jersey, New York, Pennsylvania, and Maine to hold onto the presidency. Since New Jersey only had eight electoral votes, we can point to this as the first time a tipping point state was merely medium-sized, with fewer than ten electoral votes.

Contrasting 1836 and 1840

In the states where William Henry Harrison had run, the overall popular vote margin shifted by 7.8% in favor of the Whigs. In states where Hugh L. White had run, the popular vote margin shifted by 7.3% towards the Whigs. One major exception was White's home state of Tennessee, which shifted *away* from the Whigs by 4.5%. In Massachusetts, where Daniel Webster had run, the shift towards the Whigs was a modest 5.8%. The most dramatic difference was in South Carolina, which had voted for North Carolinian Willie Mangum; the state legislature decided to back Van Buren instead of Harrison.

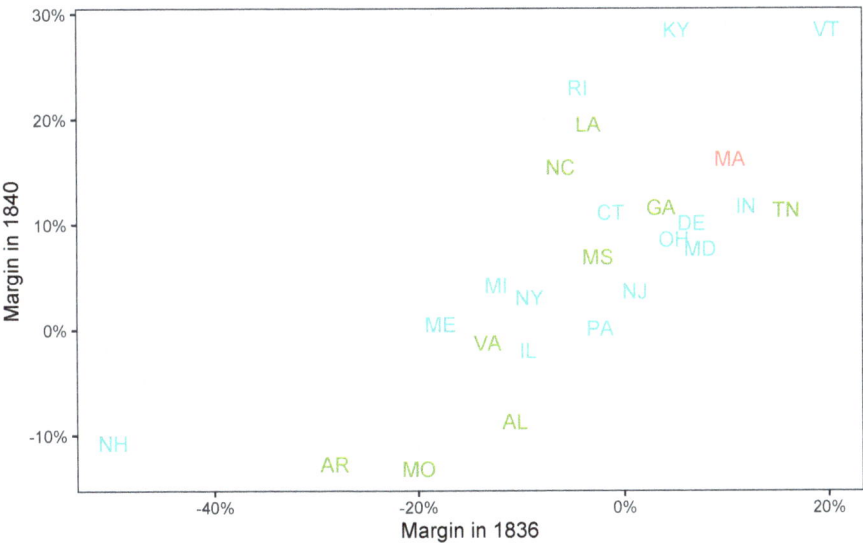

Figure 22: Comparison between vote margins in 1836 and 1840 by state.

Overall, the Whigs performed slightly better across the board, and this shift swamped any regional differences in how southern and northern Whigs were perceived by southern and northern voters.

This may have had more to do with a decline in Van Buren's political fortunes rather than increased national organization on the part of the Whigs. Two notable episodes in Van Buren's presidency were the Panic of 1837 and the forcible removal of the Cherokee to Oklahoma in 1838.[6] The panic led to years of economic difficulty, which continued through the end of Van Buren's presidency.

Following the 1840 election, William Henry Harrison assumed office, gave a lengthy inauguration speech, caught an illness, and quickly died, setting a record for the shortest presidency. His running mate, John Tyler, had nearly a full term in office until the election of 1844.

1844-1848 and the first spoilers

In the mathematical study of voting systems, one of the most well-known results is Arrow's Impossibility Theorem,[7] which lays out a set of five reasonable-sounding criteria that a voting system ought to satisfy, and then shows that no voting system satisfies all five of those criteria.

The most difficult of those criteria to satisfy is called the *independence of irrelevant alternatives*. This criterion is that between two candidates, how well they perform in the election relative to each other shouldn't change if a third candidate chooses to withdraw or enter the race. Mathematically speaking, all voting systems[8] violate this criterion to a greater or lesser degree. Notably, various types of run-off elections help minimize the impact of the spoiler effect; if the Electoral College actually functioned as expected by the Framers,[9] then the system would resist spoilers to some degree.

The spoiler effect, where a non-viable candidate decides the election by pulling votes away from one of the viable candidates, is one example of how this criterion is violated. Without a majority runoff, a plurality system is highly vulnerable to spoilers; contrary to the occasional misguided assertion to the contrary by those who defend the Electoral

---

[6]One pamphlet titled *The Contrast, or, William Henry Harrison Versus Martin van Buren* (1840) by Richard Hildreth alludes to the Cherokee removal thusly: "His Indian treaties were not like those which have since disgraced the country, by which the Indians have been cajoled, threatened and cheated into cessions which they never intended to make."

[7]First presented in "A Difficulty in the Concept of Social Welfare" (1950) by Kenneth Arrow.

[8]Excluding "trivial" voting systems like dictatorships, which most people would agree aren't actually voting systems.

[9]I.e., as a nominating body.

College system,[10] the Electoral College system is highly vulnerable to spoiler effects; a "spoiler" candidate can decide the election in a single key state.

The first time that the Electoral College was decided between two major candidates by a minor third-party spoiler candidate effect was in 1844.[11]

1844 election

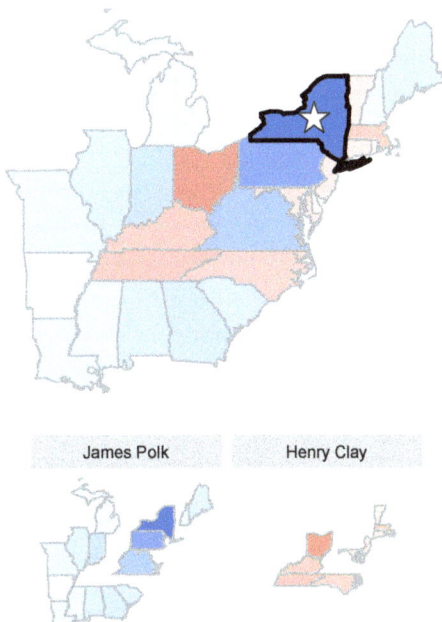

Figure 23: The 1844 presidential election.

Electoral vote: 170-105
Popular vote: 50%-48%
Pivotal state: New York
Critical state: New York
Crucial state: New York

The short-lived president William Henry Harrison was succeeded by his vice president John Tyler. Tyler was thrown out of the Whig Party, which instead ran Henry Clay (who had previously run in 1824 and 1832). His opponent was Democrat James Polk, a slave owner from Tennessee.

---

[10]See, for example, Chapter 12 in *Picking the President: Understanding the Electoral College* (2017) by Eric Burin.

[11]Arguably, the election of 1824 also featured spoiler effects, but between major candidates.

Both candidates won some New England states and some southern states, making this election one of the less regionally polarized ones.

Polk won the election by a narrow margin, and his victory depended entirely on winning New York, which was both the pivotal state and the only critical state in this election. Polk won New York by a margin of about five thousand votes out of nearly half a million votes. However, Polk did *not* earn a majority of votes in New York, and probably was not preferred to Henry Clay by a majority of New York's voters. This brings us to the first case in which a minor candidate "spoiled" the election.

James G. Birney: The first spoiler candidate

In 1840, Martin Van Buren, the incumbent Democratic president, ran for re-election, and lost soundly to popular general William Henry Harrison, earning 46.8% of the vote to 52.9%. If we add together these two numbers, we find that 0.3% of the vote is missing.

This tiny share of the vote went to abolitionist James G. Birney of the Liberty party, who had no expectation of having any influence on the outcome of the election. He was a protest candidate, and the votes for him were protest votes, a method of drawing attention to the cause of abolition. That 0.3% margin had no effect on the results in 1840, so Birney was not a spoiler in 1840. In 1844, the Liberty party again nominated Birney, again with no expectation whatsoever of victory - or of any effect on the election at all. Abolitionists simply hoped to gain publicity and advance their cause.

In the 1844 election, however, things were critically different. Birney earned 2.3% of the vote nationally – but, more importantly, 3.2% of the vote in New York, which was decided by a slender margin of 1%. So, New York's 36 electoral votes (12% of the total number of electoral votes) went to slave owner and expansionist James Polk. Polk had previously served as Speaker of the House, and while Speaker, strictly enforced a gag rule against discussing the abolition of slavery on the floor of the House.

Polk's opponent in that election was Henry Clay. As we mentioned in discussion of the 1824 election, Henry Clay had a moderate stance on slavery; he favored gradual emancipation. Henry Clay and James Birney knew each other personally; shortly after graduating from school, Birney became close friends with Clay, accompanying him during campaigns for office. Birney's connection to activist abolitionist organizations, ironically, can be traced to Henry Clay, who introduced him to Josiah Polk of the Colonization Society in 1829. Clay and Birney had a major falling-out over the issue of slavery later on.

For years afterward, some of Clay's supporters would vocally blame Birney for the loss. In a biography titled *James G. Birney and His Times: The Genesis of the Republican Party with Some Account of Abolition Movements in the South Before 1828* (1890), written by his son William Birney, you can find a vocal defense of James G. Birney's Liberty Party runs for president. In the book, William Birney gives an argument that may sound very familiar, as it has been echoed by many other principled third-party candidates defending their decision to run: He points out that while if all the Liberty party voters had voted for Clay, it would have prevented the election of Polk, it was also true that if all of Clay's supporters had voted for Birney, then Birney would have won.

Abolitionists arguably cost the Whigs the election in 1844; on the slavery issue, Clay's views were significantly closer to the abolitionists' views than Polk's views were. However, the consequences of the election did not stop there. While President Polk only served one term in office, his actions while in office impacted the nation quite significantly - as well as the struggle between abolitionists and those who favored slavery.

1848 election in summary

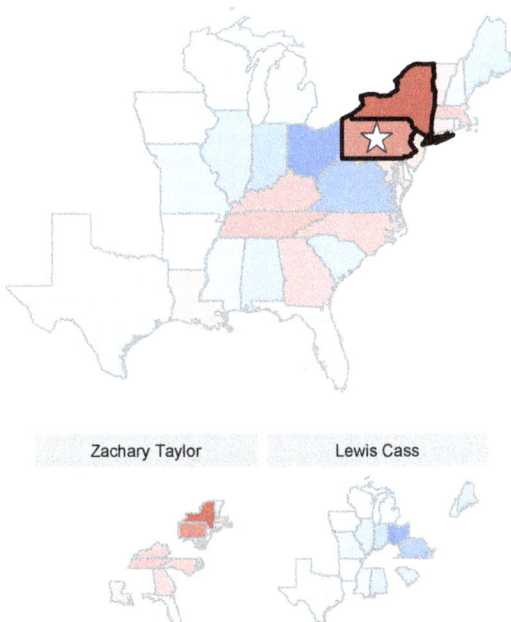

Figure 24: The 1848 presidential election.

Electoral vote: 163-127
Popular vote: 47%-42%

Pivotal state: Pennsylvania
Critical states: New York, Pennsylvania
Crucial state: Pennsylvania

Incumbent James Polk declined to run for re-election. Former president Martin Van Buren, frustrated with the direction of the Democrats, came out of retirement and ran as the Free Soil candidate, earning a significant share of the vote in several states but no electoral votes. This was the second and final election won by the Whig Party, which fielded Zachary Taylor against Democrat Lewis Cass.

The Electoral College margin between Taylor and Cass was close enough to be reversed either by Pennsylvania or New York. Both of those states were battleground states, but Pennsylvania was closer, with a margin of about thirteen thousand votes in Pennsylvania.

The spoil[er]s of the Mexican-American War

With the success of the Mexican-American War (1846-1848), the political issue of slavery crystallized into a crisis. The United States had just become much larger - almost doubling its total territorial claims - and the country was deeply divided over the topic of whether or not the newly-seized territories should allow slavery or not.

James Polk retired from office without running for re-election. The Whig candidate, Zachary Taylor, was a Southern slave owner, and widely perceived as the candidate most friendly to the cause of slavery. The Democratic candidate, Lewis Cass, adopted the moderate position of *popular sovereignty* – that whether or not slavery would be legal in a territory should be left up to the citizens of that territory to decide.[12]

Neither of these positions was acceptable to abolitionists, who wanted to see the institution contained within the existing slave states at a minimum and preferably completely eliminated. The candidate who stepped into this political void was former President Martin Van Buren. Backed by the anti-slavery faction of the Democratic Party, he ran on the Free Soil ticket. Ironically, Martin Van Buren's position as president had been too moderate for abolitionists' tastes in 1840, provoking James G. Birney's first run for president in 1840. To some degree, Van Buren's views on slavery had evolved over time; abolitionists had also become more desperate.

Martin Van Buren received 10.1% of the national vote, a little over twice as much as the national margin of 4.8%. His candidacy potentially took as

---

[12]This remained the moderate position on slavery through the election of 1860, when it was espoused by northern Democratic candidate Stephen Douglas.

many as 54 electoral votes from Lewis Cass in New York, Massachusetts, and Vermont. New York was a key perennial battleground state in those times, often decided by small margins (as had happened in 1840 and 1844); Vermont and Massachusetts in particular were staunchly anti-slavery, voting for anti-slavery candidates by consistently large margins in every election. They numbered among the few states won by anti-slavery Whig Winfield Scott in 1852 and anti-slavery Republican John Fremont in 1856.

Since Democrats held a majority of state delegations in the House, a swing of 18 electoral votes from Massachusetts and Vermont bringing the Electoral College to a 145-145 tie would have likely been enough to make Cass president in a contingent election. A swing of 36 electoral votes from New York would have given Cass an outright majority in the Electoral College. All things considered, it is likely that if Van Buren had not been on the ballot in those three states, Cass would have won.

In both 1844 and 1848, the candidate seen as friendlier to slavery was elected without a majority of the popular vote and apparently as the result of a spoiler effect. Even though the abolitionists arguably "spoiled" both the popular vote and electoral vote, the share of electoral votes potentially "spoiled" by the abolitionist candidate (12% and 19%, respectively) was much larger than the share of popular votes potentially "spoiled" by the abolitionist candidate (3% and 10%, respectively).

The chaotic behavior of the Electoral College system makes it easy for a non-viable candidate to "spoil" an election with almost no national support; it is sufficient to divide the vote in one or two key states. Advocates of the Electoral College system sometimes claim that the fact that it makes it difficult to elect third-party candidates provides a stabilizing influence; nevertheless, even completely non-viable candidates like Birney can decide an election by their presence or absence.

While it is easy to forget minor candidates who had no chance of victory, third and fourth-place candidates have earned enough votes to tip the balance between the two most popular candidates about a third of the time – usually, as in 1844 and 1848, to the detriment of their own cause. While this feature is *not* unique to the Electoral College system, the chaotic nature of the Electoral College means that the spoiler effect needs to only tip the result in a single state in order to tip a national election.

1852 election

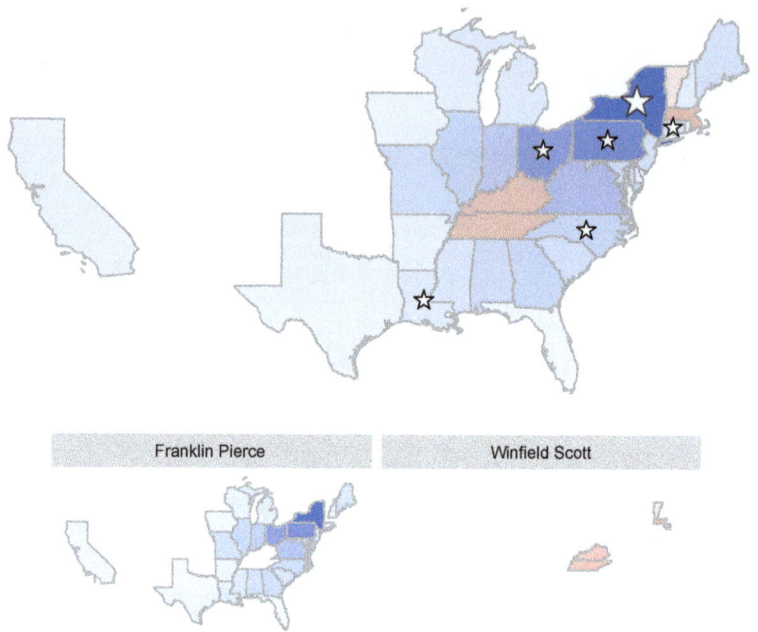

Figure 25: The 1852 presidential election.

Electoral vote: 254-42
Popular vote: 51%-44%
Pivotal state: New York
Critical states: None
Crucial states: New York, Pennsylvania, Ohio, Connecticut, Louisiana, North Carolina

President Taylor died in office and was succeeded by his vice president, Millard Fillmore, who – like former Whig vice president John Tyler – was not nominated for re-election by the Whig Party. The Whigs instead backed Winfield Scott, notable as a general. Democrat Franklin Pierce won by a large electoral vote margin with only 51% of the vote.

The pivotal state in this election was New York; had the Whigs remained popular enough to win in New York, they could have continued to win presidential elections. This would be their last election as a major force in American politics, however. The divisions within the Whig Party were too deep, and America's second version of a national two-party system was on its last legs.

The end of the Jacksonian era

The Whigs had come together as a party in opposition to Andrew Jackson. They did not remain an effective electoral force for long after Jackson's death, and the political terrain of the country was also changed by the addition of the new western territories taken from Mexico. While the Electoral College continued to operate mainly by the unit rule, what happened in the next several elections is complex enough to deserve its own chapter. The elections of 1856-1864 marked the beginning of a new party system with a new major political party.

CHAPTER 6

Civil War, minority rule, and slavery (1856-1864)

From 1861 to 1865, the United States was embroiled in a bloody civil war, known today simply as *the* American Civil War. No other conflict has caused as much death or destruction on American soil. The opening prelude to the war - including declarations of secession and early military preparations by the South - happened during the administration of President Buchanan. The immediate trigger for secession was the election of Abraham Lincoln. Both presidents were elected with an alarmingly narrow base of support.

From a deeper mathematical perspective, both the 1856 and 1860 elections showed the same dangerous flaw: A spoiler effect is *not necessary* to elect a president with minority support. Deep regional divisions can be sufficient. Many assign a significant share of the blame for the Civil War to President Buchanan,[1] so both election results can be seen as contributing to the eruption of the bloodiest war in American history.

---

[1] This gives him a reputation as a worst president, e.g., as asserted recently in *The Worst President–the Story of James Buchanan* (2015) by Garry Boulard and *Worst. President. Ever.: James Buchanan, the POTUS Rating Game, and the Legacy of the Least of the Lesser Presidents* (2016) by Robert Strauss.

Three elections in brief

1856: Setting the stage

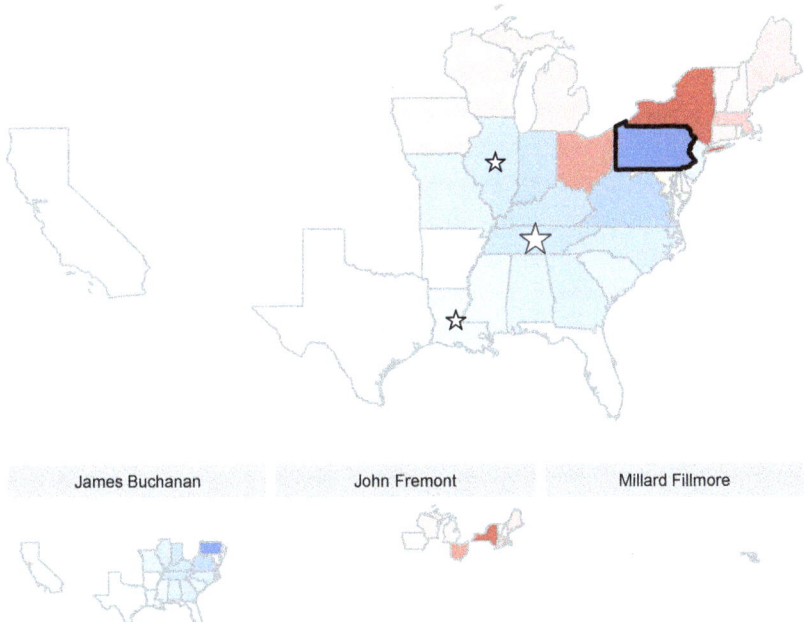

Figure 26: The 1856 presidential election.

Electoral vote: 174-114-8
Popular vote: 45%-33%-21%
Pivotal state: Tennessee
Critical state: Pennsylvania
Crucial states: Tennessee, Illinois, Louisiana

The Democrats declined to re-nominate the incumbent president, Franklin Pierce. Instead, they chose James Buchanan, who at that point in time was Minister to the United Kingdom. The newly-founded Republican Party nominated John Fremont, who had been military governor of California and briefly a senator for California. A third major candidate, former Whig president Millard Fillmore, ran as a Know-Nothing.

With the disintegration of the Whig Party complete, Buchanan was able to win with only 45% of the vote. Buchanan's Electoral College majority was fragile: A shift of 17,000 votes in Tennessee, Illinois, and Louisiana would have sent the election to the House of Representatives, with uncertain results.

1860: A nation divided

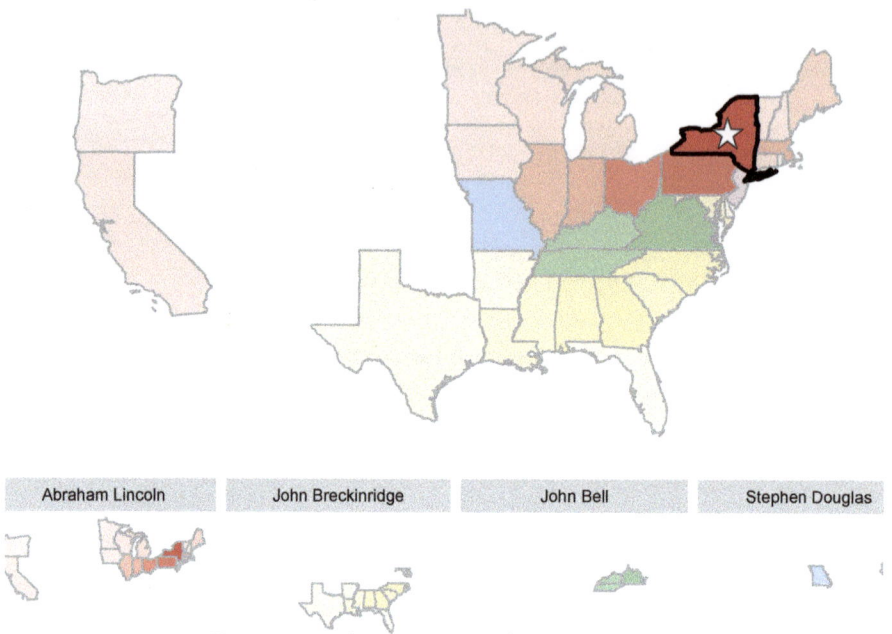

Figure 27: The 1860 presidential election.

Electoral vote: 180-72-39-12
Popular vote: 40%-26%-21%-33%
Pivotal state: New York
Critical state: New York
Crucial state: New York

The election of 1860 featured four major candidates, with Republican Abraham Lincoln emerging victorious over a fractured Democratic Party. Northern Democrat Stephen Douglas placed second in the popular vote, while Southern Democrat John Breckinridge earned the second-most electoral votes.[2] John Bell ran under the banner of the freshly-formed Constitutional Union Party, which was dedicated to staving off a civil war; he won significant support in border states that could expect to be on the front lines of any military conflict.

Although exceptionally interesting for a wide variety of reasons, the analysis of electoral power in 1860 is fairly simple. Just like in 1844, New York occupied a uniquely decisive position. New York's 35 electoral

---

[2] Exact popular vote percentages reported in various sources vary based on how one tries to account for anti-Lincoln fusion ballots in four states, which accounted for 12% of the national vote. 21% of the electorate voted for Douglas alone, and 33% of the electorate voted for an electoral slate that included at least one Douglas elector.

CIVIL WAR, MINORITY RULE, AND SLAVERY (1856-1864)   87

votes were necessary for Lincoln's electoral majority, and New York occupied the political median of the nation. If Lincoln had lost New York's electoral votes to the fusion slate of his opponents, and those fusion electors individually voted as they were expected to, there would have been a contingent election between him, Bell, and Breckinridge; with Lincoln unacceptable to the South and Breckinridge unacceptable to the North, it is likely that Bell would have won the contingent election process as a compromise candidate.

1864: A wartime election

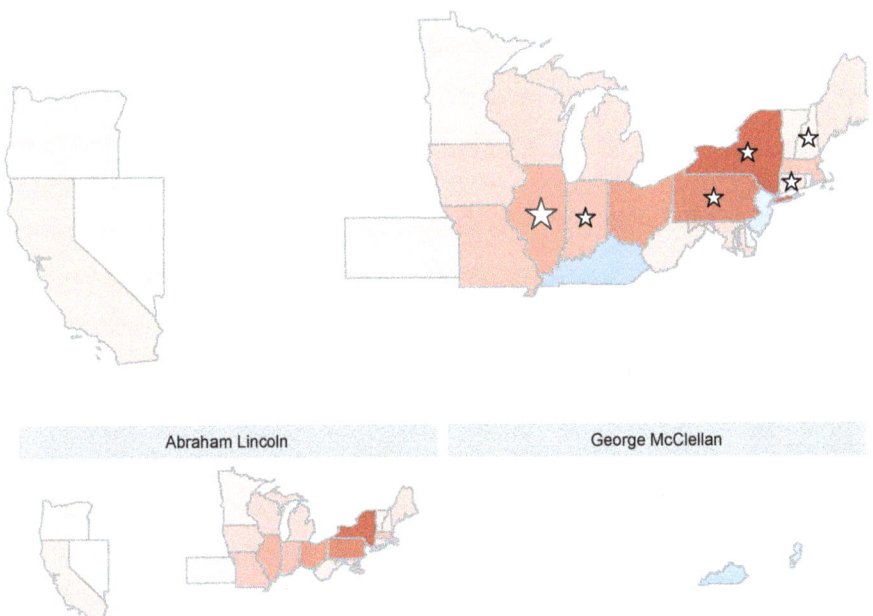

Figure 28: The 1864 presidential election.

Electoral vote: 212-21
Popular vote: 55%-45%
Pivotal state: Illinois
Crucial states: Illinois, Michigan, Indiana, Pennsylvania, New York

A factional split among Republican insiders led to incumbent Abraham Lincoln running as a National Union candidate rather than a Republican candidate, with a Democrat - Andrew Johnson as his running mate. An opposing branch of the Republican Party nominated John Fremont, but he withdrew before the election took place.

With the South having seceded, Lincoln won re-election by a significant margin against Democratic challenger George McClellan. Within the political spectrum of the Union states, we can identify Illinois, Lincoln's home state, as pivotal. Had the South participated in the election and voted unanimously against Lincoln, Lincoln still would have won re-election, albeit possibly with a minority of the popular vote, as we will discuss below.

It is worth noting Nevada was a newly-admitted state with a very small population. Due to difficulties related to travel, only two of Nevada's three designated electors were able to assemble to cast votes; Lincoln, therefore, won only two electoral votes from Nevada.

Minority rule resistant to spoiler effects

In 1844 and 1848, we saw two likely examples of the spoiler effect in the Electoral College. In both cases, a third-party abolitionist candidate probably unintentionally caused the election of a slave-owning Southerner who earned less than an outright majority of the total popular vote. By contrast, in 1856 and 1860, even though no candidate earned a majority, the result was *not* determined by a spoiler effect.

In general, whenever the highest popular vote total is less than 50%, the candidate who won the most votes might not have the support of a majority of the voters over the next most popular candidate, and we should suspect that a spoiler effect played a role. It is usually hard to prove or disprove that a spoiler effect was decisive, but whenever neither candidate has the support of a majority of the population, it makes sense that a spoiler effect is a possible factor.

However, within the Electoral College, it is possible to secure a clear majority of electoral votes in the Electoral College by winning narrow majorities in key battleground states while losing deeply in other states. In spite of the fact that the elections of 1856 and 1860 involved three or four major candidates, with no candidate receiving a majority of the vote, these elections were very clearly *not* decided by a spoiler effect. Instead, the winners, in both cases, won narrow majorities in key battleground states.

It is very important to consider that both the elections of 1856 and 1860 were decided in a very similar way *in spite of* significant differences in the two winning candidates. James Buchanan and Abraham Lincoln were very different presidential candidates, with very different views on the role of slavery in the United States of America. Buchanan was the most pro-slavery candidate in 1856; Lincoln was the most anti-slavery

CIVIL WAR, MINORITY RULE, AND SLAVERY (1856-1864)   89

candidate in 1860. Experts generally view Buchanan as one of the worst presidents, and Lincoln as one of the best.[3]

The structure of a minority victory

In 1856, Democratic candidate James Buchanan was elected with only 45% of the vote with three major candidates. However, he won an outright majority of the Electoral College vote, which allowed them to avoid a House contingent election. Yet despite winning only 45% of the vote, his Electoral College victory was not due to a spoiler effect! Four years later, in 1860, the Republican candidate, Abraham Lincoln, would perform a similar feat, winning a secure Electoral College coalition with about 40% of the total vote.

Both elections featured strong regionalization of support. For both Buchanan and Lincoln, there were only three states that they won by a plurality rather than a majority. In 1856, those three states were California, New Jersey, and Illinois; in 1860, the three states were California, New Jersey, and Oregon. The rest of their electoral votes were secured by an outright majority of the vote, in many cases a fairly narrow majority.

The 1856 election gives us an example of a way in which a candidate could have easily lost the popular vote by a resounding 45% to 55% margin while winning a slender majority in the Electoral College. The 1860 election gives us an even more dramatic example of a candidate who could lose the popular vote by a 60%-40% landslide while still earning an Electoral College majority.

How do you lock down a majority of electoral votes with a minority of the total vote? By winning narrowly and losing deeply. Buchanan won 52.4% of the vote in states that gave him electoral votes, but only 37.3% of the votes in states that did not award him electoral votes. For Lincoln, the difference is even more dramatic: While he won a narrow 53.7% victory in the states that awarded him electoral votes, he earned only 2% of the vote in the states that didn't award him electoral votes.[4]

---

[3]In 2014, a survey of political scientists placed Buchanan last and Lincoln first. See "Presidential Greatness and Political Science: Assessing the 2014 APSA Presidents and Executive Politics Section Presidential Greatness Survey" (2017) by Brandon Rottinghaus and Justin S. Vaughn. Most surveys of historians or political scientists have placed Lincoln in the top three and Buchanan in the bottom four.

[4]It's worth noting that Lincoln was not even a candidate in many Southern states ... but also that he earned about 1% of the vote in Virginia, where he was a candidate.

Positions on slavery in brief

As we saw in Chapter 5, abolitionist candidates running on the Liberty ticket may have caused the election of President Polk, and Martin Van Buren's run as on the Free Soil ticket may have caused the election of President Taylor. Both presidents were Southern slave owners, and their victories were both considered setbacks for the abolitionist cause to a greater or lesser extent. While Zachary Taylor's presidency was not particularly impactful, the election of Polk was particularly important in leading up to the Civil War.[5]

In 1844, the United States consisted of twenty-six states. Only three of those states (Louisiana, Arkansas, and Missouri) had been formed from territory added to the United States after the ratification of the Constitution; nine had been formed from the territory previously governed by existing states, and one (Vermont) had briefly existed as an independent republic. Then President Polk was elected, and in the next four years, the United States increased in size by somewhere in the range of 60% to 100%.[6]

The territorial expansions under Polk included the annexation of Texas and Oregon as well as most of the northern half of Mexico, combining to roughly 1.2 million square miles in a combination of peaceful and violent expansion - more territory than added by any other president. The massive expansion of the United States out to the Pacific coastline opened a heated political debate over whether or not the newly acquired territory should be one in which slavery was allowed or not. At stake was whether slavery, as an institution, would be contained or expanded. The stakes were high and imminent.

The mainline Democratic position on the issue was referred to as "popular sovereignty," because it invoked the principle of popular sovereignty. Rather than having the federal government decide whether or not slavery would be legal in a territory, that decision would be left up to the people of the territory. Popular sovereignty was introduced to the Democratic platform by Lewis Cass in 1848 and remained a feature of the Democratic platform through 1860, with varying degrees of success in implementation.[7]

The mainline Republican position on the issue, held by John Fremont in 1856 and Abraham Lincoln in 1860, was that slavery should be banned

---

[5] One of a number of explorations of the importance of this can be found in "Rethinking the Coming of the Civil War: A Counterfactual Exercise" (2003) by Gary Kornblith.

[6] Precise accounting will vary depending on how one treats disputed claims and "Indian country" that the federal government recognized by treaty as outside of its control.

[7] See in particular the violence that took place in Kansas 1854-1859.

in territories that were administered by the Federal government. This would confine slavery to the South.

Both elections featured a major candidate who tried to be neutral on the issue of slavery. Their priority on the issue of slavery was holding together the country rather than trying to contain or abolish slavery. In 1856, this was former president Millard Fillmore, on the Know Nothing ticket; in 1860, this was John Bell, on the Constitutional Union ticket. These candidates did badly in terms of popular votes, and even more poorly in the Electoral College - even though each represented a natural compromise between the two extremes.[8]

In 1860, a fourth position was added to the mix – the adamant demand from Breckinridge that slavery should be permitted in the territories and that northern states should cooperate in the enforcement of fugitive slave laws.

Civil War

The presidential election of 1860 should be considered one of the most historically significant elections in the history of the United States. Its immediate consequences included four years of bloody civil war, a conflict so central to the history of the United States that *antebellum*, a word literally meaning "before the war," now refers to the period that ended with 1860. It is difficult to overstate the importance of the American Civil War in American history.

The immediate trigger for the war was the election of 1860, and as I mentioned, the particular quirks of the Electoral College played a visible and critical role in this. While an American civil war over the divisive issue of slavery may have occurred without the Electoral College system, we can trace the proximate roots of the war that actually happened to quirks in the Electoral College system.

Many defenders of the Electoral College system[9] say that the Electoral College system was designed to push candidates to build broad coalitions by forcing presidential candidates to fight for votes across the entire country rather than favoring one region over another. This is incorrect. As seen in both 1856 and 1860, as well as in other elections featuring three or more candidates, the Electoral College system strongly favors polarizing candidates with regional or sectional bases of support, and strongly penalizes candidates who have broad appeal across the entire country.

---

[8] A "center squeeze" effect is a problem for plurality voting in general, but this problem is exacerbated in the Electoral College.

[9] E.g., Judith Best and Tara Ross.

Since in most elections, we have only two major candidates who receive electoral votes, it's hard to distinguish which candidates are more sectional and more national,[10] but 1860 is one of the exceptions. In 1860, there were four major candidates, and it is not difficult to identify which candidates were regionally polarizing (Abraham Lincoln, John Breckinridge), which candidate had the broadest coalition of support spread across the entire country (Stephen Douglas), and which candidate had the most neutral position on the divisive issue of the day (John Bell).

Republican candidate Abraham Lincoln won with slightly less than 40% of the popular vote. Radically anti-slavery compared to the other candidates, he was not even on the ballot in most Southern states. In Virginia, the only future Confederate state in which he had been on the ballot, he earned 1.1% of the vote; it is unlikely he would have earned more than 1% of the votes in the states of the Confederacy even if he had been on the ballot. To add to this, Southern states had lower voter turnout overall, and South Carolina's state legislature still directly appointed presidential electors rather than holding a popular vote. In the hypothetical scenario of a four-way national popular vote, it is plausible that Lincoln's share would have been slightly lower than his historical total of 39.8% due to the larger number of votes cast in the South.

Lincoln won without a single electoral vote from any of the 15 states in which slavery was legal. In three states where slavery was illegal (California, New Jersey, and Oregon), he won his electoral votes through the spoiler effect. However, he won the other 15 free states with more than half of the vote. Lincoln's victory in 1860, much like Buchanan's victory in 1856, was not due to the spoiler effect; it was instead due to the fact that he was able to win narrow majorities in battleground states like New York and Ohio while completely disregarding the South.

Lincoln did not build a national coalition. He won as a sectional candidate whose section of the country was large enough to give him victory, and the disregarded section of the country took his victory badly enough to secede.

The impact of the Electoral College on slavery

Many critics of the Electoral College system say that the Electoral College system was designed to protect slavery.[11] Some go as far as claiming that

---

[10] This may seem strange, but if the vote in a particular state is a landslide victory for one candidate, it's hard to say if the voters were motivated more by voting *for* one candidate or *against* another candidate.

[11] See, for example, "The Proslavery Origins of the Electoral College" (2001) by Paul Finkelman.

CIVIL WAR, MINORITY RULE, AND SLAVERY (1856-1864)   93

the Electoral College system has protected slavery.[12] Others correctly point out that the Three-Fifths Compromise helped motivate some opposition to reforms.[13] We discussed the origin of the system in Chapter 2. It's worth repeating that the system originated with (and was most strongly supported by) the Pennsylvania delegation - and that the delegations from the Carolinas were the only ones to vote against the final version of the system. Support for a national popular vote was also clearly present among prominent slave owners both at the time (e.g., James Madison) and later (e.g., Andrew Jackson). Now that we have reached the election of 1860, we are in a position to discuss the *effect* of the system on slavery.

This touches on the same issue that I've discussed above regarding the way that the Electoral College rewards more divisive candidates; slavery was the most divisive regional issue in the antebellum United States. In Chapter 2, we saw that protecting slavery was not a motivating factor in the design or adoption of the Electoral College system, though it played a role in the broader opposition to a national popular vote. In our intervening discussion of elections from 1788 to 1864, we've seen that the quirks of the Electoral College system sometimes favored abolitionists and sometimes backfired against abolitionists.

What remains to be discussed is what would have happened *without* the Electoral College in place. There are two major alternatives to consider: The parliamentary alternative and a national popular vote. The most common two forms of a national popular vote are a simple plurality election and a plurality election with a majority runoff.

The parliamentary alternative

As discussed in Chapter 2, the major alternative to the Electoral College system at the Constitutional Convention was election by Congress. This was subject to the infamous Three-Fifths Compromise in *exactly the same way* that the Electoral College was since electoral votes are based on the number of congressional representatives.

In what elections would the incoming Congress have chosen a president of a different party, from 1788 to 1864? Out of those twenty elections, there were three in which the president was not elected alongside a clear Congressional majority from the same party: 1824, 1848, and 1860.[14]

---

[12] E.g., *The Constitution Today: Timeless Lessons for the Issues of Our Era* (2016) by Akil Amar.
[13] E.g., *Why Do We Still Have the Electoral College?* (2020) by Alexander Keyssar.
[14] In the case of 1824, the Democratic-Republicans fragmented and the realignment of a new party system was in progress. In the other two cases, no single party held a majority of all seats in Congress.

CIVIL WAR, MINORITY RULE, AND SLAVERY (1856-1864)

In the elections of 1824 and 1860, the candidate who was chosen through the Electoral College system was the one most firmly opposed to slavery. It is difficult to imagine how the election of abolitionist John Quincy Adams over the four slave-owners contending for high office - Andrew Jackson, Henry Clay, William Crawford, and John C. Calhoun[15] - constitutes protection of slavery, except in a very indirect fashion. The election of Abraham Lincoln, as we have mentioned above, led directly to a chain of events that led to the complete abolition of slavery.

In the election of 1848, the most pro-slavery candidate, Zachary Taylor, won. However, Zachary Taylor died early in his term in office; his successor, Millard Fillmore, was less friendly to the institution of slavery; and the runner-up of the presidential election, Lewis Cass, was a moderate on the issue of slavery. The losing Democratic platform of 1848 shared the doctrine of popular sovereignty with the winning Democratic platforms of 1852 and 1856. It's hard to see a significant effect from the election of 1848, so on the balance, it's very hard to see how the adoption of the Electoral College system over the parliamentary-style alternative has had the effect of protecting slavery.

A direct vote alternative

It's worth repeating that, as I noted in Chapter 2, the most energetic backers of the Electoral College system at the Constitutional Convention also supported a national popular vote, notably James Wilson, Gouverneur Morris, and James Madison. A national popular vote was too radically democratic in 1787, and the Electoral College system was the closest they could get at the Constitutional Convention. While election by Congress was the major alternative in 1787, the major alternative *now* is a national popular vote.

From a historical perspective, looking at each election, the analysis is similar. The first point to consider is that the elections of 1796 and 1800 were very close. Since few states held a popular vote, it's hard to be sure which candidate would have won in either election. However, considering the available information, 1796 seems more likely to have been reversed by a national popular vote than 1800.

Why? John Adams won more votes via legislative appointment, while Thomas Jefferson won more votes via popular election. Adding in the fact that Adams's Electoral College margin in 1796 was due to the bonus "senator" electors, it seems possible that Adams could have lost a national popular vote in 1796. While the Federalists did carry a majority of

---

[15]Technically Calhoun was a vice presidential candidate. As I noted earlier, he did have a potential path to the presidency through failure of the House contingent election process.

House seats in the elections for the 5th Congress, Adams's support among southern Federalists was weak,[16] and his vote total probably would have lagged behind that of local Federalist candidates.

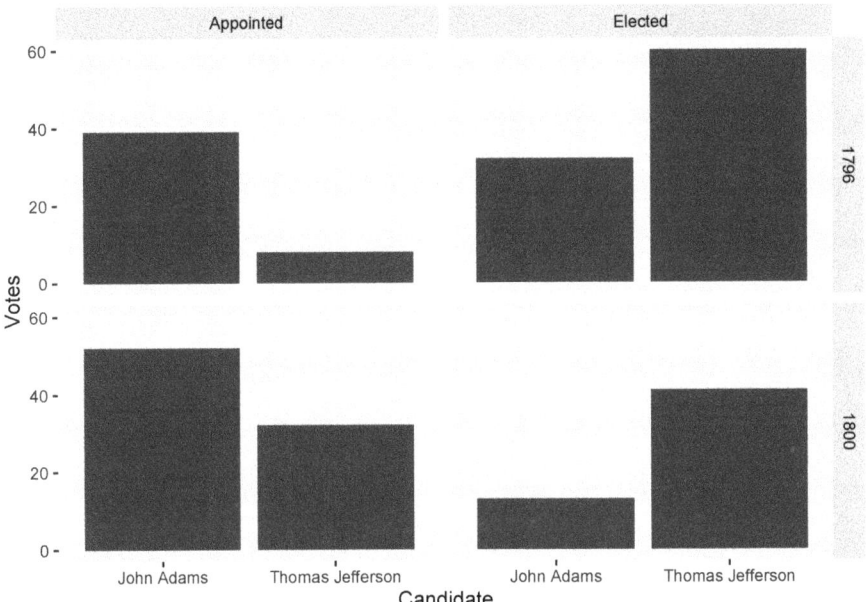

Figure 29: Electors for Adams and Jefferson by selection method in the 1796 and 1800 elections.

It's true that Jefferson's Electoral College margin in 1800 can be ascribed to the extra electors due to slave states by the Three-Fifths Compromise,[17] but this only tells us that Adams would have won if the election had been carried out by an Electoral College unhampered by the Three-Fifths Compromise. Between the concurrent House results for the elections filling the 7th Congress and Jefferson's apparent edge in more direct forms of election, there are few good reasons to believe that Thomas Jefferson would have lost a national popular vote to John Adams in 1800.

That said, it seems unlikely to me that either election would have been reversed; I just think that it is more likely that a popular vote would favor Thomas Jefferson over John Adams. The only other antebellum election in which the winner of the presidential election earned fewer votes than another candidate was the election of 1824. As I mentioned before, though, the winning candidate in 1824 (the second President Adams) was an abolitionist, and his opponent (Andrew Jackson) owned slaves. If we

---

[16] For a pointed example, see South Carolina's Federalist electors in 1796.

[17] As noted by Akil Amar in *The Constitution Today: Timeless Lessons for the Issues of Our Era* (2016) and others.

compare the Electoral College to a simple plurality vote by the people who were allowed to vote at the time, the effect of the Electoral College system has been if anything hostile to slavery.

Majority runoff voting

Many of the countries that use a direct vote for a president require a runoff election if no candidate earns an outright majority. If we consider a national popular vote with a majority runoff, we can call into question the elections of 1844, 1848, 1856, and 1860. We've already discussed the election of 1848 and seen an argument for why the impact of Taylor's victory was at best ambiguous. We have also already discussed the elections of 1856 and 1860. In both 1856 and 1860, the top two candidates were a northern Democrat and a Republican.

Given that it is unlikely that *any* voter who voted for Breckinridge would have voted for Lincoln in a runoff election, Lincoln would have needed to win over about 80% of Bell's supporters to win a runoff election. Similarly, Fremont would have needed to win over about 80% of Fillmore's supporters to win a runoff election. The secondary preferences of voters in the 1860 election have been studied extensively, and a majority runoff likely would have prevented the election of the Great Emancipator himself in 1860.[18] It is not similarly clear that a majority runoff would have prevented the election of James Buchanan in 1856.[19]

If we go back further, however, the elections of 1844 and 1848 seem more likely to be reversed than the election of 1856. It's not clear if Lewis Cass winning in 1848 would have advanced the abolitionist cause at all; he was a fan of the doctrine of *popular sovereignty*, and unlikely to curb the expansion of slavery into the territories.

In the election of 1844, it seems likely that the supporters of Birney would have coalesced behind Henry Clay, blocking the election of Polk. President Polk was largely responsible for the Mexican-American War and therefore the subsequent series of crises over the future of slavery in the West. *If* we are to compare the Electoral College system to a well-functioning plurality vote with a majority runoff, we can identify one presidential election in which the Electoral College system was responsible for a major victory for the pro-slavery faction.

---

[18] See particularly "Would the Borda Count Have Avoided the Civil War?" (1999) by Alexander Tabarrok.

[19] It is possible that in the different electoral environment of a national vote, Fillmore might have placed second and gone to a runoff with Buchanan.

A modest impact?

In light of the three most likely alternatives, we can now attempt to weigh the impact of the Electoral College on the institution of slavery itself. On the one hand, we have the election of 1844, which clearly could have gone better for abolitionists with a majority runoff vote. On the other hand, we have the elections of 1796, 1824, and 1860, all won by anti-slavery candidates who could have easily lost if not for the quirks of the Electoral College.

It's *possible* that a victorious Henry Clay would have been able to curb Southern attempts to expand slavery and put into effect his plans for gradually emancipating slaves. He would have first needed to gain the support of most of the abolitionists who voted for James Birney in a run-off election. Then he would have needed to push his plans through a Congress controlled by Democrats. Perhaps more plausibly,[20] Clay would have failed to provide fuel for a rising sectional conflict as Polk did, reducing sectional tensions.

If we are optimistic enough to think that Henry Clay would have spearheaded a movement for gradual emancipation as president, we might *also* revisit the election of 1824: Henry Clay first ran for president in 1824, and in a runoff election or parliamentary negotiation, he could have easily emerged from the chaos as a strong compromise candidate between Jackson and Adams. It is not a coincidence that in both 1824 and 1860, the two most polarizing candidates placed first and second in the Electoral College, while the more moderate candidates that could have been agreeable to a broader coalition underperformed.

The fact that the Electoral College first aggregates votes within a state rewards candidates with more sectionally concentrated bases of support, and penalizes candidates whose support is spread more broadly. Eventually, the election of one second highly polarizing candidate after another triggered a civil war, which led to the end of slavery.

---

[20] C.f. "Rethinking the Coming of the Civil War: A Counterfactual Exercise" (2003) by Gary Kornblith.

CHAPTER 7

Lincoln's Electoral College (1868-1916)

After the Civil War ended, the 13th, 14th, and 15th Amendments were passed, abolishing slavery and giving former slaves and all other born citizens the right to vote.[1] This significantly expanded the number of people allowed to vote for president, although African-Americans' ability to exercise their right to vote was soon limited in many Southern states.

From 1868 to 1944, the Southern wing of the Democratic Party stayed united with the main part of the party. Once the military governors left the former Confederate states, the region became a reliable bastion of support for the Democratic Party. New York was the major center of power in the Electoral College during this period, and the political parties evolved significantly.

The Reconstruction Era

The first several elections following the Civil War were marked by an assortment of irregularities directly related to the aftermath of the Civil War. Since African-American voters were briefly able to vote in large numbers in the period between the passage of the 15th Amendment and

---

[1] The 14th Amendment also provided a reason for stripping voting rights from former Confederate soldiers.

LINCOLN'S ELECTORAL COLLEGE (1868-1916)

the imposition of poll taxes, literacy tests, et cetera, this period also had markedly different political geography than previous or subsequent elections.

1868: A partially re-united country

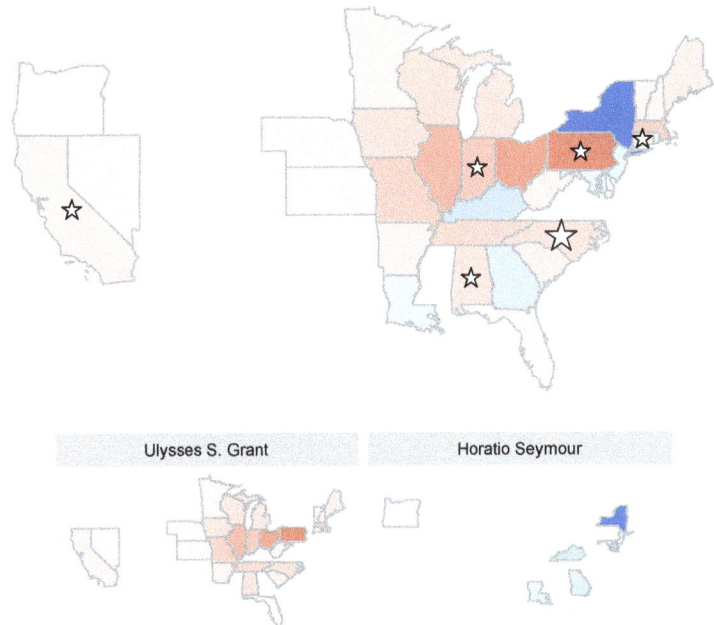

Figure 30: The 1868 presidential election.

Electoral vote: 214-80
Popular vote: 53%-47%
Pivotal state: North Carolina
Critical states: None
Crucial states: North Carolina, Pennsylvania, Connecticut, Indiana, Alabama, California

Impeached but not removed from office, incumbent president Andrew Johnson was not nominated for re-election by the Democratic Party, which chose to run Horatio Seymour instead - a former governor of New York. Republican Ulysses S. Grant, who had been the general in charge of the Union's army at the end of the war, won by a large margin in the Electoral College, despite an unexceptional popular vote margin. The Southern electorate was temporarily very different due to the inclusion of African-American voters and the exclusion of some whites who had supported the Confederacy, and this helped push him over the edge in North Carolina and Alabama in particular.

Texas, Virginia, and Mississippi had not been yet re-admitted to the Union, and there was no presidential election in these states. The pivotal state in this election was North Carolina. This marked the second election in which a state with fewer than ten electoral votes (North Carolina had nine) held a pivotal position in a presidential election.

1872: A dead man in the running

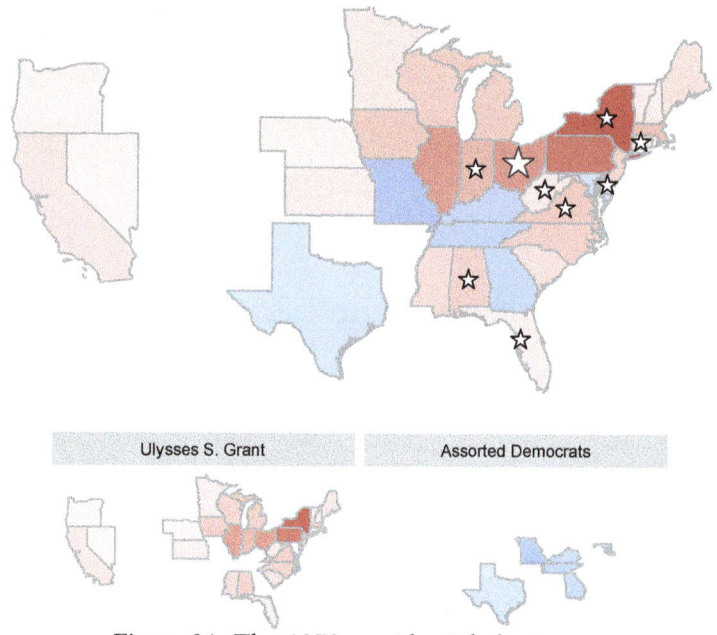

Figure 31: The 1872 presidential election.

Electoral vote: 286-0-47-5-5-3-3-1-1-1
Popular vote: 56%-44%
Pivotal state: Ohio
Critical states: None
Crucial states: Ohio, Florida, New York, Indiana, Alabama, Connecticut, West Virginia, Delaware, Virginia

Republican incumbent Ulysses S. Grant won re-election by a relatively large margin against Democratic challenger Horace Greeley, who was best known as a newspaperman but had also been in Congress. Initially, it appeared as though Grant would win by 300-66 in the Electoral College.

However, there were major irregularities that resulted in a very different vote total, with Grant earning 286 electoral votes and Greeley earning 0 electoral votes.

First, Horace Greeley died after the electors were chosen but before the electors voted. Most of the 66 electors pledged to support Greeley cast their votes for a variety of other candidates. Three attempted to vote for Greeley, and their votes were rejected by Congress as invalid. This set an important precedent for future elections; if a presidential candidate dies after electors are chosen but before electors vote, electors *must* either support an alternate candidate or have their votes discarded.[2]

Second, Congress rejected the legitimacy of Grant's electors in Arkansas and Louisiana on the grounds of widespread fraud, reducing Grant's total electoral vote from 300 to 286. It's worth noting that if Grant had died, rather than Greeley, the likely result of the election would have been a massive constitutional crisis as Republican electors scrambled for a replacement candidate to support. However, because the deceased candidate was also clearly the losing candidate, an electoral crisis was averted.

1876: Uncertainty and fraud in the Electoral College

The centennial year of the United States' existence saw one of the most contentious elections in its entire history. The election of 1876 was not won at the ballot box nor by presidential electors; it was resolved by a combination of political maneuvers, luck, partisanship, and fraud.

---

[2] Some states have laws that bind electors to vote in a particular fashion and do not address scenarios where a presidential candidate dies. As of 2020, the Supreme Court has affirmed that these binding laws are legal in *Chiafalo v. Washington* (2020), but did not specifically address whether or not binding laws can force an elector to cast an invalid vote for a dead candidate.

The 1876 election in brief

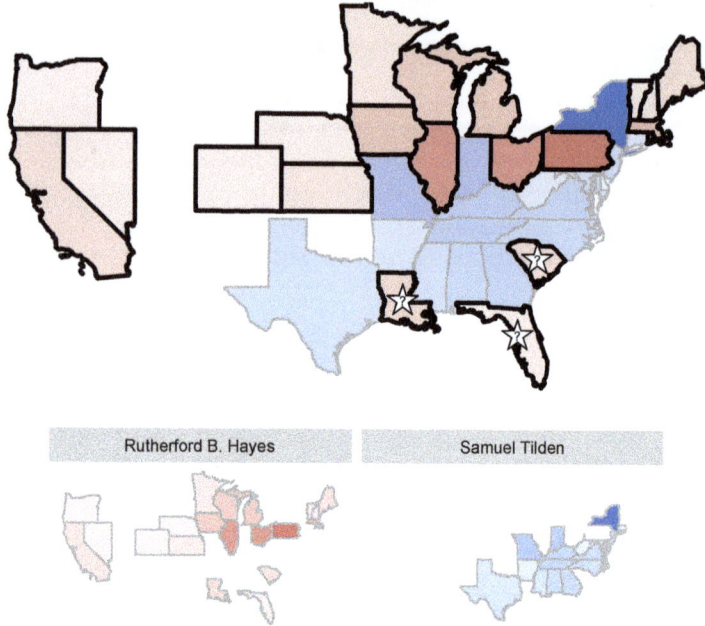

Figure 32: The 1876 presidential election.

Electoral vote: 185-184*
Popular vote: 49%-51%
Pivotal state: South Carolina or Louisiana or Florida
Critical states: All states won by Hayes
Crucial state: South Carolina or Louisiana or Florida

Republicans nominated Rutherford B. Hayes of Ohio; Democrats nominated Samuel Tilden of New York. There were three states whose results were contested: South Carolina, Louisiana, and Florida. It is clear that one of those states was therefore pivotal. It is not clear which state had the narrowest margin in terms of actual votes cast. South Carolina had the narrowest official margin of the three contested states, although it is possible that more voters voted for Tilden in any or all of the three disputed states. Whichever of the three disputed states we call pivotal, this election marked the *only* time that a state with fewer electors than average has been both pivotal and critical.[3]

In considering scenarios in which Tilden could have won, it is worth noting that Tilden won his home state of New York by a relatively narrow

---
[3] New Hampshire came close to this achievement in 2000, but Florida's margin was narrower.

margin; without New York, Tilden would have simply decisively lost in the Electoral College, rendering the disputes over presidential electors in Florida, Louisiana, South Carolina, and Oregon moot. Tilden's home state advantage in New York would have been critical in any Tilden victory and was very close to pivotal.

This was the first election in which the candidate with the most votes in the Electoral College was not also the candidate with the most votes overall in the nation. It was the second election in which the bonus "Senate" electors provided a decisive margin, as Hayes won a number of small states in the west.[4] As of the writing of this book, this was the final election in which a state legislature appointed presidential electors directly – since those electors voted for Hayes, it was the only election after 1824 in which state legislatures' appointees played a critical role, with Colorado's three electors being appointed by its Republican state legislature.

Fraud and uncertainty

To this day, nobody truly knows who the legitimate winner of the election of 1876 would have been if the election had been conducted fairly and freely. Across the entire South, results were marred by a combination of voter suppression, voter intimidation, misconduct by election officials, deceptive ballot design, and blatant fraud. Dirty tricks were not limited to the South. Corruption and electoral malpractice were significant and widespread outside of the South, but most of the controversies of the election of 1876 took place in the South.

In three key Southern states still occupied by federal troops, initial returns – as in all other former Confederate states – favored the Democratic candidate, Samuel Tilden. Republican officials in those three states, backed by military force, disqualified the returns from just enough counties to tip the balance in favor of the Republican candidate, Rutherford B. Hayes.

Even without the returns from those key counties, Tilden won an apparent majority of the national popular vote, with a margin of about 3%. In the broader historical context, Tilden's recorded share of the vote was typical for a winning presidential candidate; from 1828 to 2020, the winning presidential candidate earned a smaller share of the popular vote than Tilden in twenty-four out of forty-nine presidential elections.

One notable electoral irregularity that occurred outside of the South: The Democratic governor of Oregon declared that John Watts, a Republican

---

[4]The first time this happened was in 1796; it happened again in 2000.

elector, could not stand for office. The reason was that as a postmaster, Watts qualified as a "Person holding an Office of Trust or Profit under the United States," and was thus ineligible to serve as a presidential elector under Article II, Section 1 of the Constitution. Watts then resigned from his position shortly before the date for the meeting of the electoral colleges. Once the dust had settled in Oregon, all four states submitted two competing sets of votes from their electoral colleges.

The case of Oregon is particularly complex, involving bribery as well as conflicting votes between the House and Senate on the issue of whether or not the electoral vote of Watts could be counted as legitimate.[5]

Under existing rules, Tilden was expected to win a House contingent election held to resolve an election in which no single candidate had a majority.[6] Instead of resolving the election by contingent election, as would be appropriate when neither candidate had a legitimate claim to a majority of the vote from the various electoral colleges, Democrats and Republicans in Congress agreed to resolve the dispute in a novel way.

A special electoral commission

In order to resolve the dispute, the two parties put together a special electoral commission. This consisted of five representatives, five senators, and five Supreme Court justices. The original intent was to create a panel consisting of seven Republicans, seven Democrats, and one independent, which would be therefore seen as non-partisan. Justice David Davis was supposed to be that independent;[7] however, Democrats attempted to buy the vote of the anticipated independent Supreme Court justice by appointing him to the Senate, and he resigned from the Supreme Court – which meant that a Republican justice, Joseph P. Bradley, was appointed to the commission in place of the independent judge.

The electoral commission then resolved each of the four cases in favor of the Republicans by a party-line 8-7 vote, declaring that the Republican governors had the authority to declare the final election results, but that the Democratic governor had exceeded his authority by disqualifying

---

[5] See "Corruption and the Disputed Election Vote of Oregon in the 1876 Election" (1966) by Harold Dippre for a detailed treatment of this. Attempts to bribe or persuade key figures were not limited to the case of Oregon; for example, there was a documented effort to persuade James Russell Lowell of Massachusetts to vote for Tilden. See Chapter 13 of *James Russell Lowell: A Biography* (1901) by Horace Scudder.

[6] In the outgoing House of Representatives, Democrats held majorities in 24 out of 38 state delegations.

[7] For one nicely detailed account of this, see "How Not to Count Votes" (2004) by John Nagle.

Watts. As a result of this, Rutherford B. Hayes was elected by the margin of a single electoral vote, 185-184.

Following this ruling, efforts to reconstruct the South ended. Historians are divided on whether this was part of a behind-the-scenes bargain made to get Democrats to accept the Hayes presidency or not.[8]

The consequences

It is difficult to be sure if Tilden's apparent national majority was legitimate. The Republican vote totals in all former Confederate states were almost certainly reduced by a concerted effort to drive down participation by African-American voters.[9] The 1876 election did inspire the creation of the Electoral Count Act of 1887, which established a consistent set of rules for Congress to follow in resolving disputes involving the Electoral College.

This specific factor is not unique to the 1876 election; the measures taken by southern Democrats to reduce African-American participation in elections led to remarkably low turnout levels across the entire region until after the passage of the 24th Amendment and Voting Rights Act in 1964. Grover Cleveland's pluralities in 1884, 1888, and 1892, along with Wilson's plurality in 1916, are similarly of suspect status, narrow enough that they could have been reversed with greater participation by African-American voters in Southern states.

While Tilden's national popular vote majority can be seen as somewhat dubious, it remains less dubious than Hayes's electoral vote majority, which was adjudicated by the narrowest possible partisan margin based on four separate individually questionable decisions. It is not likely that Hayes had a greater actual vote total in all three disputed Southern states. The Watts decision was also of dubious logical merit. While in line with the will of the voters of Oregon, allowing an elector to meet eligibility requirements retroactively after being elected made a mockery of the Framers' intention to prevent conflicts of interest. Additionally, this last decision was at odds with the logic employed by the commission in the case of the other three states, which determined that the governor's certification was decisive in resolving which of a pair of disputed electoral returns was legitimate.

---

[8]The thesis of a compromise was introduced in *Reconstruction and Reunion: The Compromise of 1877 and the End of Reconstruction* (1951) by C. Vann Woodward. For the debate, see briefly "Was There a Compromise of 1877" (1973) by Allan Peskin, Woodward's rebuttal "Yes, There Was a Compromise of 1877" (1973), et cetera.

[9]This is widely documented in many sources, but see perhaps "Joseph E. Brown and the Florida Election of 1876" (1962) by Derrell Roberts and "A Most Corrupt Election: Louisiana in 1876" (2001) by Ronald King.

The South did not rise again in response to the election. Rutherford B. Hayes, dubbed "Rutherfraud" by his detractors, served a single term in office, with limited policy successes. It is by no means clear that Hayes was a superior choice to Tilden in any regard; he did little to stem the tide of corruption or the rise of Jim Crow in the South. Interestingly, a presidential candidate with a profile very similar to Tilden would be elected in 1884; Grover Cleveland was also a reform-minded Democrat from New York with enemies in Tammany Hall.

The era of the Empire State

The period from 1880 to 1908 is marked by a few curious occurrences. Republicans won six out of these eight elections. Unusually, it was Democrats who fielded fewer distinct candidates (four), nominating Grover Cleveland three times (he won twice) and William Jennings Bryan three times (he never won).

This also marked the peak of New York's power in presidential politics. New York had always been important in presidential elections and would remain so through 1976. The Empire State had a clear and incontestable claim to being *the* decisive political battleground in 1880, 1884, and 1888. New York was on the winning side of every presidential election from 1880 to 1912. From 1876 to 1908, there was only one winning ticket that didn't include a New Yorker.[10]

[10] McKinley / Hobart in 1896.

1880: The closest popular vote

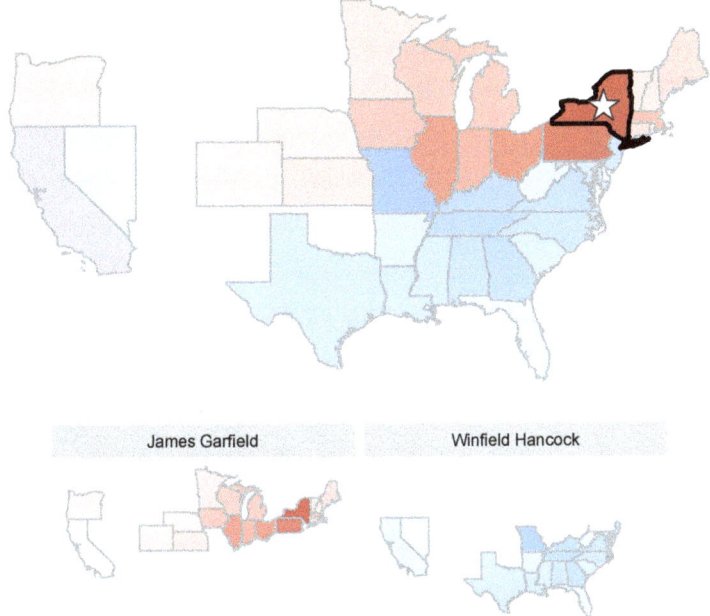

Figure 33: The 1880 presidential election.

Electoral vote: 214-155
Popular vote: 48%-48%
Pivotal state: New York
Critical state: New York
Crucial state: New York

Incumbent Rutherford Hayes had never intended to run for re-election. In his place, the Republicans nominated a congressional representative from Ohio, James Garfield, who won a narrow victory over Democrat Winfield Hancock, a general with a lengthy military career including both the Mexican-American War and the Civil War. Both candidates received almost exactly the same number of votes; the popular margin has been reported in various sources as between two thousand and ten thousand. Given the likely presence of some errors in counting, we can't even be sure that Garfield earned more votes; the two were essentially tied.

For this reason, the election of 1880 is noteworthy for featuring the smallest popular vote margin in the history of American presidential elections. It is the *only* election where the Electoral College was decided by a larger margin of votes than the popular vote; it was nevertheless a close election in the Electoral College as well. Garfield won New York by a little over twenty thousand votes, and New York was by any measure the key state that decided the election. New York was the pivotal state, and also the unique critical state; had Hancock won twenty thousand more votes in New York, he would have won the election.

This is the *only* election where the national popular vote was within the margin of normal counting error, although there are other elections where the national popular vote margin has been contested on the basis of divided electoral slates[11] or by the scope of election fraud.[12]

1884: A new Democrat

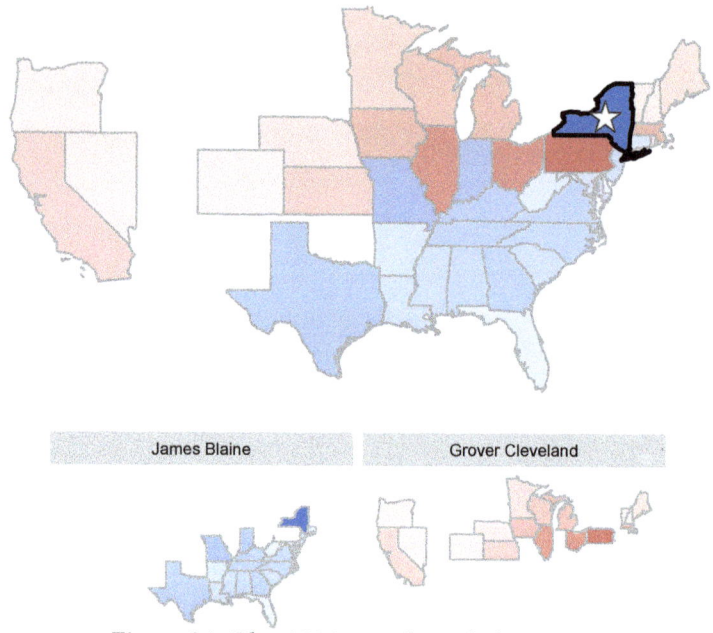

Figure 34: The 1884 presidential election.

Popular vote: 49%-48%
Electoral vote: 219-182
Pivotal state: New York
Critical state: New York
Crucial state: New York

Incumbent president Chester A. Arthur (James Garfield had died in office) was unable to secure nomination by the Republicans, who instead nominated James Blaine. The Democrats nominated New York governor Grover Cleveland.

---

[11] See in particular Alabama in the 1960 election.
[12] See both the 1876 and 1960 elections.

LINCOLN'S ELECTORAL COLLEGE (1868-1916) 109

This was a close election by any measure, but was ultimately decided by a margin of about one thousand votes in New York; Grover Cleveland, as the sitting governor of New York, ultimately was responsible for certifying the narrow victory of his own electors. This would have been more suspicious if Grover Cleveland did not have a reputation for honesty and the enmity of the Tammany Hall machine. He was the first Democratic president elected since James Buchanan in 1856.

Presidential historians today often regard Grover Cleveland as a better president than the other presidents who served after Abraham Lincoln but before McKinley.[13] As mentioned earlier, Grover Cleveland had a very similar political profile to Samuel Tilden (Democratic reformer from New York, enemy of Tammany Hall).

1888: The Republicans strike back

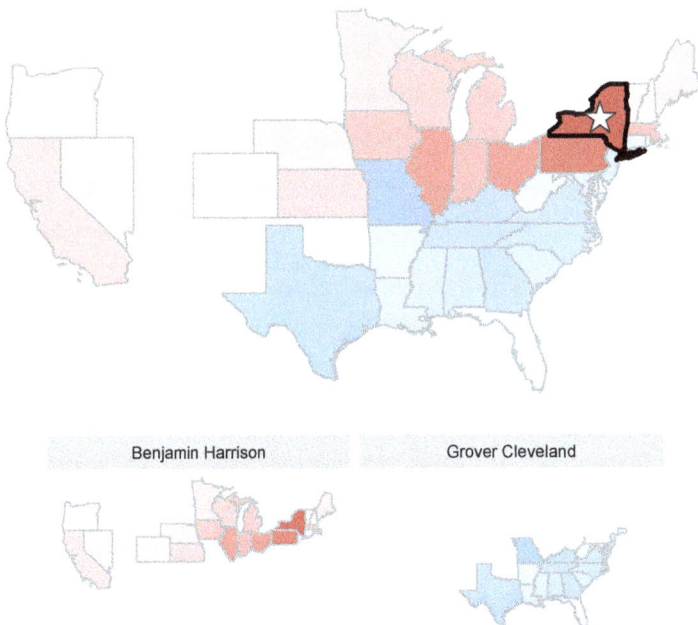

Figure 35: The 1888 presidential election.

Electoral vote: 233-168
Popular vote: 48%-49%
Pivotal state: New York
Critical state: New York
Crucial state: New York

---

[13]See, for example, "America's Presidents: Greatest and Worst: Siena's 6th Presidential Expert Poll 1982-2018." (2018) by Douglas Lonnstrom and Thomas Kelly.

Incumbent Grover Cleveland won more votes nationally than Republican challenger Benjamin Harrison; however, for the second time in the electoral history of the United States (and the second time in only twelve years), the direction of this margin was reversed in the Electoral College. Ultimately, this election was decided by a narrow margin in New York (about fourteen thousand votes). This was the third time in a row in which New York was the key decisive state of the election. However, this was not the end of Grover Cleveland's political career, as we will see shortly.

Harrison, as the grandson of the short-lived William Henry Harrison, was the second dynastic president. He is poorly regarded by most presidential historians; so are the two presidents who were sons of previous presidents (Adams and Bush). While it is true that Harrison's numbers in the South were likely reduced by the effects of Jim Crow laws on African-American voter turnout, his numbers in key battleground states (notably New York) were inflated by fraud. It's not clear if Harrison had persuaded more New Yorkers to vote for him or simply had the backing of a more effective political machine with fewer scruples.

Boss Quay, who had come up from Pennsylvania to bend the vote in critical New York City, suggested that many people had risked prison to make sure that Harrison defeated Cleveland, though Harrison was unaware.[14] Other records suggest that Harrison was aware of a vote-buying scheme; what blew the scheme open was a letter intercepted on its way to New York from Indiana which outlined a "blocks of five" scheme in which voters would be bribed in groups of five, giving one member of the group both the money and responsibility for insuring the others voted correctly.

The publication of the letter was an open admission of election fraud not matched in its overt corruption before or since. The *New York World* estimated that, based on the sums of money involved, the number of votes bought in New York was in excess of 100,000 - in other words, more than seven times the margin of victory. As Harrison was apparently aware of this scheme, Harrison was nearly the first president to be charged with election fraud.[15]

---

[14] An early account of this can be traced back to *Old Time Notes of Pennsylvania: A Connected and Chronological Record of the Commercial, Industrial and Educational Advancement of Pennsylvania, and the Inner History of All Political Movements Since the Adoption of the Constitution of 1838* (1905) by A. K. McClure. Matt Quay (also known as Boss Quay) is attributed the quote "Providence hadn't a damned thing to do with [Harrison's victory]", which has then been repeated in many other sources.

[15] See *Life of Walter Quintin Gresham, 1832-1895* (1919) by Matilda Gresham for details on the "blocks of five" case, including the full text of the letter in question and discussion of Harrison's apparent levels of awareness.

1892: The return of Cleveland

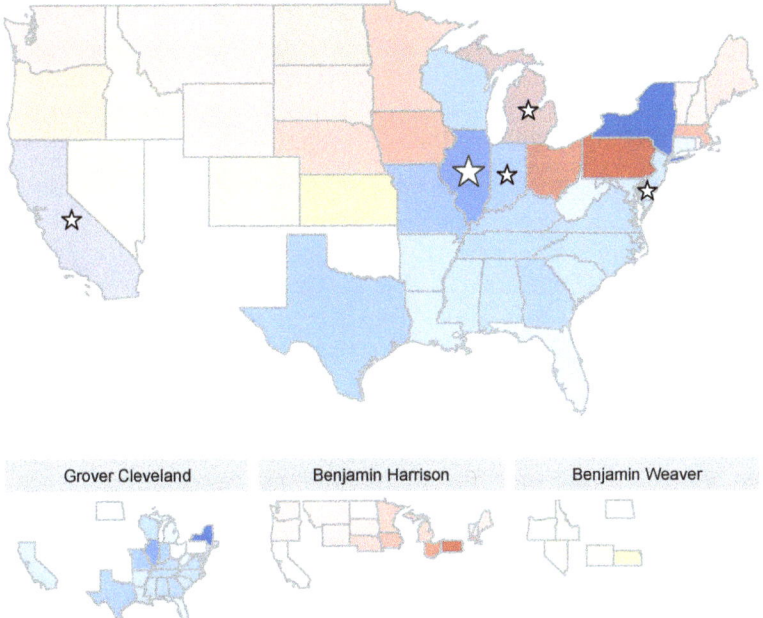

Figure 36: The 1892 presidential election.

Electoral vote: 277-145-22
Popular vote: 46%-43%-9%
Pivotal state: Illinois
Critical states: None
Crucial states: Illinois, West Virginia, Wisconsin, Indiana

For the third time in a row, Democrat Grover Cleveland won a relatively narrow plurality of the popular vote against his Republican opponent, who was in this case the incumbent Benjamin Harrison. Benjamin Weaver of the People's Party carried several Western states. Cleveland also won in the Electoral College, making him the first (and so far only) president to serve non-consecutive terms.

This time, Cleveland won New York and also the election; although he won New York by a large enough margin that we would call Illinois the pivotal state. He won the Electoral College by a large enough margin that even losing New York's votes would not have cost him the election. The shift of margin in New York might partly be attributed to the fact that Harrison had lost the support of Boss Quay and some other key machine politicians. The battleground status of New York and the poor state of election integrity meant that whichever party did a better job of cheating in New York City could carry the state.

As I noted previously, Cleveland is generally regarded as a better president than Harrison, and he was more popular than Harrison at the time he held office. Grover Cleveland's mixed electoral record wasn't the result of any systematic effect in the Electoral College that gave a real and enduring advantage to either Democrats or Republicans. This was just chaos; Cleveland's initial win in 1884, his loss in 1888, and his second victory in 1892 were differentiated by small shifts in voting behavior.

In either 1884 or 1888, the result could very easily have been decided by machine politics at work in New York City itself. Those two elections were well within the margin of fraud or even unintentional error, and the potential spoiler effect of Weaver as a third-party candidate was quite significant in 1892. Either the Electoral College failed by electing Harrison in 1888, or it failed *twice* by electing Cleveland in 1884 and 1892.

1896: An election without a New York candidate

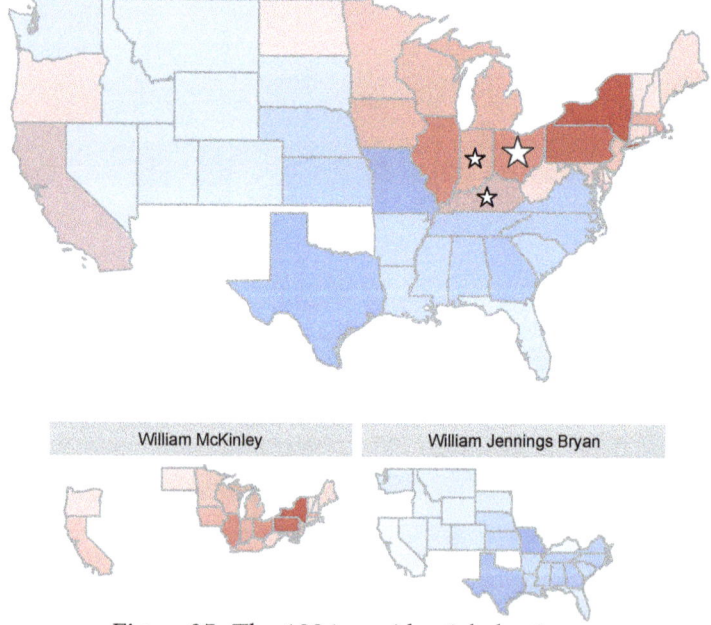

Figure 37: The 1896 presidential election.

Electoral vote: 271-176
Popular vote: 51%-47%
Pivotal state: Ohio
Critical states: None
Crucial states: Ohio, Indiana, Oregon, and California

Republican William McKinley faced off against William Jennings Bryan, who was jointly nominated by both the People's Party and Democratic Party (with two different vice presidential running mates). McKinley won by a comfortable margin.

Ohio, the home state of McKinley's running mate Garret Hobart, was the pivotal state in this election; if Bryan won Ohio, Indiana, Oregon, and California, he would have won the election. This was the closest that William Jennings Bryan came to winning the presidency out of three attempts. This was also the only election from 1876 to 1908 in which the winning ticket did not include either a presidential or vice presidential candidate from New York.

1900: A re-match

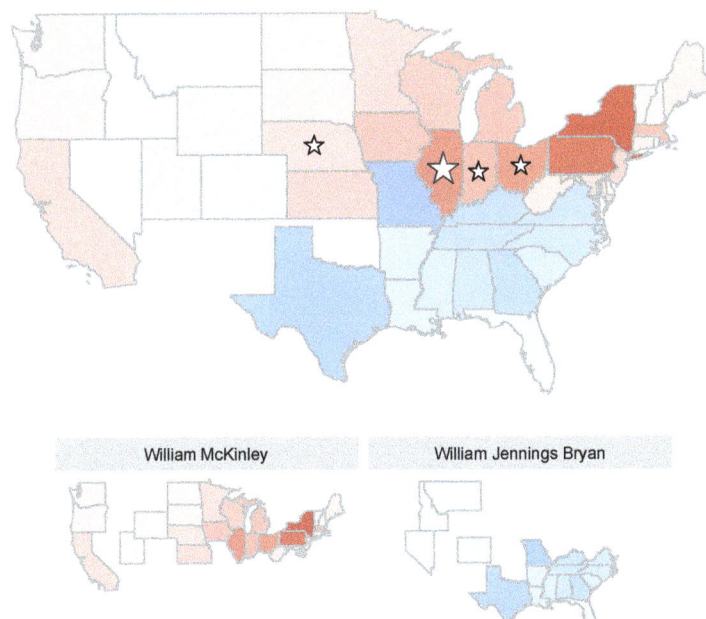

Figure 38: The 1900 presidential election.

Electoral vote: 292-155
Popular vote: 52%-46%
Pivotal state: Illinois
Critical states: None
Crucial states: Illinois, Ohio, Kansas, Indiana

Incumbent William McKinley chose a new running mate, New York Governor Theodore Roosevelt, a choice that would prove important later. McKinley easily defeated William Jennings Bryan in this rematch election, carrying several additional states. In this election, Bryan crucially lost his home state of Nebraska. Ohio and New York remained close to the national median, but Illinois can be identified as the pivotal state in this election.

1904: A popular vice presidential successor

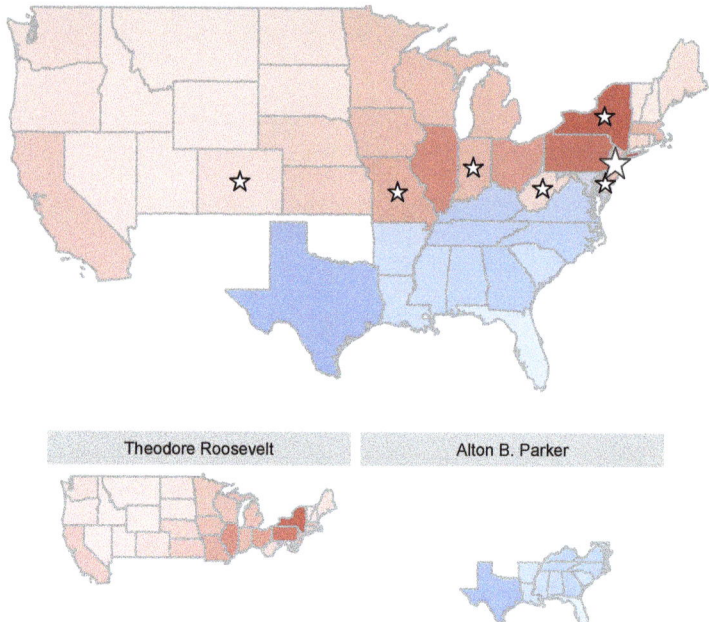

Figure 39: The 1904 presidential election.

Electoral vote: 336-140
Popular vote: 56%-37%
Pivotal state: New Jersey
Critical states: None
Crucial states: New Jersey, Colorado, Indiana, West Virginia, New York, Delaware, Missouri

Theodore Roosevelt ascended to the presidency following the assassination of McKinley. Unlike all previous vice presidential successors,[16] Theodore Roosevelt was very popular both within his party and the nation at large. He was renominated by his party and won by a large margin against Democratic challenger Alton B. Parker. Since

---
[16]John Tyler, Millard Fillmore, Andrew Johnson, and Chester A. Arthur.

LINCOLN'S ELECTORAL COLLEGE (1868-1916) 115

Roosevelt had become president in the wake of McKinley's assassination, this made Roosevelt both the first vice presidential successor to be renominated for his party and the first to win re-election.

The pivotal state in this election was New Jersey, which had previously been critical in 1840; New York, though not critical, was crucial. Every state won by Parker was south of the Mason-Dixon line.

1908: The last run of William Jennings Bryan

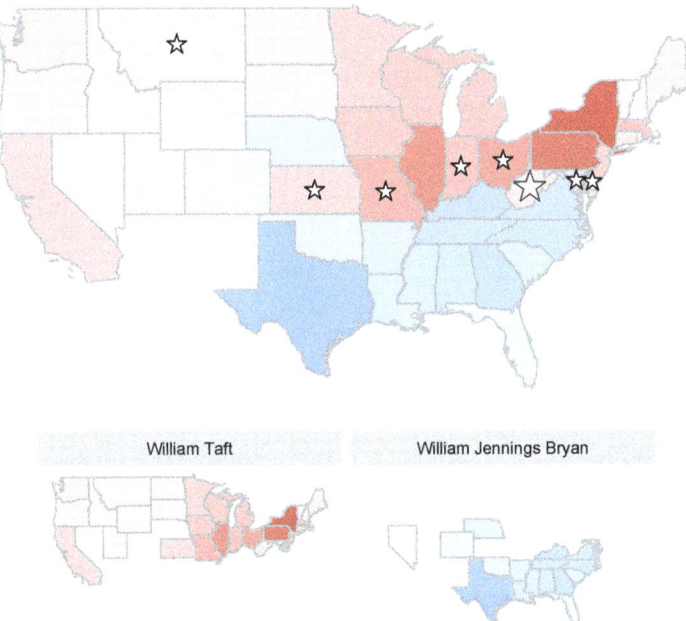

Figure 40: The 1908 presidential election.

Electoral vote: 321-162
Popular vote: 52%-43%
Pivotal state: West Virginia
Critical states: None
Crucial states: West Virginia, Kansas, Ohio, Delaware, Montana, Indiana, Maryland, Missouri

The Republican Party nominated Theodore Roosevelt's chosen successor, Secretary of War William Taft. The Democrats nominated William Jennings Bryan for a third time.[17] While the popular vote margin in this election was considerably smaller than the margin in the

---
[17] Amusingly, this meant the third William versus William contest since 1896.

1904 election, the electoral map was very similar; Bryan only added his home state of Nebraska and two small Western states to the Democratic column.

The pivotal state in this election was West Virginia, which at seven electoral votes is one of the smallest pivotal states on record - although many more than just West Virginia's seven electoral votes would have been needed to flip the election.

Woodrow Wilson and the Condorcet problem

The 1912 election featured one of the periodic breakdowns of the two-party system, and possibly the most significant spoiler effect seen in an American presidential election. Much as in 1860, one of the major parties split, with different wings of the party supporting different candidates; also as in 1860, the main branch of the party did worse in the Electoral College.

The 1912 election in brief

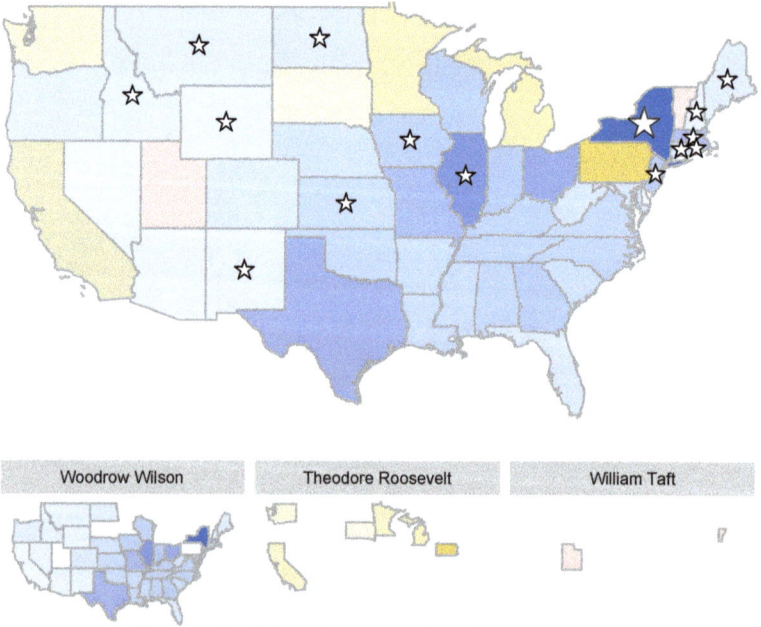

Figure 41: The 1912 presidential election.

Electoral vote: 435-88-8
Popular vote: 42%-27%-23%
Pivotal state: New York
Critical states: None
Crucial states: New York, Nevada, Oklahoma, Wisconsin, New Jersey, Oregon, Montana, Kansas, New Mexico, Iowa, North Dakota, Massachusetts, Illinois

In 1912, there were three major candidates: Former president Theodore Roosevelt, incumbent president William Taft, and Democratic challenger Woodrow Wilson. Perennial candidate Eugene Debs also ran, earning 6% of the vote, the most he earned in any of his five bids for the presidency. The standard story about the election of 1912 is that Wilson won due to a divided Republican vote. While this is true on a certain level, the fact that Woodrow Wilson had a strong concentrated regional base of support was a significant advantage.

Taft's running mate, James Sherman, died. The eight Republican electors voted for Nicholas Butler as a group instead.

The falling-out between Theodore Roosevelt and his former protege William Taft led Roosevelt to run under the banner of the Progressive Party. The Democrats nominated Woodrow Wilson under more ordinary and less dramatic circumstances. The pivotal state was New York; had the contest been a two-way contest instead of a three-way contest, New York would have assumed the same outsized importance in the outcome that it frequently did from 1860 to 1888.

The 1916 election in brief

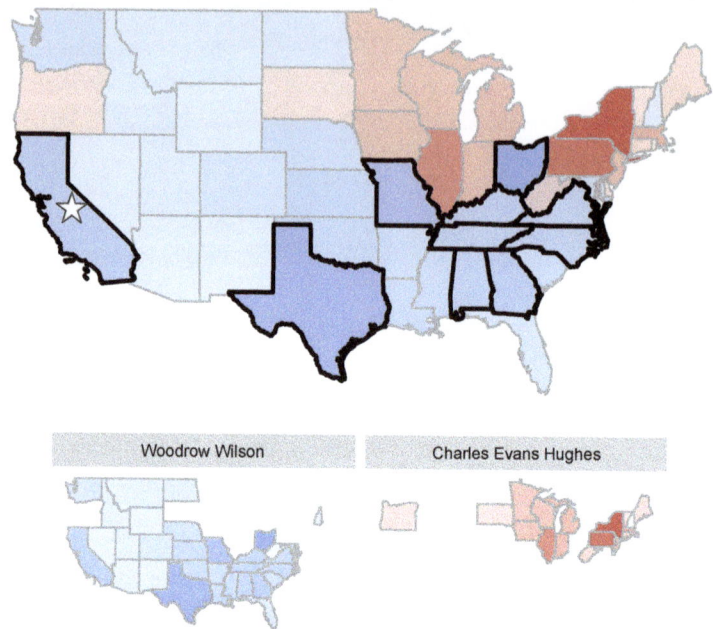

Figure 42: The 1916 presidential election.

Electoral vote: 277-254
Popular vote: 49%-46%
Pivotal state: California
Critical states: California, Alabama, Georgia, Kentucky, Missouri, North Carolina, Ohio, Tennessee, Texas, Virginia
Crucial state: California

Republicans nominated Charles Evans Hughes, a former New York governor and at the time a justice on the Supreme Court, to challenge incumbent president Woodrow Wilson as the Great War (later known as World War I) engulfed Europe. Woodrow Wilson was, if anything, a bit more popular than he had been in 1912; however, without the benefit of a massive spoiler effect, he came quite close to losing the election. While his popular vote margin was not unusually close, his victory in the Electoral College was one of the narrowest on record, with ten critical states. Losing any one of those ten states would have lost Wilson the election.

Out of these ten critical states, his margin was narrowest in California (less than four thousand out of a million votes), which was therefore the pivotal state of the election. This was the first election since the disputed election of 1876 in which New York (the most frequent pivotal state) voted for the losing candidate; the ninth election in which the pivotal state was also critical; and only the third election in which a state other than New York was both critical and pivotal.

Setting the stage for spoilers

In Chapter 5, we noted that spoiler effects can play a significant role. In Chapter 6, we noted that when there are three or four major candidates, the separation of the electoral colleges by state helps candidates who have strong sectional bases of support and harms candidates with broad support across the entire country, leading in the most extreme cases to spoiler-proof minority victories.

Finally, as we noted near the beginning of this chapter, African-American voters' ability to participate in elections was sharply limited across the South following the end of Reconstruction. Following the election of President Hayes and the withdrawal of federal troops from the last three occupied Southern states, Democrats had uncontested control of the South.

An Electoral College landslide without a popular foundation

Woodrow Wilson won 435 electoral votes out of a total of 531. This was a larger electoral margin than seen in *any previous contested election*.[18] He did so with only 41% of the vote – the second-smallest share of the popular vote of anybody winning a majority in the Electoral College, and the third-smallest share of the popular vote of any successful candidate.[19]

The election of 1912 has some clear similarities to the election of 1860. The winner received about the same share of the popular vote (40% in 1860, 41% in 1912). The other major party was divided; in 1860, the Republican candidate won against a pair of Democratic candidates. In 1912, the Democratic candidate won against a pair of Republican candidates. In addition to the three candidates coming out of the two major parties, both elections featured prominent candidates outside of the two major parties; the other candidates received 13% of the vote in 1860 and 8% of the vote in 1912.

---

[18] George Washington won by unanimous vote in 1788 and 1792; James Monroe won all but one electoral vote in 1820, thanks to a "faithless" elector who voted in an unexpected way.

[19] John Quincy Adams, with 31% of the vote, had been elected by the House of Representatives in 1824, and drew a significant share of his electoral vote from electors appointed by state legislatures. Abraham Lincoln, with 40% of the vote, had a relatively fragile majority in the Electoral College, one that depended on winning a key state – New York – by a narrow margin.

Another major similarity is that both Wilson and Lincoln were firmly placed on one end of the political spectrum, apart from the other candidates. The Republicans were firmly opposed to the spread of slavery and were deeply unpopular in the South. In 1912, the two Republican candidates were formerly close political allies, and even the minor party candidates (running on Socialist and Prohibition tickets) were champions of specific progressive causes.

Given the political spectrum of the day, it is likely that almost all of the voters who voted for a candidate other than Wilson would have preferred either Roosevelt or Taft over Wilson, just as in 1860, it is likely that almost all of the voters who voted for a candidate other than Lincoln would have preferred either Bell or Douglas over Lincoln.[20]

The vote against Abraham Lincoln was divided between three major candidates; the vote against Woodrow Wilson was mostly divided between two major candidates, with two minor candidates who did not earn electoral votes. Both earned a similar share of the total popular vote. Both were also similarly polarizing. How is it, then, that Abraham Lincoln won by electoral vote narrowly, while Woodrow Wilson won by a large margin? The difference lies in the fact that their *opponents* were not as sectionally polarizing relative to one another. John Bell and John Breckinridge had regions of clear separate support; Theodore Roosevelt and William Taft did not.

Sectionalism and the Electoral College

In 1860, the candidates who placed third and fourth in the popular vote placed second and third in the Electoral College. Breckinridge had a strong concentrated base of support in the South. Bell's base of support was slightly less concentrated, but was still concentrated in states where slavery was legal.[21] He had particularly strong support in border states where avoiding war was a high priority. Stephen Douglas, on the other hand, had broad support across the entire country - and therefore won electors in only two states, Missouri and New Jersey.

In 1912, Woodrow Wilson had a concentrated regional base of support in the South; however, his opponents lacked a similar natural base of support. The result was that both of them performed similarly to Stephen Douglas, earning disproportionately few electoral votes. If Taft and

---

[20] For a possible counterexample, there might have been Southerners unwilling to vote for *anyone* on a Republican ticket, but who were willing to vote for Roosevelt on the Progressive ticket. It's not clear how many of this type of voter actually existed, however.

[21] Bell came close to earning electors in New Jersey and New York thanks to a "fusion" ticket; those were the last two Northern states to abolish slavery.

Roosevelt had been sectional candidates, similarly popular but more regionally polarizing, the election could have gone very differently.

While it is tempting to ascribe Wilson's sectional support in the South to his status as the first southerner[22] nominated by a major party since 1860, the fact is that the South voted similarly strongly for every Democratic presidential candidate since federal troops were withdrawn after the 1876 election. The share of the vote for William Jennings Bryan in 1908 is very strongly correlated with the share of the vote for Woodrow Wilson in 1912 - with William Jennings Bryan earning a slightly larger share of the vote overall.

The Condorcet problem and spoiler effects

Like Abraham Lincoln and John Breckinridge in 1860, Woodrow Wilson had a significant advantage as a candidate with a concentrated regional base of support (the South). Unlike Lincoln, though, Wilson only faced candidates who had broad national appeal. The result is that in most states, the election was decided by a spoiler effect.

In the 1860 election, 169 out of Abraham Lincoln's 180 electoral votes came from states where he won an outright majority of the vote, including the critical state of New York. By contrast, the only states in which Wilson earned more than half of the vote were the eleven states of the former Confederacy, with a total of only 126 out of the 435 electoral votes. Roosevelt earned an outright majority in only one state,[23] and Taft didn't earn a majority of the vote in any state.

Four hundred electoral votes from thirty-six states were within the numeric margin of a potential spoiler effect - more than in any previous presidential election, and only matched subsequently by the 1992 election. When we consider the political spectrum of the day, the very similar map of Democratic support in 1908 and 1920, and Wilson's comparatively narrow re-election in 1916, it seems very clear that Wilson won because of the spoiler effect. In fact, we can go as far as to say that, out of the top three candidates,[24] Wilson looked like a *Condorcet loser*.

A brief digression: Back in the late 18th century, a French mathematician by the name of Nicolas Jean Antoine Marie de Caritat (better known by his title as the Marquis of Condorcet) came up with the idea of analyzing voters' preferences by looking at how voters would cast their ballots in a

---

[22]Wilson was born in Virginia and spent much of his life in Georgia, South Carolina, and North Carolina.

[23]South Dakota, with five electoral votes.

[24]I.e., if we do not include the minor party candidates who failed to win any electoral votes.

simple head-to-head contest.[25] Thus, a candidate who loses every such contest is known as a Condorcet loser; a candidate who would win every such contest is a Condorcet winner; and if there is no Condorcet winner or Condorcet loser, then the resulting cycle of preferences is known as a Condorcet paradox.

Many voting systems, notably including the perennially popular majority runoff election, satisfy the Condorcet loser criterion, that is, they will never elect a Condorcet loser. Few satisfy the similar Condorcet winner criterion, which is that a system will always elect a Condorcet winner if one exists. A simple plurality vote can elect a Condorcet loser; the Electoral College can do so quite similarly.

Most of Roosevelt's supporters probably preferred Taft to Wilson. Most of Taft's supporters probably preferred Roosevelt to Wilson. It's even likely that most of those voting for the Socialist Party candidate Eugene Debs and the Prohibition Party candidate Eugene Chafin preferred Taft or Roosevelt to Wilson. In a two-person race against either of his two Republican opponents, it's almost certain Wilson would have lost, quite possibly by a large margin.

It's also worth noting that in spite of all the advantages that accrue to an incumbent president in a time of crisis, Wilson was only narrowly re-elected in 1916.[26]

The artificial landslide

Wilson and Lincoln earned a similar share of the vote with a similar amount of fragmentation of their opponents. The structure of Lincoln's support was strongly polarized, meaning that Lincoln was immune to the spoiler effect. However, that is not to say that Lincoln's 1860 victory was more secure than Wilson's 1912 victory.

The fusion ticket of anti-Lincoln electors in New York lost the state by a margin of only fifty thousand votes; without New York's 35 electoral votes, Lincoln would not have had a majority in the Electoral College. Taking Wilson's electoral majority away would have required reversing a combined margin of hundreds of thousands of votes across twenty different states. Wilson's landslide wasn't a product of chaos within the Electoral College; instead, it was mainly a result of a spoiler effect, with

---

[25] *Essai Sur l'application de l'analyse à La Probabilité Des décisions Rendues à La Pluralité Des Voix* (1785).

[26] Arguably "He kept us out of the war!" amounted to false pretenses, since Wilson ended American neutrality in World War I shortly after he was re-elected, but that is another argument for another time. The risk that a president chooses to change his or her tune after being re-elected is not linked to the Electoral College.

the sheer size of the landslide amplified by the disadvantage faced by candidates with broad support.

Support for Roosevelt, Taft, and even the minor party candidates was spread diffusely across the entire country. In 1860, both John Bell and John Breckinridge had strong regional concentrations of support, respectively in the border states that would have the most to lose from a civil war and in the South. Stephen Douglas, by contrast, placed fourth in the Electoral College despite having about as much popular support as Lincoln's other two opponents combined. Wilson's opponents both had more Douglas-like profiles, popular but with geographically diffuse support that wasn't exceptionally strong anywhere in particular.

Historical consequences

Woodrow Wilson's presidency had major effects on both the United States and the world. Wilson had grown up in the South and lived much of his life there. While he launched his political career in New Jersey, he was arguably the only Southern Democratic president elected with the support of the South between James Polk (elected in 1840) and Jimmy Carter (elected in 1976).[27]

Because Wilson's term in office spanned major global events (particularly World War I, the worst influenza pandemic of the modern era, and the formation of the League of Nations) it is difficult to overstate the impact of the 1912 election on the course of history. While in some cases it is not clear if Roosevelt or Taft would have made very different decisions, it is worth noting that before 1913, segregation had been mostly created and enforced at state, local, and private levels: The federal government did little to create or discourage racial discrimination at the time.[28] Unlike any other president before or since, however, Wilson took substantial steps to advance segregation, particularly within the federal government.[29]

---

[27]Truman (1948) came from a border state and Lyndon B. Johnson (1964) came from Texas, but both were strongly in favor of civil rights and lost most of the former Confederate states in their respective elections.

[28]The constitutional amendments that support modern federal anti-discrimination law existed, but were not enforced in the same way. See in particular *Plessy v. Ferguson* (1896).

[29]For one account of how this developed, see "Woodrow Wilson and Federal Segregation" (1959) by Kathleen Wolgemuth.

CHAPTER 8

A coeducational Electoral College (1920-1956)

The passage of the 19th Amendment in 1920 led to another dramatic expansion of the voting franchise. Women's suffrage roughly doubled the number of eligible voters.[1]

A string of Republican landslides

In the previous several election cycles, Republicans had been more friendly to women's suffrage than men, most notably in the case of Theodore Roosevelt and the Progressives who had broken away from the party in 1912 with Roosevelt.[2] After the return of many of the breakaway Progressives, Republicans also voted for the 19th Amendment in greater numbers than Democrats. It is probably not coincidental that the next three election cycles involved landslide victories for the Republican Party.

In the case of Herbert Hoover, a large gender gap in voting was fairly well documented,[3] but it seems reasonable to assume that in spite of a paucity

---

[1] It's worth noting that in some states, women had already won the right to vote in presidential elections, so this was not an exact doubling from 1916 to 1920.

[2] C.f. *The Woman Suffrage Movement in America: A Reassessment* (2013) by Corrine McConnaughy.

[3] C.f. "Gender Gaps in Presidential Elections" (1999) by Jo Freeman.

A COEDUCATIONAL ELECTORAL COLLEGE (1920-1956)   125

of good survey data, women voters played a key role in 1920 and 1924 in what amounted to the most dramatic pair of electoral landslides since the time of James Monroe.

The 1920 election in brief

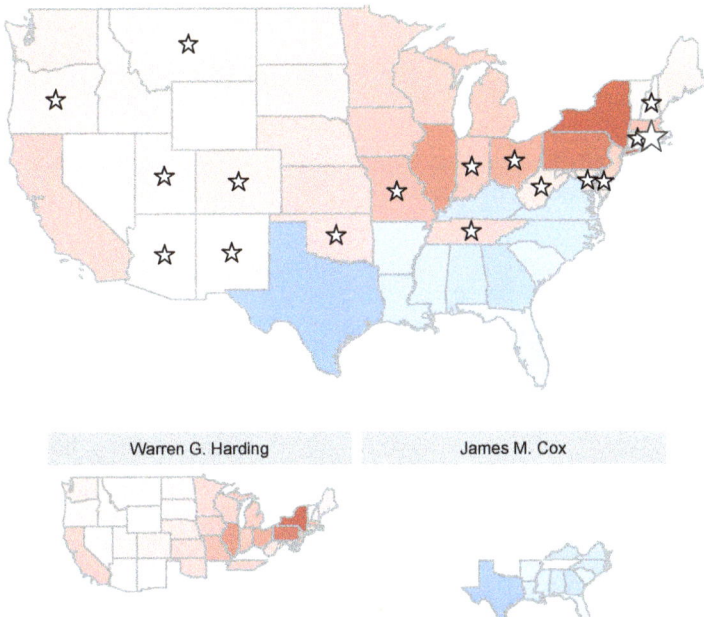

Figure 43: The 1920 presidential election.

Electoral vote: 404-127
Popular vote: 60%-34%
Pivotal state: Rhode Island
Critical states: None
Crucial states: Rhode Island, Connecticut, Montana, Oregon, Colorado, Nevada, New Hampshire, Ohio, Utah, Indiana, Delaware, Maryland, West Virginia, Missouri, Arizona, Oklahoma, Tennessee

The Republicans nominated former Ohio newspaperman Warren G. Harding; the Democrats nominated former Ohio newspaperman James M. Cox. Harding won by a landslide; no presidential candidate had the support of over 60% of voters since 1820. In spite of earning 60% of the vote, Harding's margin in the Electoral College was no larger than Wilson earned in 1912 with 42% of the vote, as the South remained firmly Democratic.

As an ironic reference point, Cox received a similar raw number of votes as Wilson in 1912 and 1916; the electorate had grown dramatically. With the passage of the 19th Amendment, women nearly doubled the electorate. Since the progressive wing of the Republican Party supported women's suffrage and the prohibition of alcohol, it is often thought that new women voters played an important role in Harding's victory. However, there is relatively little hard evidence to support or deny this claim.

It is worth noting that Cox's running mate was Franklin D. Roosevelt, who would later become a highly successful president. Unusually, the pivotal state in this election was a small state, Rhode Island, although Rhode Island was only one of a collection of seventeen crucial states that Cox would have needed to flip in order to win.

The 1924 election in brief

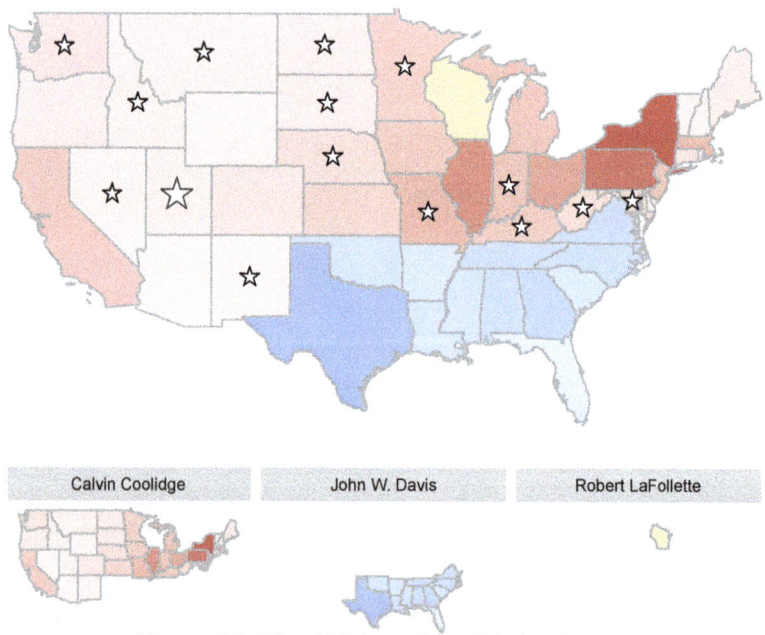

Figure 44: The 1924 presidential election.

Electoral vote: 382-136-13
Popular vote: 54%-28%-17%
Pivotal state: Utah
Critical states: None
Crucial states: Utah, Nebraska, Indiana, Washington, South

A COEDUCATIONAL ELECTORAL COLLEGE (1920-1956) 127

Dakota, Idaho, Minnesota, Missouri, Arizona, New Mexico, West Virginia, Montana, Maryland, Kentucky, North Dakota

Warren G. Harding died in office; incumbent Calvin Coolidge faced opponents from both ends of the political spectrum. Democratic candidate John W. Davis won in the South, while Progressive Robert LaFollette only took his home state of Wisconsin, leaving Coolidge to win in a landslide.

Since Congress had deadlocked on re-apportioning the House after the 1920 census, the weights in the Electoral College were starting to become unusually disproportionate.

The pivotal state in this election was Utah, which only had four electoral votes, although Coolidge would have needed to lose many more states than just Utah in order to transform his landslide victory into a narrow defeat.

The election of 1928 and the allocation problem

The 1928 election is, on one level, a profoundly uninteresting election. The two-party system was intact, no odd electoral anomalies reared their ugly head, and the election was not particularly close. However, it's noteworthy for one particular reason. This election had one of the most disproportionately assigned Electoral Colleges in history. Congress never reapportioned the House after the 1920 census, so the 1928 presidential election was carried out on the basis of the 1910 census instead.

A COEDUCATIONAL ELECTORAL COLLEGE (1920-1956)

The 1928 election in brief

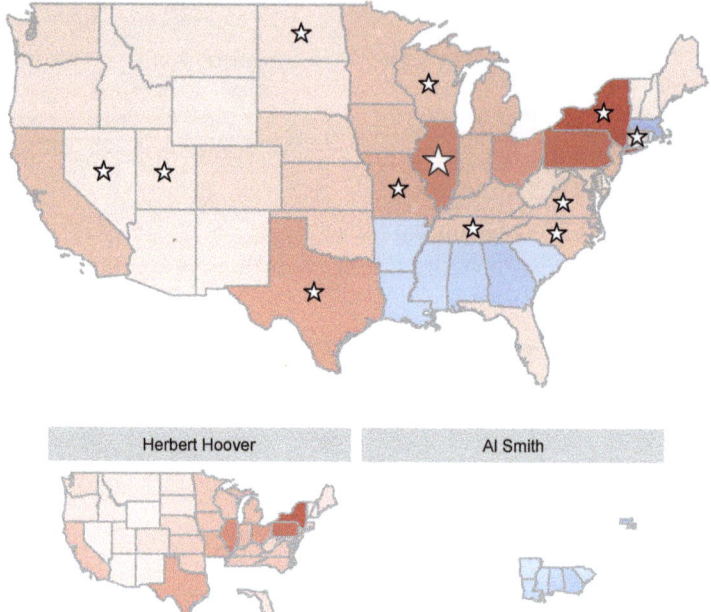

Figure 45: The 1928 presidential election.

Electoral vote: 444-87
Popular vote: 58%-41%
Pivotal state: Illinois
Crucial states: Illinois, Nevada, Missouri, North Dakota, North Carolina, Wisconsin, Connecticut, Virginia, Utah, Tennessee, Texas, New York

Republicans nominated Herbert Hoover, notable as an engineer, businessman, and recent Secretary of Commerce who had never previously held elective office. Democrats nominated Al Smith, governor of New York and an opponent of Prohibition; this marked a third straight Republican landslide. It is well-documented that women voters backed Hoover in large numbers, with a gender gap playing a role in his strong victory.

In spite of the fact that Al Smith won a higher share of votes than the previous two Democratic presidential candidates, he earned fewer electoral votes, winning the deep South, Rhode Island, and Massachusetts (failing to carry his home state of New York). The pivotal state in this election was Illinois (a large state with 29 electoral votes).

The allocation problem

The Constitution says that the number of representatives granted to each state should be based on the number of residents of each state.[4] It further requires the number of residents should be determined every ten years by a census. It does not provide a formula for translating population into representation, but instead leaves the details entirely up to Congress:

> Representatives and direct Taxes shall be apportioned among the several States which may be included within this Union, according to their respective Numbers, which shall be determined by adding to the whole Number of free Persons, including those bound to Service for a Term of Years, and excluding Indians not taxed, three fifths of all other Persons. The actual Enumeration shall be made within three Years after the first Meeting of the Congress of the United States, and within every subsequent Term of ten Years, in such Manner as they shall by Law direct.

Congress mostly addressed this problem on an *ad hoc* basis. Both the size of the House and the formula used to determine which states would get how many representatives varied significantly from decade to decade. From 1790 to 1920, there were fourteen official censuses; from 1792 to 1922, Congress passed twelve separate apportionment acts that set both the mathematical formula and size of the House for each allocation. Each act was subject to intense debates. Generally speaking, most representatives were strongly opposed to any apportionment that would reduce the size of their state's delegation; this helped steadily increase the size of the House over time.

That is not to say that Congress had not tried drawing up a long-term solution before. The apportionment act written to address the 1850 census was intended to apply to *all future censuses;* as standing law, it did manage to remained in place long enough to apply to the 1860 census.[5] In 1920, however, something new happened: Congress refused to act at all.

The basic reason for this was that the results of the 1920 census were controversial. They showed unexpectedly large population growth, concentrated heavily in a small number of states and partly driven by high immigration rates. The South, as a region, was largely left out

---

[4]Since slavery has been abolished, there are no "other persons" to count in fractional terms.

[5]This may have only happened because Congress was distracted by a civil war, and therefore too busy to start a fresh fight over seat allocations.

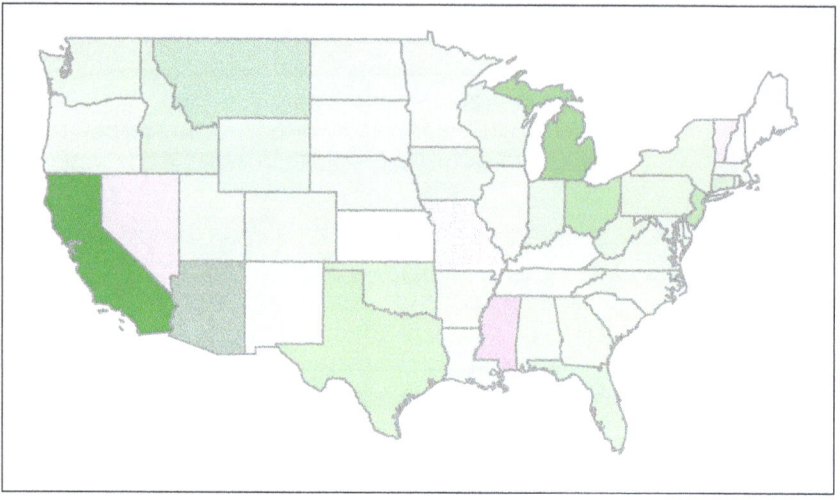

Figure 46: Changes in population from 1910 to 1920 censuses. Green indicates growth, magenta indicates population decline.

of this pattern of massive growth, and the population in California had expanded. The census conducted in 1910 provided the basis for not only the 1912, 1916, and 1920 Electoral Colleges, but for the 1924 and 1928 Electoral Colleges as well.

This made the 1928 presidential election one of the most disproportionate in history. Under ordinary circumstances, electors are based on population figures that are between two and ten years out of date; in the 1928 election, the Electoral College was based on population figures that were *eighteen years out of date.* This distortion was particularly striking for Arizona, California, and New Mexico, which had rapidly-growing populations.[6]

There are two major distortions introduced by the Electoral College other than the bonus "Senator" electors. One is that states with growing populations are underrepresented, while states with declining populations are overrepresented. Another factor is that residents who are unable to vote – a population that includes prisoners and non-citizens, and used to include slaves – inflate the population of the state without adding voters.

---

[6]Nevada was something of an outlier because Nevada's population was simply significantly lower than most other states with 1 representative.

A COEDUCATIONAL ELECTORAL COLLEGE (1920-1956) 131

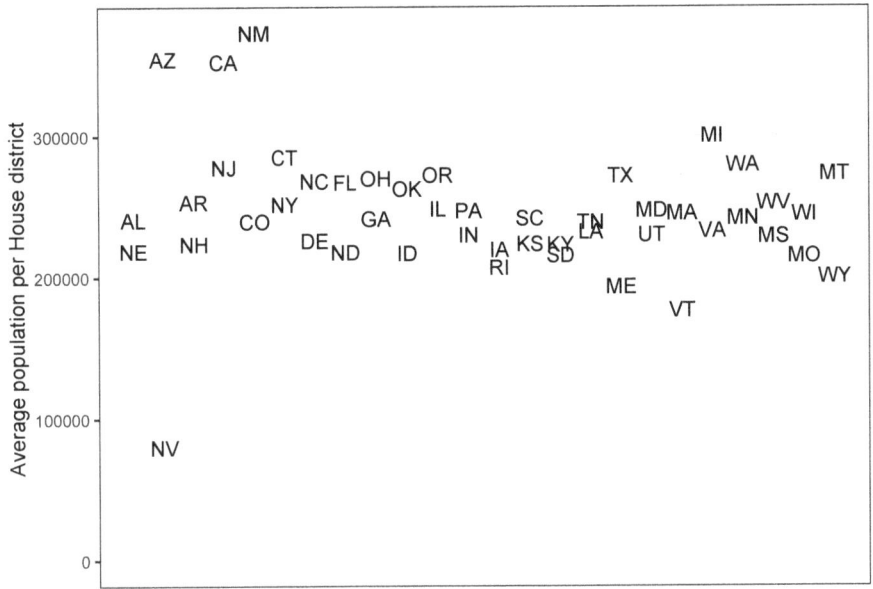

Figure 47: Allocation of House seats by population in 1928.

In 1928, 63,000 South Carolinians voted for Al Smith, translating to nine electoral votes for Al Smith; over 375,000 West Virginians voted for Herbert Hoover, which translated to only eight electoral votes for Herbert Hoover. An even more dramatic difference can be found looking at California; California experienced rapid population growth. At the time, California also had unusually high voter turnout as well.[7]

In his landslide loss, Al Smith won eight states, including Massachusetts, Rhode Island, and half a dozen states in the South, for a total of 87 electoral votes – 64 from the South and 23 from New England. In the six Southern states he won, he earned 728,488 votes out of a total of 1.1 million votes; the South's population was not growing quickly and had unusually low turnout relative to population due to the effects of Jim Crow.

In California, Al Smith earned 614,365 votes. In spite of the fact that this was close to his vote total in those six Southern states, it was not enough to win him California's 13 electoral votes. Hoover carried California with 1.1 million votes – slightly more than the number of votes cast in those six Southern states combined. Winning a majority of California's 1.8 million votes gave Hoover 13 electoral votes; winning majorities in six separate Southern states with a combined total of 1.1 million votes gave Smith 64

---

[7]This is no longer true today.

electoral votes.

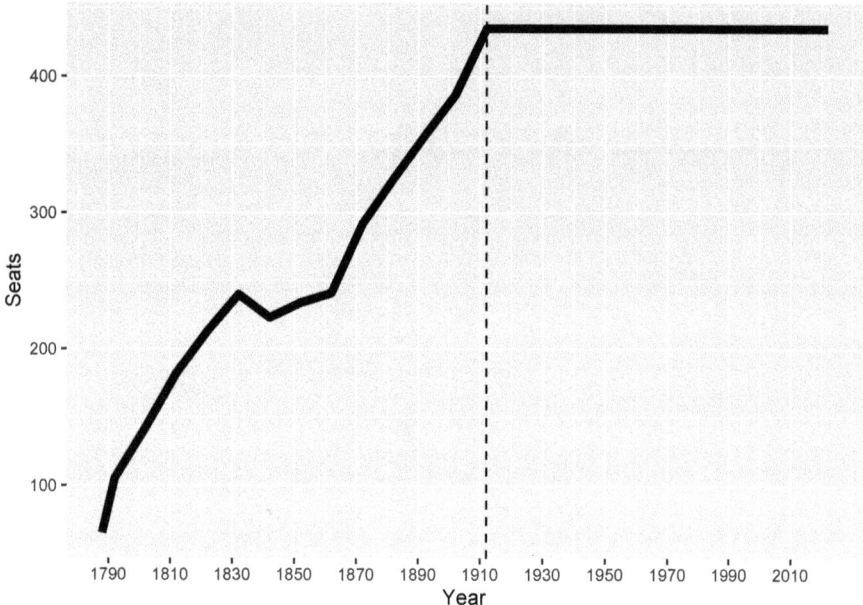

Figure 48: Seats in the House of Representatives by decennial census allocation.

From the 1930 census forward, the House has been reallocated with every census using a fixed size of the House of 435 seats. This has brought the United States further and further away from what political scientists refer to as the cube root law: Legislatures tend towards a size roughly equal to the cube root of the population.[8] The fixed size of the House means that the very smallest states tend to be slightly overrepresented compared to slightly larger states; for example, as of 2020, Montana has almost twice the population of Wyoming, but both states only have one representative in the House.

The gross inequalities between citizens and representation seen in the 1928 election is an extreme case of a consistent pattern related to population growth. In elections that happen further along in the decennial census cycle, states with faster-growing populations are underrepresented, both in the House and in the Electoral College, while states with declining populations are overrepresented. Non-citizens, prisoners, and felons unable to vote further distort the relative power of voters in different states by padding the population with those who cannot vote.

---

[8]There is a fairly simple graph optimization argument for why the cube root might give the optimal size for a working legislature, but there are numerous other arguments that can be made on the subject. See the vein of literature starting with "The Size of National Assemblies" (1972) by Rein Taagepera.

A COEDUCATIONAL ELECTORAL COLLEGE (1920-1956) 133

While the United States is not growing as quickly as it was in 1920, the relative difference between states' growth rates still has a significant effect. A more recent example is the case of Texas and New York. In every census conducted after 1970, the share of Americans living in New York has declined while the share living in Texas has grown. The result is that Texans have consistently been less well represented than New Yorkers, both in the Electoral College and in the House of Representatives. In 1980, there were 547,000 Texans for each presidential elector from Texas, but only 428,000 New Yorkers for each presidential elector from New York. In the 2000 election, Texas had 2 million more residents but fewer presidential electors.

The Roosevelt elections

Franklin D. Roosevelt won a string of four elections by exceptionally large margins. While some previous presidents had considered running for a third term in office, Franklin D. Roosevelt was the first president elected more than twice. He will likely be the only American president elected more than twice; the subsequent passage of the 22nd Amendment limited future presidents to two terms.

The 1932 election in brief

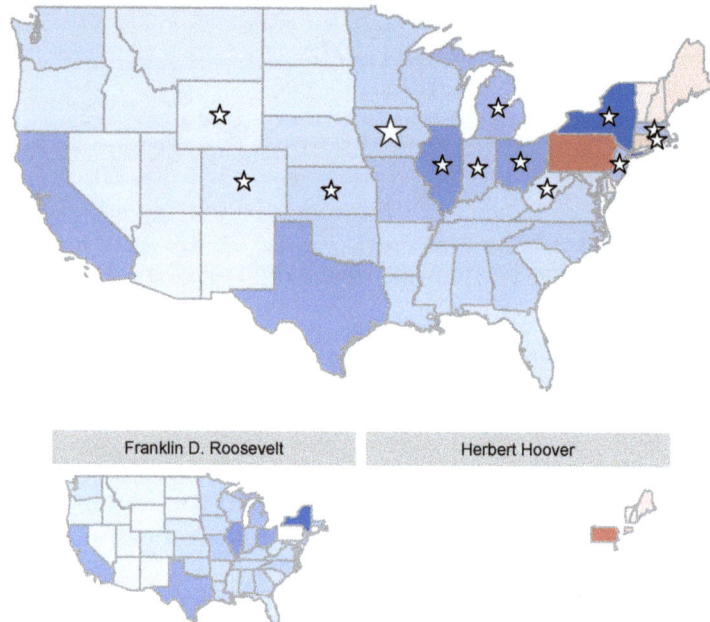

Figure 49: The 1932 presidential election.

Electoral vote: 472-59
Popular vote: 57%-40%
Pivotal state: Iowa
Critical states: None
Crucial states: Iowa, Utah, Wyoming, Colorado, New York, Indiana, West Virginia, Kansas, Michigan, Massachusetts, Ohio, New Jersey

The political landscape re-aligned dramatically with the Great Depression. Democrats nominated Franklin D. Roosevelt of New York, who ran on giving a "New Deal" to America. Incumbent president Herbert Hoover lost by a popular margin as large as the one he had won by four years previously.

While Roosevelt's popular landslide was less dramatic than Harding's 1920 landslide, he won a record 472 electoral votes, giving him the most dramatic margin in the Electoral College since James Monroe in 1820. The pivotal state in this election was Iowa, although since the election was not close, reversing the result of the election would have required Hoover victories in many other states.

A COEDUCATIONAL ELECTORAL COLLEGE (1920-1956)

The 1936 election in brief

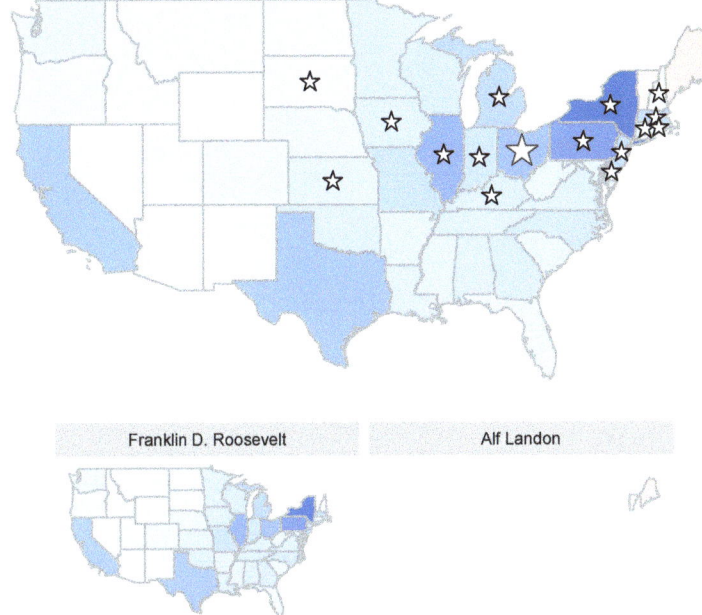

Figure 50: The 1936 presidential election.

Electoral vote: 523-8
Popular vote: 61%-37%
Pivotal state: Ohio
Critical states: None
Crucial states: Ohio, New Jersey, New York, Kentucky, Illinois, Michigan, Nebraska, Pennsylvania, Connecticut, Indiana, Rhode Island, Iowa, South Dakota, Massachusetts, Kansas

Incumbent Franklin D. Roosevelt won against challenger Alf Landon of Kansas by the largest margin in modern history, winning 61% of the popular vote and breaking his previous record with 523 electoral votes. Roosevelt's support was weakest in the northeast.

Since there was no real opponent to Washington in 1788 or 1792, and no real opponent for James Monroe in 1820, Alf Landon has the unique, if ignominious, distinction of winning fewer electoral votes than any other candidate backed by a major party. The ratio between his share of the electoral vote and his share of the popular vote is also lower than any candidate who won any electoral votes.

The pivotal state in this election was Ohio, although many other states would have been required to flip the election.

The 1940 election in brief

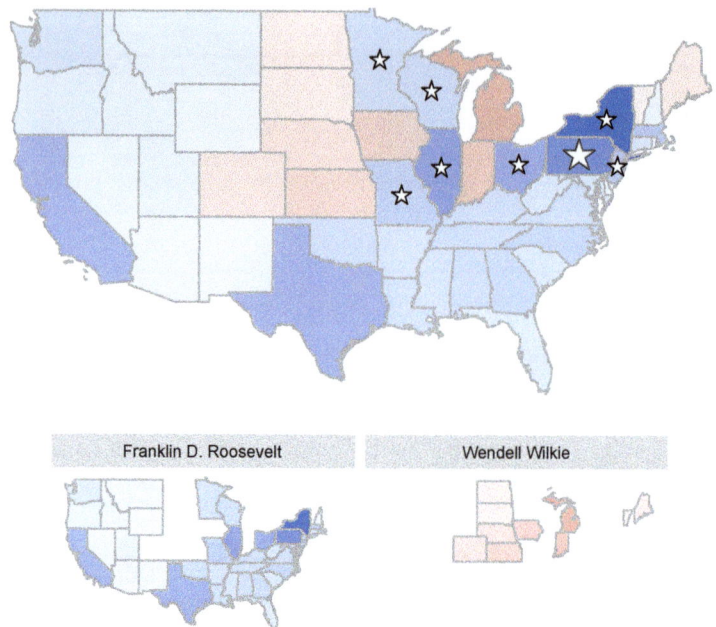

Figure 51: The 1940 presidential election.

Electoral vote: 449-82
Popular vote: 55%-45%
Pivotal state: Pennsylvania
Critical states: None
Crucial states: Pennsylvania, Massachusetts, New Hampshire, Missouri, Ohio, Minnesota, New York, Illinois

Incumbent Franklin D. Roosevelt, still resoundingly popular, won an unprecedented third presidential election against fellow New Yorker Wendell Wilkie.

The pivotal state in this election was Pennsylvania. While this election was closer than Roosevelt's previous election, Wilkie needed to also win seven other key states in order to catch up to Roosevelt in the Electoral College.

The 1944 election in brief

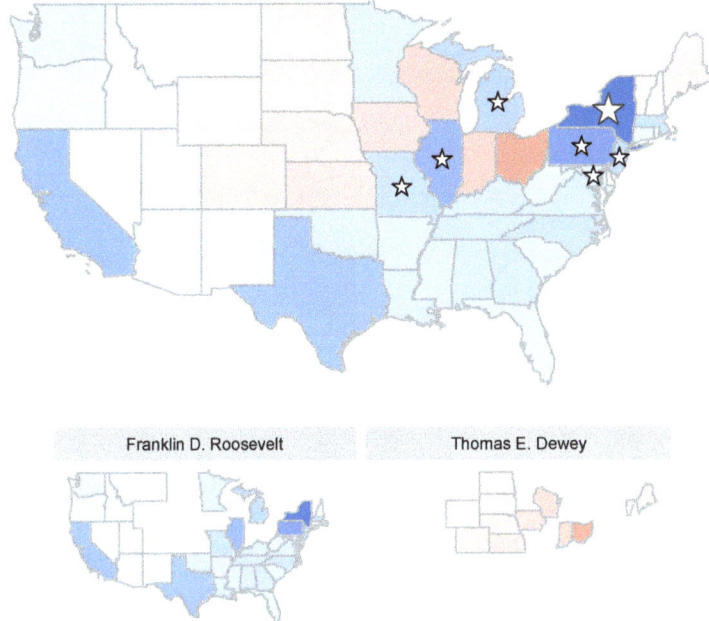

Figure 52: The 1944 presidential election.

Electoral vote: 432-99
Popular vote: 53%-46%
Pivotal state: New York
Critical states: None
Crucial states: New York, Oregon, New Hampshire, Maryland, Idaho, Illinois, Pennsylvania, New Jersey, Michigan

1944 marked a second election in a row where both major candidates were from New York, as the Republican challenger Thomas E. Dewey was from New York. Incumbent Franklin D. Roosevelt's support slid to 53%, which was still sufficient for him to win an unprecedented fourth term in office. He died early during his fourth term, however, which had interesting consequences.

A Southern strategy

From 1880 to 1944, the "Solid South" was consistently and strongly Democratic in presidential elections, even though most Democratic presidential candidates were not Southerners. In 1948, this pattern broke.

The 1948 election in brief

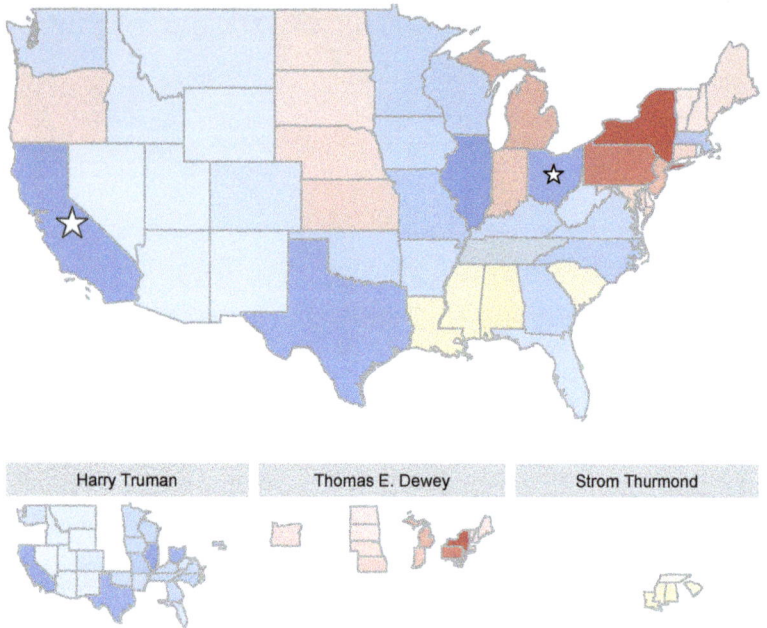

Figure 53: The 1948 presidential election.

Popular vote: 50%-45%-2%
Electoral vote: 303-189-39
Pivotal state: California
Critical states: None
Crucial states: California, Ohio

Franklin D. Roosevelt died in office in 1945, passing the office to his vice president, Harry Truman. After a contentious Democratic convention, Harry Truman faced both a Republican challenger, Thomas E. Dewey, and Dixiecrat Strom Thurmond, who had led a walkout of Southern delegates from the Democratic Convention.

Polling showed Dewey in the lead, but Truman won. The Chicago Daily Tribune famously went to press with a headline erroneously declaring Dewey the winner. Truman's margins in Ohio and California combined to less than 25,000 votes, and had he lost those two states (which had 25 electoral votes each), it would have been up to the House of

Representatives to choose the ultimate winner of the election between the three candidates. The result of this would have been uncertain; Truman would not have been able to win a majority of House delegations without support from either Republicans or Southerners.

While the popular margin was not very close nationally, the three-way electoral split caused by Thurmond came very close to throwing the election to the House of Representatives for the first time since 1824. This was part of a deliberate strategy by the Southern wing of the Democratic Party.

The segregationists' strategy

Once Reconstruction ended, the American South consistently supported the Democratic Party and consistently opposed the Republican Party. The party of Lincoln was responsible for what some Southerners insisted on referring to as the "War of Northern Aggression," and the decimation of the slavery-based Southern economy.

Southern blacks initially supported the Republican Party, but made up a small minority of voters due to various efforts to limit their participation. This included poll taxes, literacy tests, and threats of violence. Once federal troops were withdrawn, the "Solid South" was a reliably Democratic bastion. From 1880 to 1944, there were only half a dozen cases where one of the eleven former Confederate states voted for a Republican president - one state in Warren G. Harding's landslide 1920 victory, and five states in Hoover's landslide 1928 victory. South Carolina, Georgia, Alabama, Mississippi, Georgia, Louisiana, and Arkansas voted for the Democratic candidate in all nine of those presidential elections.

As president, Truman broke with Southern Democrats on the issue of segregation, fracturing the Democratic Party along regional lines. At the 1948 Democratic National Convention, Northerners added a civil rights plank to the party platform. Many Southern Democrats were furious and walked out of the Democratic National Convention. The Dixiecrats, as they became known, decided to run their own presidential candidate on a pro-segregation platform, hoping to cost Truman the election.

Strom Thurmond of South Carolina headed the ticket. He had no chance of winning a majority in the Electoral College. However, as seen dramatically in the 1860 election, polarizing candidates whose support is concentrated in a single region of the country can do disproportionately well in the Electoral College. Strom Thurmond could, and did, win electoral votes in the South in spite of obtaining only a small fraction of the national vote.

Strom Thurmond's run for president could be seen as quixotic, a symbolic move doomed to failure.[9] However, the Dixiecrats' move had two pragmatic avenues for success, even if Strom Thurmond was doomed.

First, by dividing the Democratic base, they could spoil the election in favor of the Republicans, forcing the party to either accommodate their demands or face continuing losses on the national level. Second, and more likely, if neither Truman nor Dewey received a majority of the electoral vote, the election would go to a contingent election in the House. Dixiecrats could not win a national election, but they could negotiate for political concessions during a contingent election process.

Thus, the Dixiecrats had two potential paths to political victory. Both of those paths relied on the fact that the Electoral College rewards sectional candidates; the Dixiecrats did not need to compete outside of the South in order to either win or spoil electoral votes.

What a Dixiecrat victory would have looked like

If Dixiecrats had simply spoiled the election in favor of Thomas E. Dewey, a liberal Republican from New York, it's not clear this would have helped their cause any more than abolitionists had helped their cause a century earlier by spoiling the election in favor of James Polk in 1844.[10] For the Dixiecrats, *victory* would have meant denying either candidate a pledged majority in the Electoral College, giving them leverage for negotiations in the contingent election process.

In 1800 and 1824, the contingent election process was performed by the outgoing Congress. In the outgoing 80th Congress, the Republican Party had majorities in 29 out of 48 state delegations; Democrats controlled 17, with 2 evenly split. Most of these were the 11 former Confederate states. However, thanks to changes in the scheduling of Congressional sessions and presidential elections, the contingent election would have been carried out by the 81st Congress instead of by the 80th Congress.

In the 81st Congress, Republicans controlled 19 state delegations and Democrats 25 state delegations, with 4 evenly divided. Winning would require winning a majority vote in each of 25 separate state delegations; a tied delegation is treated as an abstention. In order to be elected, Truman needed either the support of key incumbent Republican members of

---

[9]Thanks to a comparatively-popular monograph using the word in the title, this is sometimes used to refer to Progressive candidate Henry Wallace's 1948 bid, but see "Review of Truman Defeats Dewey by Gary A. Donaldson" (2000) by Bruce Kalk for one example of applying the adjective to Thurmond.

[10]See Chapter 5.

A COEDUCATIONAL ELECTORAL COLLEGE (1920-1956)   141

Congress or of the Southern wing of his own party; both groups demonstrably disliked Truman.

It would have been similarly difficult for Dewey to win unless he was willing to cut a deal with the Dixiecrats. If both major parties stuck to their candidates, and Dewey and Truman stuck to their principles, it is entirely possible that the entire House contingent election process would have stayed deadlocked until the deadline, at which point the vice president would have become president.

Who would the vice president have been? This would have been resolved by a contingent election in the Senate. In the 81st Congress, the Democrats had a 54-42 seat majority, but fully half of the Democratic caucus came from Southern states, putting the Dixiecrats in a potentially pivotal position. Southern Democrats would be able to resolve the election in favor of either Democrat Alben Barkley or Republican Earl Warren. At a glance, Alben Barkley, a Democrat from Kentucky, appears more likely; the Dixiecrats were conservative Democrats, while Earl Warren was a California liberal. However, political negotiations between the three factions could have resolved in either direction.

Since the contingent election for vice president is carried out between the top two candidates, with senators voting individually, either candidate could have won with as few as 49 out of 96 votes. A 48-48 tie was possible, though less likely than a tie or deadlock in the House. The 12th Amendment does require "a majority of the whole number shall be necessary to a choice," so it is also possible for the Senate election to deadlock through abstention or absence. In this case, by the 20th Amendment and the recently-passed Presidential Succession Act of 1947, the presidency would have fallen to the newly-elected Speaker of the House, Sam Rayburn. It is worth noting that the constitutionality of passing the presidency to a member of Congress has been questioned;[11] if this element of the newly-passed Presidential Succession Act had been challenged, incumbent Secretary of State George C. Marshall would have succeeded to the presidency.

How close the election was

It is very easy, when reading history, to overestimate how certain the outcome was.[12] The 1948 election was exceptionally close by any measure.

---
[11] C.f. "Preserving Our Institutions: The Continuity of the Presidency (Second Report)" (2009) by the Continuity of Government Commission.
[12] This is known as the "fallacy of inevitability."

The shocking nature of Truman's victory may have helped make his margins look more decisive: Dewey had been clearly leading in polls, and Truman seemed an unpopular incumbent. The Chicago Daily Tribune famously went to press with the (erroneous) headline "Dewey DEFEATS TRUMAN!" Some history books record Truman's 1948 victory as a landslide; doing so is a mistake on a basic mathematical level. Truman earned less than 50% of the total popular vote. While his popular margin over Dewey may look large, given the share of the vote that went to minor candidates, his majority within the Electoral College depended on a margin of about twenty five thousand votes in two states - a small fraction of a percent of the electorate.

In particular, Truman won very narrow victories in Ohio and California: 0.2% and 0.4%, respectively. California was decided by a margin of about 18,000 votes, and Ohio was decided by a margin of about 7,000 votes. Each of those states had twenty-five electors. Closer elections typically only show up once or twice in a lifetime.[13]

If we look closely at the political factors peculiar to 1948, it's worth noting that Truman's victory also depended on many electoral votes in states that routinely elected pro-segregation politicians. It is not difficult to imagine scenarios in which Strom Thurmond won a plurality of the vote in several more Southern states.[14]

This means that if Dewey had done just slightly better or if the Dixiecrats had gained the backing of political leaders in a few more southern states, the election would have been decided in the House; and as discussed above, Truman would have faced a difficult contingent election if he did not reach some sort of political accommodation with the Dixiecrats.

The lessons of 1948

The presidential election of 1948 was neither the first nor the last time the Democratic Party fractured along regional lines. This had happened in 1860; it would happen again in 1960 and 1968. While the United States has *usually* had a seemingly-stable two-party system, the parties are frequently built out of fragile coalitions that come apart at key points in history.

It's also important to realize that the most unusual and unfamiliar features of the Electoral College system - the contingent election process that

---

[13] E.g., a person born in 1889 and dying of a ripe old age of seventy in 1959 would have only lived through one closer election - that of 1916.

[14] In particular, see the Dixiecrats' efforts to capture the main "Democratic Party" line on the ballot, which succeeded in only four states - the same four states that Thurmond won. In Alabama, Dixiecrats managed to exclude Truman from the ballot.

A COEDUCATIONAL ELECTORAL COLLEGE (1920-1956)

takes over if no candidate wins a majority in the combined electoral colleges - are not impossibly remote possibilities. While no contingent election for president has occurred since 1824, there have been several close calls, including 1948. The flaws within the contingent election process are not remote possibilities, but instead, are most likely to emerge during times of political crisis.

The Eisenhower elections

The 1952 election in brief

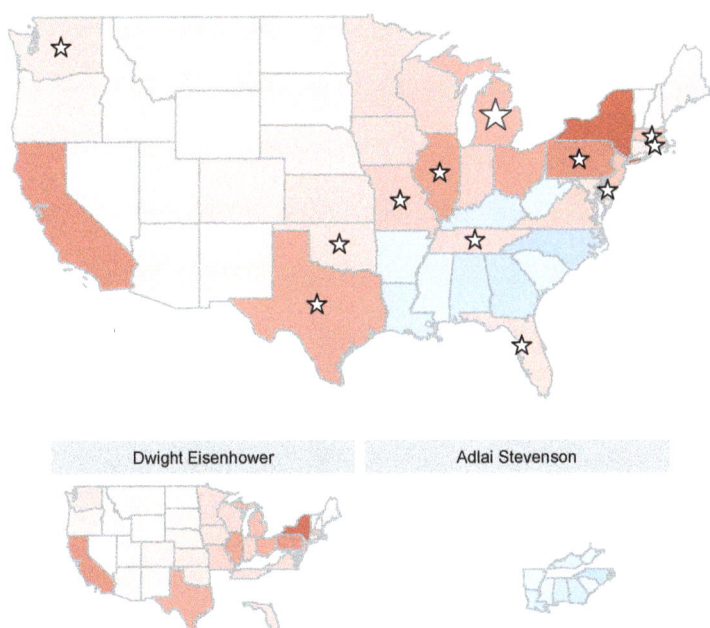

Figure 54: The 1952 presidential election.

Electoral vote: 442-89
Popular vote: 55%-44%
Pivotal state: Michigan
Critical states: None
Crucial states: Michigan, Minnesota, New Mexico, Florida, Illinois, Washington, Oklahoma, Massachusetts, Texas, Pennsylvania, Delaware, Missouri

Although not required to stand down by the recently-passed 22nd Amendment limiting future presidents to two terms, incumbent Harry

A COEDUCATIONAL ELECTORAL COLLEGE (1920-1956)

Truman was unpopular, thought very unlikely to win a second election, and chose not to run. The Democrats nominated Adlai Stevenson; the Republicans nominated Dwight Eisenhower.

Eisenhower won by a large margin; Stevenson's support was most heavily concentrated in the South, with the Dixiecrats returning to the fold.

The 1956 election in brief

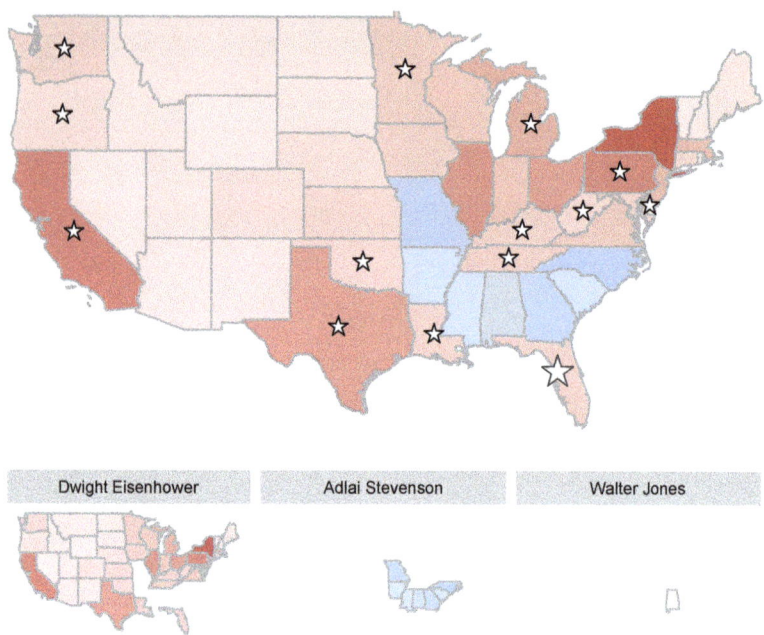

Figure 55: The 1956 presidential election.

Pivotal state: Florida
Popular vote: 57%-42%
Critical states: None
Crucial states: Florida, Montana, Louisiana, Pennsylvania, Michigan, Texas, California, Oregon, Oklahoma, Kentucky, Washington, West Virginia, Minnesota, Tennessee

Popular incumbent Dwight Eisenhower faced an easy rematch with Democratic challenger Adlai Stevenson. The pivotal state in this election was Florida, which had grown by this point to a medium-sized state with ten electors. In Alabama, one electoral vote was unexpectedly cast for an Alabama judge, Walter Jones; the elector, William Turner, shared a hometown with the judge. This lone defiant electoral vote was a warning sign: Times were changing, and many southern Democrats were no happier with the national party than they had been in 1948.

CHAPTER 9

The system in transition (1960-1968)

A series of major changes rocked the foundation of the presidential election system (and the political system as a whole) between the election of 1960 and the election of 1972. Many of these changes were linked to an active and successful civil rights movement. This included a string of landmark court cases, federal civil rights legislation, three constitutional amendments impacting the right to vote, and significant changes to the nomination process carried out by the political parties.

The 23rd Amendment, ratified in 1961, added presidential electors for the District of Columbia. This was the second successful constitutional amendment directly targeting the Electoral College system. Presidential elections were also affected by the 24th Amendment, ratified in 1964, which eliminated the use of poll taxes. Finally, the 26th Amendment, ratified in 1971, lowered the minimum voting age to eighteen. While many of the changes in this period were individually limited in scope, their cumulative effect was quite significant.

On top of the legal changes in who was allowed to participate in general elections, significant reforms to the nomination processes used by the major political parties also took place during this period; the modern presidential primary system may be very impactful, but it is only around fifty years old. This period marked a turning point in the strained relations between the northern and southern wings of the Democratic Party, with many conservative Democrats shifting to the Republican Party after the Dixiecrats' electoral gambits failed.

The uncertain election of 1960

The 1960 election in brief

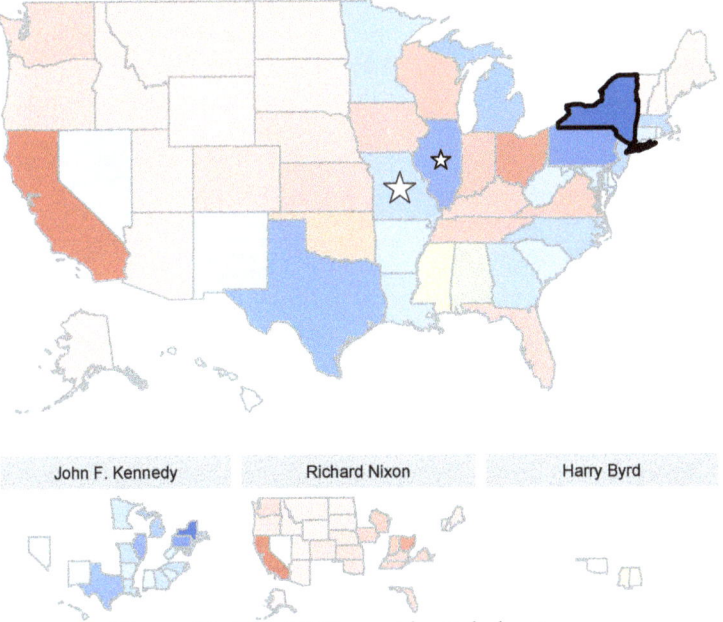

Figure 56: The 1960 presidential election.

Electoral vote: 303-219-15
Popular vote: 50%-50%
Pivotal state: Missouri
Critical state: New York
Crucial states: Missouri, Illinois, Hawaii

The Democrats nominated sitting senator John F. Kennedy; the Republicans nominated sitting vice president Richard Nixon. Southern Democrats, unhappy with the party's national platform, nominated unpledged electors in several states; these unpledged electors earned about 0.4% of the national vote. Fourteen unpledged electors and one Republican elector in Oklahoma voted for Harry Byrd; the Republican elector engaged in a letter-writing campaign to try to get other Republican electors to vote for Byrd.

The 1960 election featured what is generally considered the second-smallest margin in the popular vote. Because of the complications involved with trying to count votes for separate

Democratic electors for different candidates in the same state, the popular vote margin varies based on which source of data is used.

A difference of 19,000 votes in Missouri, Illinois, and Hawaii would have been sufficient to throw the election into the House; a reversal of the vote in Texas and Illinois would have been sufficient for an outright victory by Nixon in the Electoral College. Although Kennedy won New York by a larger margin, New York was a critical state in his coalition; the election was close enough that New York could have decided the victor.

The narrow margin of victory & fraud

Initial returns had Kennedy winning California and Nixon winning Hawaii, but the final results were reversed in both of these states.[1] Republicans challenged the results, alleging fraud in both Illinois and Texas. These allegations were not groundless; there were irregularities. In the case of Chicago, evidence of widespread election fraud was detected in a partial recount.[2]

Many Republicans on the losing side contended that the election had only been won via fraud. While Republicans challenged results in eleven states, the most prominent allegations of fraud focused on Texas near the Mexican border and Chicago. There were enough documented irregularities in both places to lead to a handful of criminal charges.

Winning those two key states (where the evidence of fraud was strongest) would have been enough to tip the election in Nixon's favor. There were numerous other close states, including one (Hawaii) where a recount resulted in a flipped outcome; when we consider the possibility of undetected election fraud or even simply widespread errors in counting, there were multiple paths by which Nixon could have easily been accepted as the legitimate victor. After Election Day was over, the nation was on the cusp of a national crisis, with Republicans ready to challenge the legitimacy of Kennedy's likely victory.

In the modern day, most of us associate Nixon with the Watergate scandal. It is worth underlining that this scandal had not yet taken place:

---

[1] For further details, see "The 1960 Election in Hawaii" (1961) by Daniel Tuttle and "The 1960 Election in California" (1961) by Eugene Lee and William Buchanan.

[2] See "The State's Attorney and the President: The Inside Story of the 1960 Presidential Election in Illinois" (1978) and "Was the 1960 Presidential Election Stolen? The Case of Illinois" (1985) by Edmund Kallina for a detailed exercise in trying to estimate the likely impact of fraud from those numbers. Kallina concludes the presidential election was likely not stolen; however, the numbers he comes up with show Kennedy's Illinois victory was definitely within the *potential* margin of fraud and error combined, particularly considering the possibility that precincts with voting machines had higher rates of election fraud or error.

THE SYSTEM IN TRANSITION (1960-1968)

Nixon was quite popular and widely respected as a politician. In this particular case, Nixon placed the stability of the country over his own personal interest in getting elected, graciously conceding the election to Kennedy and opposing recounts.

In retrospect, considering what we know of the less savory aspects of Nixon's character in the modern (i.e. post-Watergate) era, it is terrifying to think that in 1960, the stability of the country depended on Nixon taking the high road. Nixon chose not to contest an election that he sincerely believed had been stolen by Democratic fraud. Pragmatically, a recount would have been impossible in Texas and difficult in Chicago. Investigation of irregularities in the election did eventually lead to criminal charges for election officials in both Texas and Illinois.

Who really won the popular vote?

The election of 1960 is one of three elections in American history where we cannot confidently identify the winner of a plurality of the popular vote. The other two were the elections of 1876, which featured widespread fraud and contested vote totals, and 1880, where the national margin was exceptionally narrow. Recall that there were the documented irregularities in Texas and Illinois, which could easily have been sufficient to tip the Electoral College; adding in the possibility of fraud and simple counting error in other states, and the popular vote could be considered uncertain.

As was the case with the 1876 election, the legitimacy of the Electoral College vote is more doubtful than the legitimacy of the popular vote winner; however, in the case of 1960, there are additional technical issues related to the popular vote total that make identifying the plurality winner difficult. Some experts classify the election of 1960 as a "misfire" election where the candidate with more votes lost, but this depends on the method of accounting for votes.[3]

Southern Democrats in several states, desperate to preserve segregation and deeply disappointed in the progressive wing of the Democratic Party, chose to nominate electors who had not pledged to support any candidate. In Louisiana and Mississippi, these unpledged electors ran on a separate slate; in Alabama, the official Democratic slate was split between six unpledged electors and five Kennedy electors.

The mixed slate in Alabama, divided between Kennedy electors and unpledged segregationist electors opposed to the election of Kennedy,

---

[3] This is discussed by Robert Alexander in *Representation and the Electoral College* (2019) and George Edwards in *Why the Electoral College Is Bad for America* (2019).

makes it difficult to count votes in Alabama as votes for any one candidate in particular. If we use the highest vote total of any elector as the total for a candidate, Kennedy earned about 113,000 more votes than Nixon nationwide or about 0.33% of the national vote. An alternate method of counting the votes for a mixed slate is to count them as 5/11 of a vote for Kennedy and 6/11 of a vote for Byrd; under this alternative accounting, Nixon won the equivalent of about 61,000 more votes nationally, a margin of 0.18%.[4]

In either case, this would be the second-smallest national popular margin, but still larger than the effective popular margin within the Electoral College system. A shift of 9,000 votes in Illinois and 10,000 votes in Missouri (or 46,000 votes in Texas) would have denied Kennedy a safe majority in the Electoral College. Thus, while there is some room for uncertainty in whether Nixon or Kennedy would have won in a direct popular vote, with or without a majority runoff, the legitimacy of the result in the Electoral College was *even less* certain.

The return of a Southern strategy

The strategy of the rebellious Southern Democrats was similar to their strategy in 1948. As in 1948, the strategy was nearly successful; Kennedy's majority in the Electoral College was very fragile, as noted above, and possibly due to election fraud by corrupt officials in the Texas borderlands and Chicago.[5] Also as in 1948, there were electoral votes not won by either major candidate. In this case, the votes were cast by unpledged electors who voted as a bloc for Harry F. Byrd of Virginia.

If neither Nixon nor Kennedy eked out a majority in the Electoral College, Southern segregationists would have been in a pivotal position in the Electoral College, able to deny either major candidate from receiving an outright majority unless their demands were met. Similarly, they would have been in a pivotal position in a House contingent election; neither Nixon nor Kennedy would be able to get a majority in the Electoral College without cooperation from Southern Democrats. If the House contingent election process deadlocked between the top three eligible candidates, the presidency would go to the vice president.

As noted in the earlier discussion of the 1948 election, ties in the Senate contingent election process choosing a new vice president are

---

[4] Slightly different figures for these margins can be seen in various different sources. Some states had multiple versions of their returns due to recounts. In this case, I have relied on the figures from David Leip's "David Leip's Atlas of US Presidential Elections, Datasets" (2017).

[5] See again Kallina's work on the subject.

THE SYSTEM IN TRANSITION (1960-1968)

much less likely. Like Albus Barkley had been in 1948, the Democratic vice presidential candidate, Lyndon B. Johnson, was from a Southern state (Texas) and had a history as a Democratic leader in the Senate. In 1948, the Republican vice presidential candidate was Earl Warren, a liberal Republican from California; the 1960 Republican nominee for vice president, Henry Cabot Lodge, was a liberal Republican from Massachusetts. Cabot had openly pledged that Nixon would nominate an African-American to the Cabinet. At a glance, Johnson appears the more likely victor.

If the House contingent election process deadlocked, the winner of the Senate contingent election would then have automatically become president by default, a scenario we had to discuss with regard to the 1948 election. If both elections deadlocked, the current Speaker of the House, Sam Rayburn, could have become president.[6]

In discussing 1948, I noted that it seems unlikely that either Dewey or Truman could have reached an easy accommodation with Southern Democrats. However, there are reasons to think that Nixon might have been able to reach an accommodation with Southern Democrats without too much difficulty.

Modern political commentators frequently credit Nixon with bringing disaffected southerners into the Republican Party. He also notoriously engaged in numerous ethically questionable activities in order to become president. This included attempts to sabotage peace talks in Vietnam leading into the 1968 election as well as the events leading to the Watergate scandal. The full consequences of such a bargain in 1960 are murky and complex; the amount of political change in the United States that can be traced to the Kennedy and Johnson administrations (1961-1968) is truly momentous.

---

[6]As noted in the previous discussion of the 1948 election and in "Preserving Our Institutions: The Continuity of the Presidency (Second Report)" (2009) by the Continuity of Government Commission, the constitutionality of a member of Congress succeeding to the presidency is contestable and might have been contested; in that case, incumbent Secretary of State Christian A. Herter would have then become president.

The 1964 election and the Voting Rights Act

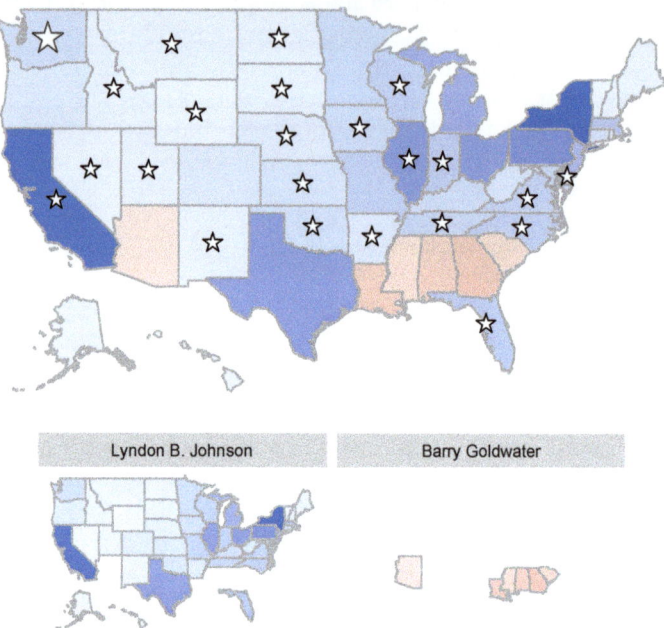

Figure 57: The 1964 presidential election.

Electoral vote: 486-52
Popular vote: 61%-38%
Pivotal state: Washington
Critical state: None
Crucial states: Washington, Wisconsin, Iowa, Colorado, Delaware, New Mexico, Illinois, Montana, California, Nevada, North Dakota, Wyoming, Arkansas, Indiana, North Carolina, Oklahoma, South Dakota, Tennessee, Utah, Kansas, Virginia, Nebraska, Florida

The Democrats nominated incumbent president Lyndon B. Johnson, who had succeeded to the office after the assassination of John F. Kennedy. The Republicans nominated sitting senator Barry Goldwater of Arizona. Interestingly, the resulting electoral map was almost the opposite of the previous two-candidate race in 1956. Arizona and Louisiana were the only two states that voted Republican in both 1956 and 1964; North Carolina, Missouri, and Arkansas were the only three states that voted Democratic in both 1956 and 1964.

Lyndon B. Johnson earned a higher share of the popular vote than any other presidential candidate on record since the uncontested re-election of James Monroe in 1820. Also notably, Goldwater's performance in the Electoral College was only a little better than the performance of Strom Thurmond in 1948 (with 2.4% of the vote) and of George Wallace in 1968 (with 13.5%); those three candidates won most of the same states.

The Voting Rights Act

Following his re-election, Lyndon B. Johnson helped to push for further civil rights legislation. One of the most significant successes of the civil rights movement during the 1960s was the Voting Rights Act of 1965. The Voting Rights Act eliminated many of the barriers that had been erected to keep African-American voters away from the polls. Combined with other legislation and numerous court cases that removed unconstitutional barriers to minority voting, this created a significant shift in the electorate, particularly in the South.

In addition to causing an uptick in African-American turnout, the successes of the civil rights movement also fueled a political shift among white voters, particularly in the South. The days of the "Solid South" were over.

1968: The presidential election system reshaped

1968 was an exceptionally eventful year, both in the United States and abroad.[7] The American presidential election of 1968 was no exception, and provided the impetus for significant reforms to how the political parties nominated presidential candidates. Democrats were fractured not only between northern and southern wings but also between younger and older voters. The incumbent president wasn't re-nominated, and one of the other major contenders for the nomination was assassinated. The political establishment of the Democratic Party picked a nominee who was unacceptable both to the segregationists and to younger activists within the party.

After the election, the 26th Amendment would lower the voting age to 18, and the McGovern-Fraser Commission would take up the question of how to fairly nominate presidential candidates without facing popular backlash. The Electoral College itself nearly fell victim to this wave of reforms, with both Republicans and the main part of the Democratic Party willing to cooperate in putting an end to the Dixiecrat strategy, but conservatives from the South were able to successfully lead a filibuster of

---

[7] C.f. *1968: The Year That Rocked the World* (2005) by Mark Kurlanski.

the Bayh-Celler amendment, enlisting the help of enough key allies who felt they also benefited from the existing system.

The 1968 election in brief

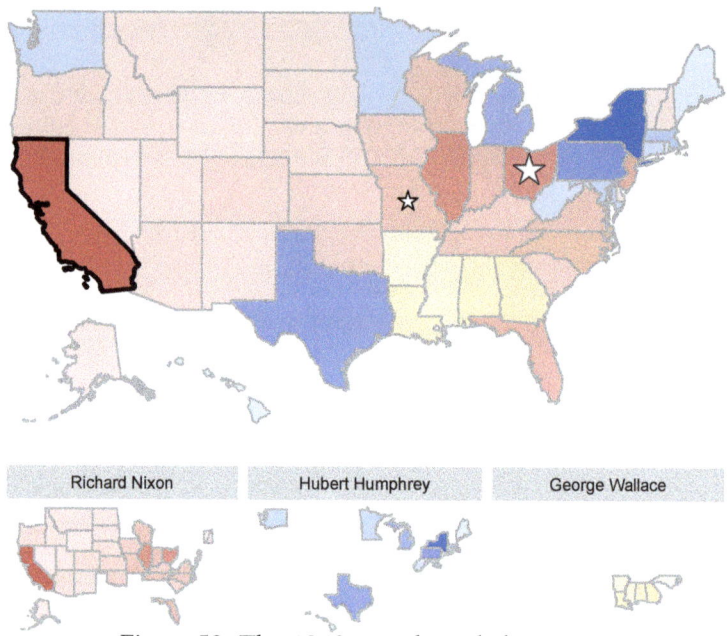

Figure 58: The 1968 presidential election.

Electoral vote: 301-191-46
Popular vote: 43%-43%-14%
Pivotal state: Ohio
Critical state: California
Crucial states: Ohio, Missouri

The incumbent president, Lyndon B. Johnson, decided not to run for re-election after facing significant challenges from within his own party. The Democrats nominated incumbent vice president Hubert Humphrey after a very contentious nomination process during which one of the major candidates for office died.[8] The Republicans nominated former vice president Richard Nixon.

The election featured a significant third-party bid by segregationist George Wallace, who won several states as well as a single additional vote from an independent-minded elector in North Carolina.[9] The additional

---
[8] Robert F. Kennedy, aka Bobby Kennedy.
[9] Dr. Lloyd Bailey of Rocky Mount.

vote was challenged in Congress but counted nonetheless.

This can be seen as a recurrence of the strategy used by Southern Democrats in 1948 and 1960; just as in those two cases, the attempt nearly worked, coming within a narrow margin of forcing a House contingent election.

Segregationists strike back

Although the popular vote margin was very close between Nixon and Humphrey, the electoral vote count was not close; Humphrey had trouble winning states in the South, especially since the race featured a strong regional candidate, George Wallace, a pro-segregation Southerner. As in 1948 and 1960, the strategy of the southern candidate was not one aimed at winning, but at denying either major-party candidate a majority. Also as in 1948 and 1960, they were very close to success. From a statistical perspective, considering how narrowly all three elections were decided, it is remarkable that the southerners' strategy failed all three times.

Had Nixon lost both Ohio and New Jersey to Humphrey, or his home state of California, the election would have been decided either by political negotiation before the assembly of the various electoral colleges, or by a contingent election in the House. In either case, segregationists, with little loyalty to either national party but strong loyalty to their own cause, would have been in a strong position to negotiate for policy concessions. While Nixon had no personal fondness for segregationists, it is not clear that he would have been unwilling to strike a bargain for power over principle.

If the segregationists' gambit had succeeded in forcing a contingent election and negotiations failed badly enough to lead to a deadlock in the House contingent election process, the set of possible resulting presidents would have included Edmund Muskie (Humphrey's running mate), Spiro Agnew (Nixon's running mate), John McCormack (the Democratic Speaker of the House), and even Dean Rusk (the incumbent Secretary of State).[10]

---

[10]The reason for this is that the constitutionality of allowing a member of Congress to succeed to the presidency is questionable. See in particular "Preserving Our Institutions: The Continuity of the Presidency (Second Report)" (2009) by the Continuity of Government Commission.

The Bayh-Celler Amendment

The fact that 1968 marked another close call for this strategy was a warning sign for both major parties; most of the political insiders in both major parties were old enough to remember 1948, and Nixon in particular had been a candidate in two of the three episodes. After the election, Republicans and northern Democrats engaged in a bipartisan effort to abolish the Electoral College, with the support of newly-elected president Nixon, who did not want his upcoming re-election bid to be held hostage by Southern Democrats.

The resulting proposed amendment was known as the Bayh-Celler amendment. This came closer to passing Congress than any other effort to abolish the Electoral College system in a long history of attempts.[11] The plan was intended to create a single-round presidential election system and encourage the preservation of the existing two-party system. Votes would be counted for a joint ticket of president and vice president; the ticket receiving the most votes would win, provided that the ticket received at least 40% of the total vote. In the rare event that no ticket received 40% of the vote, a run-off election between the top two tickets would resolve the election.[12]

This amendment passed the House by the requisite 2/3 margin, with scattered opposition from representatives in some southern and western states. Support for the bill was broadly bipartisan, with the opposition mostly consisting of a combination of conservative Southern Democrats and conservative Republicans from outside the South. Southerners like Strom Thurmond were also able to recruit some support for the Electoral College among politicians representing or drawn from urban minority populations; at this point in time, the nation's largest five cities were all located in key battleground states, and key urban minorities had significant potential leverage in presidential elections as a result.[13]

The Bayh-Celler amendment was filibustered by Southern Senators in a clear effort to preserve the distinctive Southern strategy employed

---

[11] See *The People's President: The Electoral College in American History and the Direct-Vote Alternative* (1968) by Neal Pierce and Lawrence Longley, *Electoral College Reform: Challenges and Possibilities* (2016) by Gary Bugh, and most recently *Why Do We Still Have the Electoral College?* (2020) by Alexander Keyssar for detailed accounts of those attempts.

[12] Personally, I think a run-off election would be warranted any time the top ticket received less than a majority; the cost of having a second round of elections is vanishingly small compared to the cost of electing the wrong person to the presidency.

[13] See in particular the contemporary discussion in *The Case Against Direct Election of the President: A Defense of the Electoral College* (1975) by Judith Best, but also discussion of the episode in recent work such as *Why Do We Still Have the Electoral College?* (2020) by Alexander Keyssar and *Let the People Pick the President: The Case for Abolishing the Electoral College* (2020) by Jesse Wegman.

THE SYSTEM IN TRANSITION (1960-1968)

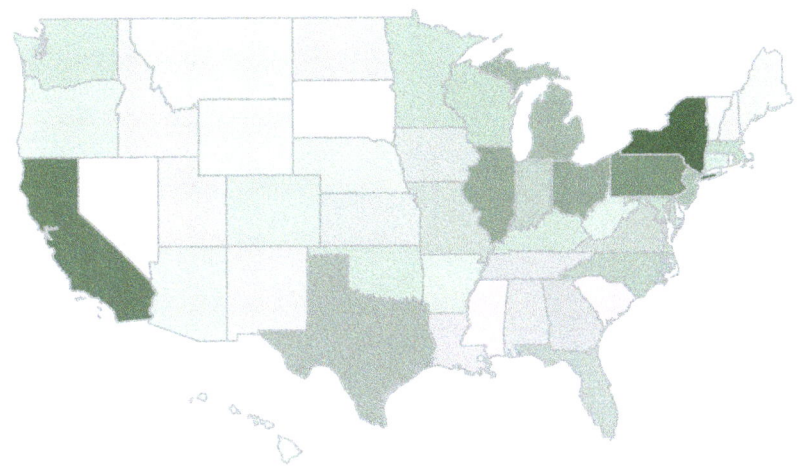

Figure 59: House vote on the Bayh-Celler amendment by state - green for votes in favor, magenta for votes against. Grayish tones indicate delegations with split votes.

in 1948, 1960, and 1968. They were joined by some Republican senators, mainly by conservatives from sparsely populated western states. Proposing a Constitutional Amendment requires a 2/3 majority of the Senate; the bill failed two cloture votes by narrow margins (with 34-36 senators voting against it). In every other way that mattered, segregationists lost the fight in the Senate eventually; however, they were able to successfully block electoral reforms that would have prevented them from running a regional third-party candidate to great effect in the future.

Despite their success in preserving the option for future use, segregationists have not made another attempt to force a House contingent election since 1968.

The creation of a new nomination system

In 1968, only fourteen of the fifty states held primaries, and many of those primaries were not contested. Most delegates to the Democratic and Republican national party conventions in charge of selecting candidates were chosen by political insiders, as they had been since the early days

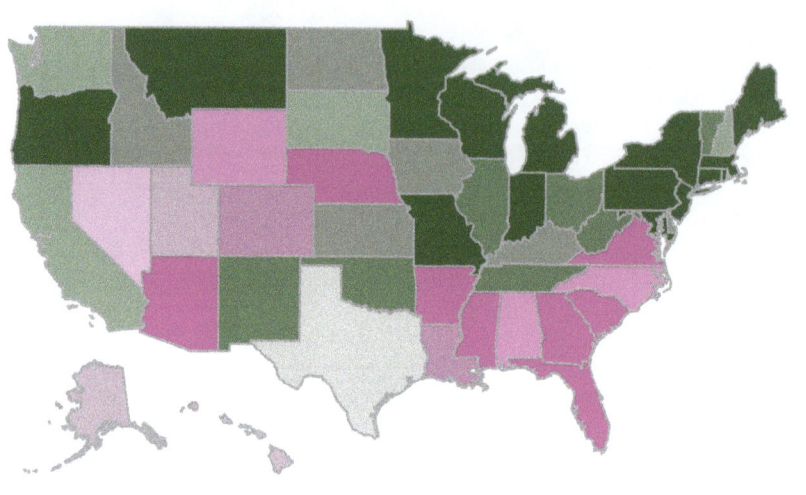

Figure 60: Senate cloture votes on the Bayh-Celler Amendment by state. Both cloture votes are combined in this figure. Lighter shades show some abstentions; muddy colors indicate split votes.

of party conventions.

Incumbent president Lyndon B. Johnson, who had won by a landslide in 1964, declined to run for re-election. Robert F. Kennedy, the brother of the late president John F. Kennedy, ran for the Democratic nomination; he was assassinated in June. Incumbent vice president Hubert Humphrey, who had declined to compete in any of the thirteen state-wide primaries, was selected as the Democratic Party nominee.

There were riots in Chicago, the site of the Democratic National Convention. Robert F. Kennedy had been a favorite among the young and radical; Hubert Humphrey had been a prominent member of the Democratic establishment for 16 years, starting with his national political debut at the 1948 Democratic National Convention. Interestingly, this marked the second time that Hubert Humphrey had been involved with a firestorm at the Democratic National Convention. The first time was in 1948, when, as a first-time Senate candidate, he gave an impassioned speech in favor of adopting a civil rights plank in the Democratic Party platform.

The contentious nomination of Hubert Humphrey led to a complete reworking of the process by which the two major parties selected nominees. The Democratic Party formed a commission (known to history as the McGovern-Fraser Commission) to rework the party's presidential nomination process. The major changes made by the commission had the effect of pushing primary elections to the forefront of the nominating process. Before, most delegates to the national conventions were selected by local party leaders; after, most delegates were chosen through the primary election process as supporters of a particular presidential candidate.

Although these reforms were designed by Democratic leaders, the nomination process for Republicans was similarly altered. Primary elections are governed by state laws, and states that shifted to using presidential primaries generally did so for both major parties. The primary system and its evolution are topics that deserve entire books by themselves, and many books have been written on those subjects; they are, however, peripheral to the Electoral College system except for a couple of interesting natural analogies, which I would like to discuss briefly before we continue.

One of the major reforms implemented by the Democrats was the elimination of the *unit rule* for primaries. Under the unit rule, the candidate earning the most votes would win the state's slate of elected delegates, in a clear parallel to how the Electoral College operates. However, while the use of the unit rule maximized the importance of winning the support of voters in a particular state, it led to more chaotic and less representative outcomes, and the Democrats wanted a nomination process that was both orderly and representative of the will of Democratic voters.

There is a lesson in that; in designing their own rules for an electoral system, Democrats tried and discarded a system that operated like the modern Electoral College. Republicans have been slower to make similar adjustments, but have done so for similar reasons.

The 26th Amendment

The 26th Amendment, ratified in 1971, required states to allow citizens as young as eighteen to participate in elections. This followed shortly on the heels of the 1970 Voting Rights Act, which required states to allow eighteen-year-olds to participate in federal elections. It is worth noting that the 14th Amendment required states to allow twenty-one-year-olds to participate in federal elections; just as the 14th Amendment did not bar states from letting eighteen-year-olds vote, the 26th Amendment does not prevent states from granting sixteen-year-olds voting rights.

CHAPTER 10

The modern system (1972-2020)

From 1960 to 1971, very rapid changes took place to the presidential election system. This included changes in who was allowed to vote through the 23rd, 24th, and 26th Amendments as well as the reforms associated with the Voting Rights Act of 1965. It also included a massive change to the major parties' nomination process in the aftermath of the 1968 election and the reforms of the McGovern-Fraser Commission.

From 1972 to the present, the ground rules for presidential elections have remained the same. No new constitutional amendments have expanded the franchise, and no major political reforms to the major parties' nomination process have taken place. However, even as the rules have remained constant, the political terrain has shifted between the major parties. Political polarization has steadily increased, and both parties have become significantly more ideologically uniform - and the amount of trust placed in election processes has declined. Significant portions of the losing party's base in each presidential election have refused to accept the results as legitimate.

There's also been a rise in the perception that the Electoral College reliably favors one side over another. The 2000 election left many believing that Republicans had an unfair advantage in the Electoral College; the 2004 election demonstrated they did not, and by the later Obama years, the myth of the "blue wall" had grown, with some Democrats confidently believing Republicans could no longer win presidential elections. After 2016, the belief that Republicans had a large and enduring advantage in the Electoral College became quite popular.

1972: The first modern presidential election

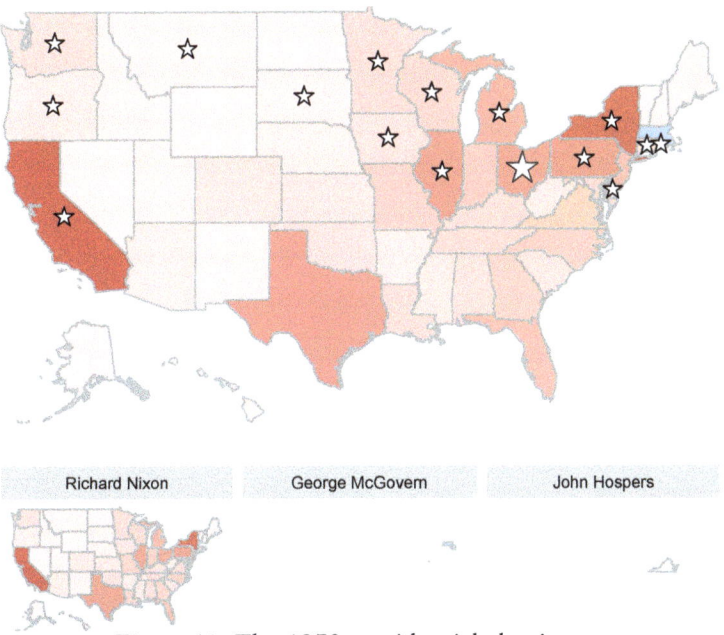

Figure 61: The 1972 presidential election.

Electoral vote: 520-17-1
Popular vote: 61%-38%
Pivotal state: Ohio
Critical states: None
Crucial states: Ohio, Delaware, Montana, Pennsylvania, Illinois, Connecticut, Washington, New Mexico, Iowa, Michigan, California, Oregon, Wisconsin, South Dakota, Rhode Island, Minnesota

Using their new presidential nomination process designed by Senator George McGovern and other members of the McGovern-Fraser Commission, Democrats nominated McGovern. McGovern was very liberal, had made many enemies within the Democratic establishment thanks to his role in reforming the party process, and initially selected fellow Senator Thomas Eagleton of Missouri as his running mate. Two weeks after the Democratic convention, Eagleton admitted to a history of mental illness and was replaced by diplomat Sargent Shriver.

Arguably, McGovern had an unfair advantage in the nomination process, since he was more familiar with how the newly designed primary system worked, but the Democratic nomination process was highly competitive. Republicans uneventfully nominated incumbent president Richard Nixon. The Libertarian Party nominated John Hospers, who unexpectedly earned one electoral vote from a Republican elector in Virginia despite receiving only 3,674 votes.

Nixon won by a strikingly large margin. However, it soon emerged that Republican operatives had been illegally spying on key Democrats. The burglary at the Watergate Hotel and subsequent attempts by the Nixon administration to cover up the scandal ultimately led to the resignation of Nixon. The most ironic part of this was that given the disorganized nature of the Democratic nomination process in this cycle, intelligence gathered before the Democratic National Convention was probably of little value to the Nixon campaign - and given Nixon's blowout margins, he probably would have won the election without resorting to illegal spying.

The 1976 election in brief

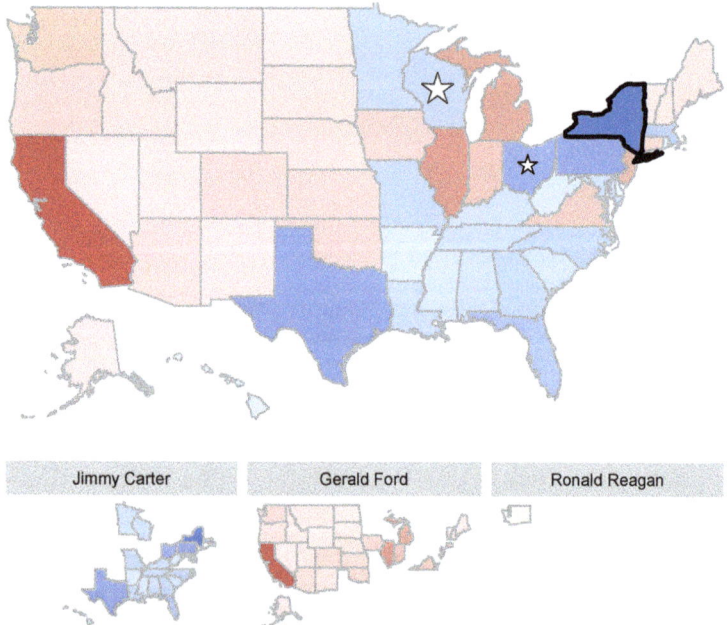

Figure 62: The 1976 presidential election.

Electoral vote: 297-240-1
Popular vote: 50%-48%
Pivotal state: Wisconsin

THE MODERN SYSTEM (1972-2020)

Critical state: New York
Crucial states: Wisconsin, Ohio

Following the resignation of the elected president and vice president, the offices were filled by Gerald Ford and Nelson Rockefeller. Incumbent president Gerald Ford successfully overcame a primary challenge from Ronald Reagan, the Republican governor of California. In an attempt to appease the conservatives within his own party, however, he chose Senator Bob Dole (a conservative from Kansas) as his running mate instead of Nelson Rockefeller (a moderate from New York).

After a contentious Democratic nominating process, Georgia governor Jimmy Carter emerged as the Democratic nominee. In the general election, Carter won a narrow victory with barely over 50% of the vote; his victory was even narrower in the Electoral College. A shift of fewer than 50,000 votes in Wisconsin and Ohio could have tipped the result of the election.

Another plausible path to a Ford victory lies in the fact that Ford lost New York by a margin of about 4% in New York - not the closest margin, but close enough that his loss may have been due to his apparent snub of New York's most popular Republican politician, Nelson Rockefeller. New York was a critical state in Carter's winning coalition, with enough electoral votes to tip the election by itself.

It is difficult to be sure, however, and Ford's worries about conservatives deserting him were well-founded. In fact, one Republican elector in Washington chose to vote for Ronald Reagan instead of Gerald Ford.

The 1980 election in brief

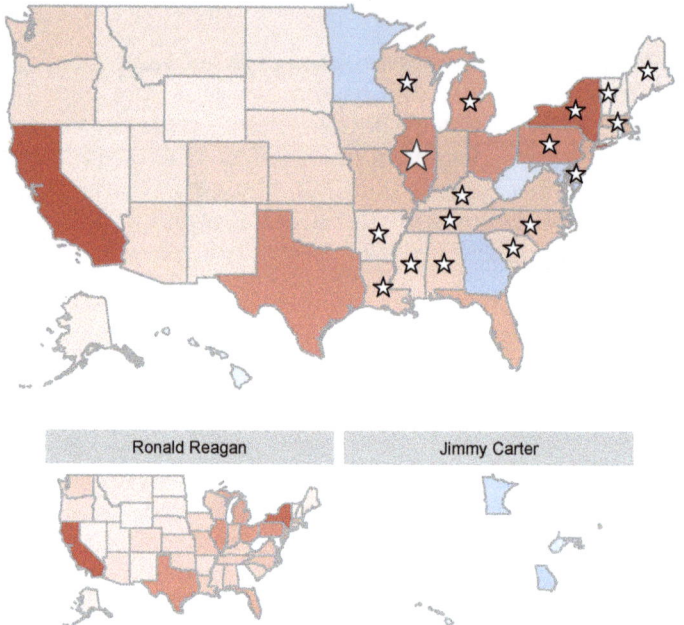

Figure 63: The 1980 presidential election.

Electoral vote: 489-49
Popular vote: 51%-41%-7%
Pivotal state: Illinois
Critical states: None
Crucial states: Illinois, Pennsylvania, Missouri, Michigan, Vermont, Louisiana, Wisconsin, Maine, New York, North Carolina, South Carolina, Kentucky, Mississippi, Alabama, Arkansas, Massachusetts

Democrats nominated incumbent president Jimmy Carter. After a contentious nominating process, Republicans nominated Ronald Reagan. One of the more moderate Republican candidates, John Anderson, chose to run as an independent candidate after losing the primary, earning 6.6% of the national vote. Additional minor-party candidates accounted for another 1.6% of the vote.

The election of 1980 is frequently framed as an electoral landslide. Reagan won over 90% of all electoral votes and an outright majority of 50.7% of the vote. Outgoing president Jimmy Carter won only half a dozen states, plus the District of Columbia. What is frequently overlooked about the election of 1980, however, is that *if* all of the votes against Reagan had gone to the same candidate, Reagan would have lost the Electoral College while winning the popular vote.

Reagan was a beneficiary of a significant spoiler effect; he entered office unpopular with not only Democrats but also a significant branch of his own party. Reagan was too conservative for many Republicans, especially in the northeastern part of the country. If Reagan had earned the same 50.7% of the vote against a single opponent earning the same 49.3% of the vote that was distributed between his opponents, he would have lost the vote in the Electoral College by a narrow 254 to 284 margin.

We may typically think of the structure of the electoral map of 1980 as favoring Reagan and Republicans because of Reagan's apparent landslide, but in order to secure a victory against a single opponent with his particular geographic patterns of support, Reagan needed more than 51% of the popular vote in order to surpass 50% of the electoral vote. Reagan won not because of an Electoral College advantage but in spite of a modest Electoral College disadvantage.

The 1984 election in brief

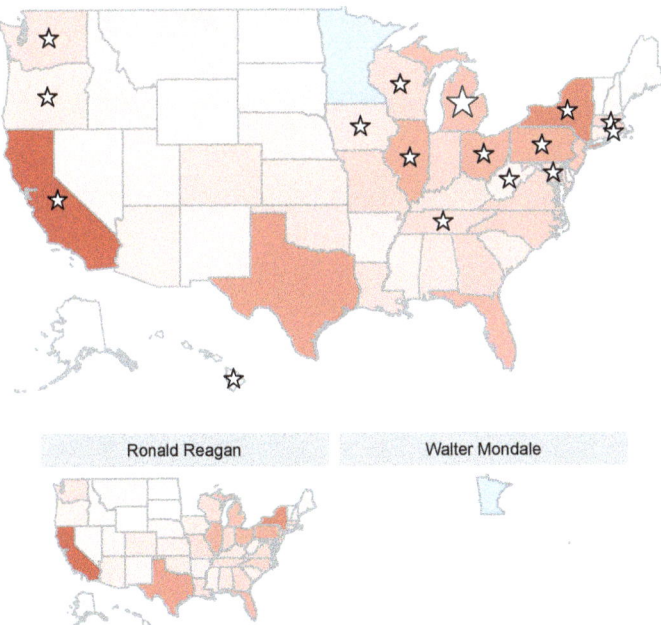

Figure 64: The 1984 presidential election.

Electoral vote: 525-13
Popular vote: 59%-41%

Pivotal state: Michigan
Critical states: None
Crucial states: Michigan, Ohio, Vermont, Tennessee, California, Washington, Illinois, Oregon, Hawaii, West Virginia, Wisconsin, New York, Iowa, Pennsylvania, Maryland, Massachusetts

Democrats nominated former vice president Walter Mondale to run against the Republican incumbent, Ronald Reagan. Reagan earned a little less than 60% of the vote, winning every state except for his opponent's home state of Minnesota. (The three electors of the District of Columbia also voted for Mondale.) In Electoral College terms, this was the most dramatic victory since 1936. Reagan also set a new age record for a major party nomination at 73, a record that would be later broken by both major parties in the 2020 election.

The 1988 election in brief

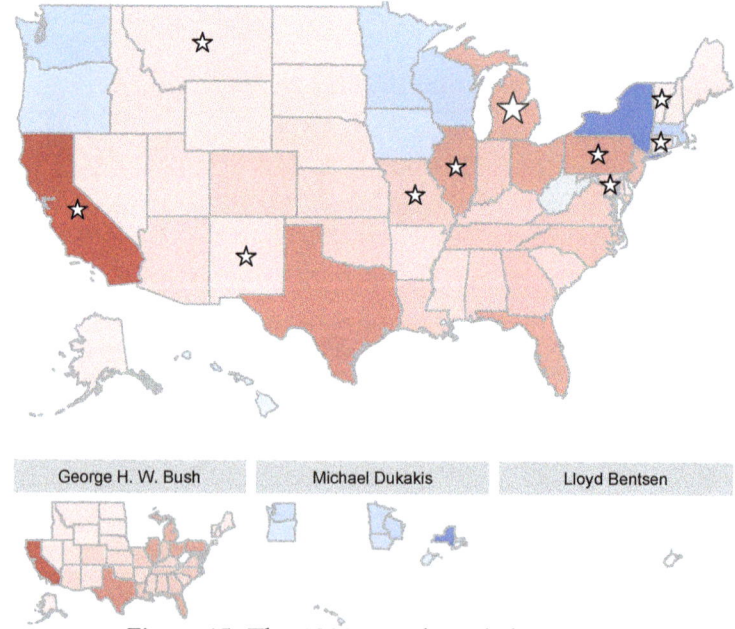

Figure 65: The 1988 presidential election.

Electoral vote: 426-111-1
Popular vote: 53%-46%
Pivotal state: Michigan
Critical states: None

THE MODERN SYSTEM (1972-2020)

Crucial states: Michigan, Colorado, South Dakota, Montana, Connecticut, New Mexico, Missouri, California, Vermont, Pennsylvania, Illinois

Republicans nominated incumbent vice president George H. W. Bush. Democrats nominated Massachusetts governor Michael Dukakis. Thanks in large part to the continued popularity of departing incumbent Ronald Reagan, Bush won a clear majority of the popular vote. This was the first election in which New York could be said to be clearly not a battleground state. It had clearly been a key battleground state when Carter won it in 1976; Reagan had won it in 1980 and 1984.

One elector in West Virginia deliberately switched her votes, casting a vice presidential vote for Michael Dukakis and a presidential vote for his running mate, Lloyd Bentsen.

Broad coalitions versus regional factions

The 1992 election in brief

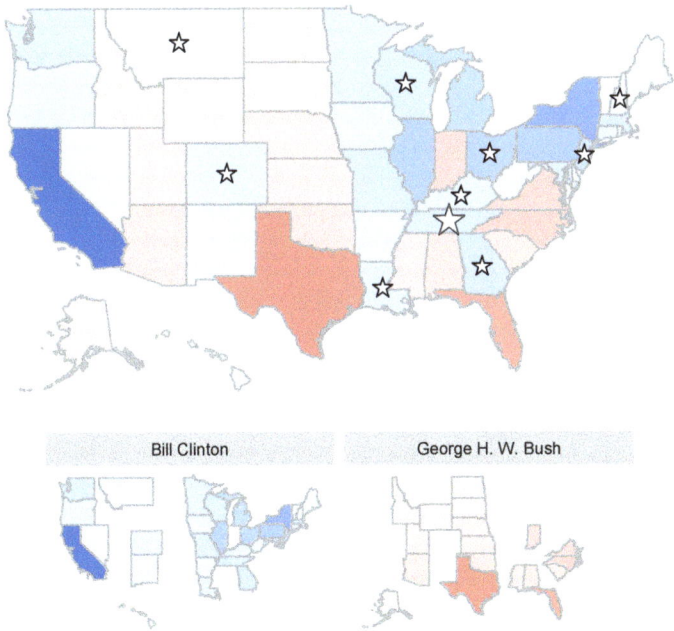

Figure 66: The 1992 presidential election.

Electoral vote: 370-168
Popular vote: 43%-37%-19%

Pivotal state: Tennessee
Critical states: None
Crucial states: Tennessee, Louisiana, Wisconsin, Colorado, Kentucky, Nevada, Montana, New Jersey, Ohio, Georgia

George H. W. Bush's popularity flagged following a financial crisis, the first Iraq war, mounting deficits, and an economic recession. Democrats nominated Arkansas governor Bill Clinton. Texas businessman Ross Perot ran as an independent candidate on the issue of the national debt, at some points leading other candidates in the polls, but his support collapsed late in the race after temporarily suspending his campaign.

Bill Clinton won the three-way contest by a narrow popular margin and a safe Electoral College margin. This marked only the second occasion that a small-state politician successfully ran for president, the previous occasion being Franklin Pierce of New Hampshire in 1852. Another interesting footnote to this race: The pivotal state was Tennessee, the home state of the winning Democratic vice presidential candidate, Al Gore.

The 1996 election in brief

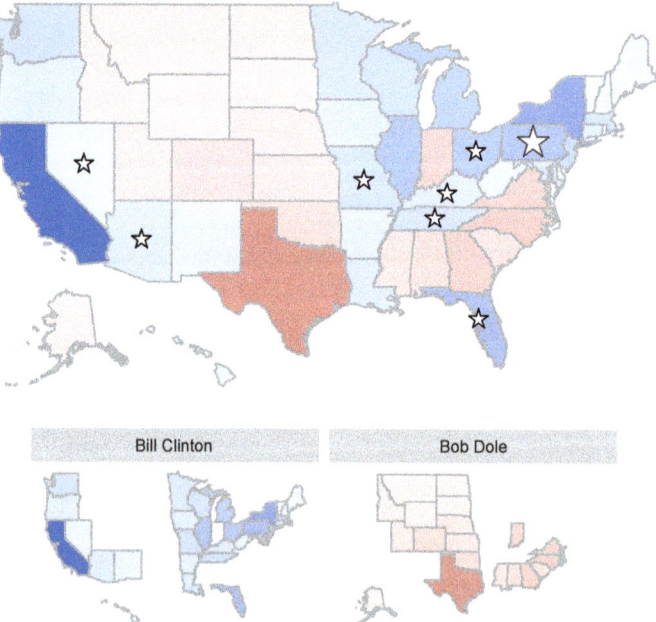

Figure 67: 1996 presidential election.

Electoral vote: 379-159
Popular vote: 49%-41%-8%
Pivotal state: Pennsylvania
Critical states: None
Crucial states: Pennsylvania, Oregon, New Mexico, Ohio, Missouri, Florida, Tennessee, Arizona

Incumbent president Bill Clinton ran for re-election. Republicans nominated Kansas senator Bob Dole. Ross Perot reprised his third-party candidacy on the ticket of what was now known as the Reform Party, earning a smaller but still significant share of the popular vote without earning any electoral votes - more than many of the regional candidates who have earned electoral votes, such as Strom Thurmond in 1948.

It's worth noting that two years later, Jesse Ventura won the Minnesota election for governor running as a Reform party candidate, a narrow victory that demonstrated what could happen if polling continued to show a third party candidate viable through the day of the election.

A possible split-party victory

What if Bill Clinton placed third in the Electoral College?

Democrats controlled majorities in both the House and Senate and so would have been able to control the contingent election process if no candidate won a majority in the Electoral College. This means that in a scenario where no single candidate earned a majority of the vote, Clinton could have won the presidency on the basis of partisan loyalty by legislators. However, while the House is allowed to choose between the top three presidential candidates, the Senate can only choose between the top two vice presidential candidates.

If the Democratic ticket placed third in the Electoral College, even by a narrow margin, Democrats in the Senate would have been forced to choose between the Reform and Republican vice presidential candidates. The president and vice president have not come from different tickets since the election of 1796, but if the party holding a majority of state delegations places third in the presidential race, it could happen in the future *in spite* of the fact that the 12th Amendment is generally thought to *prevent* such cases.

The disadvantage of a broad coalition

The map of the Electoral College vote in 1992 doesn't look exceptional at all. It shows a seemingly solid victory for Democratic challenger Bill

Clinton over incumbent Republican president George H. W. Bush in a two-party system. There were three major candidates in this election, however - even though the third candidate did not win any states. Perot's performance in the Electoral College was disproportionately poor - the worst since Stephen Douglas placed fourth in the Electoral College with the second-largest number of votes.[1]

The most interesting thing about Ross Perot's candidacy is the contrast between his share of the popular vote and his share of the electoral vote. In terms of his share of the popular vote, he did exceptionally well for a minor party candidate - and performed well across multiple regions. However, this isn't reflected in the Electoral College map. Many third-party candidates have earned electoral votes; Ross Perot did not.

Ross Perot received almost a fifth of the vote and even led in polling at some points during the campaign.[2] Since 1788, only two third-place candidates have ever earned a larger fraction of the popular vote by themselves: Millard Fillmore in 1856 and incumbent president William Taft in 1912.[3] Perot was the second-most popular third-party candidate ever to challenge a two-party system; only Teddy Roosevelt, a popular former president, earned a larger share of the vote.[4]

In 1856, the new two-party system hadn't finished forming yet: The Whig Party had just disintegrated. The Know Nothing and Republican parties were both in contention to replace the dying Whig Party. In the congressional elections of 1854, the Know Nothings and Whigs both won more seats than the Republicans. In 1912, Roosevelt's run as a Progressive was more of a revolt from within the Republican Party than an independent bid.

Within the Electoral College, however, Ross Perot failed to receive a single vote. Unlike many other third and fourth-party candidates, from Free Silver to Dixiecrat, his support was spread fairly evenly across the entire country instead of concentrated in a single region. Perot's support was broadly enough distributed that in 49 states, neither Clinton nor Bush received a majority of the vote.[5]

---

[1] If we include fusion votes, Douglas had the support of 33% of voters but only earned 3.6% of the votes in the Electoral College.

[2] E.g., the *New York Times* described him as having a "clear lead" in a short piece on June 11th.

[3] Notably, Roosevelt placed second in 1912 as a third-party candidate. Also note that in 1860, the third and fourth place candidates earned more votes if we give them full credit for fusion ballots.

[4] The candidate coming the closest to Perot's share of the vote without earning any electoral votes was yet another former president, Martin Van Buren. The fact that Perot performed so well as a third-party candidate *without* being a former president is remarkable.

[5] Clinton did win Washington, D.C. with 84% of the vote and its three electors, and his home state of Arkansas and its six electors with 53% of the vote.

THE MODERN SYSTEM (1972-2020)   171

This had never happened before. There have been three elections in which the field of candidates was more strongly fragmented, but in all of them, at least one candidate had a strong regionalized base of support.[6] In a two-candidate race, neither Bush nor Clinton could have won against Perot without winning over some of the other party's loyal voters.

However, because Ross Perot was a centrist with support spread diffusely across the country, he received no electoral votes. Aside from cases in which presidential electors have decided to exercise their free will rather than in concordance with the will of the voters, there have been ten elections in which candidates from three or four different parties earned the vote of at least one entire state's slate of electors.[7] In eight of these cases, the electoral votes for the third and fourth-place candidates can be attributed to strongly regionalized (or even localized) patterns of support.

Was Ross Perot a viable candidate?

It is easy to cast Perot's candidacy as a doomed quixotic effort from a billionaire with money to burn and use his poor Electoral College performance as evidence of his inevitable failure, but all indications are that victory was entirely possible. As I mentioned before, during polling leading up to the election, Ross Perot was in the lead at some points. It seems clear that voters' opinions on Ross Perot shifted substantially over the course of the campaign.

He made some mistakes; notably, he briefly suspended his campaign, leading to a sudden collapse in his polling numbers. His support collapsed further leading into the election, as voters decided that the election was likely to come down to Bush versus Clinton. Had either Clinton or Bush been the trailing candidate in the polls shortly before the election, as they had earlier in the campaign, they would likely have experienced a similar late-stage collapse in support.

Was there a spoiler effect?

It's unclear whether or not Perot provided any sort of meaningful spoiler effect tipping the balance in Clinton's favor. While Clinton's large

---

[6] In 1824, all four major candidates won a popular vote majority in at least one state. In 1860, both Lincoln and Breckinridge won majorities in many states, while Douglas eked out only one arguable majority in New Jersey as part of a fusion ticket. In 1912, neither Taft nor Roosevelt earned a majority in any state, but Wilson earned majorities across much of the South.

[7] To be specific, 1824, 1832, 1856, 1860, 1892, 1912, 1924, 1948, 1960, and 1968.

Electoral College margin was well within the margin of Perot's possible spoiler effect, Perot ran as an outsider centrist with a singular focus on the national debt and an otherwise moderate platform, taking votes away from both Clinton and Bush from the center.[8]

Because voters' opinions of Perot seem to have varied quite substantially over the course of the campaign, it's hard to be sure whether or not Perot could have won a hypothetical two-candidate contest between him and either Bush or Clinton. There are indications that a significant number of voters were skeptical of Perot for reasons unrelated to his moderate position on the issues that differentiated Clinton and Bush. Public opinion polling was significantly more consistent in establishing that most voters preferred Clinton to Bush.

Looking back at regional versus national candidates

By most measures, 1992 is the most recent election featuring a major third-party candidate. With this in mind, we can look back at all elections featuring three or more major candidates for president. As I mentioned, there have been ten elections in which at least three candidates won the vote of at least one state each; and an additional two elections in which at least three candidates earned 10% or more of the total popular vote. These elections are important in studying the history of the Electoral College system for one very important reason: The mathematical structure of the Electoral College rewards divisive candidates and penalizes unifying candidates.

Those who seek to defend the Electoral College system often wrongly claim that the system requires candidates to seek out broad coalitions.[9] There is little if any evidence in favor of these claims. Two-candidate elections are particularly difficult to test: If one candidate receives 90% of the vote in a region and a second candidate receives 10% of the vote in that same region, we cannot say whether the first candidate or the second candidate is more responsible for the extreme polarization of the electorate in that region.

In elections with three or more major candidates, which tend to occur at critical points in the nation's history,[10] we can start to disentangle which candidates are more or less strongly polarizing by examining the structure of their support. With three or more candidates, we can also identify

---

[8] See, for example, Alexander Tabbarok's analysis in "President Perot or Fundamentals of Voting Theory Illustrated with the 1992 Election" (2001), based on an October poll of 3,536 registered voters.

[9] E.g., Judith Best, Tara Ross, et cetera.

[10] E.g., leading into the Civil War.

which candidates have taken a more moderate position on key issues, such as slavery in the 1860 election. Both methods clearly show that regionally polarizing candidates who take extreme positions do better than candidates who attempt to unify the country from a moderate position.

Ross Perot's underperformance in the 1992 Electoral College as a candidate with a broad regional coalition is not unusual. As a particularly dramatic point of contrast, Strom Thurmond did better in the 1948 Electoral College than Stephen Douglas did in the 1860 Electoral College - even though Stephen Douglas placed second in the national popular vote while Strom Thurmond placed a very distant third. Strom Thurmond's share of the vote was *an entire order of magnitude* smaller than Stephen Douglas's. It is further likely that Stephen Douglas was what voting theorists call a Condorcet winner (someone who would win in a head-to-head contest against any of his opponents) and also likely that Strom Thurmond was a Condorcet loser (someone who would lose in a head to head contest against any of his opponents).

To understand the basic mathematical properties of the Electoral College system that rewards regional candidates, it helps to start with a simple example: What happens if a candidate only competes in their own home state? If they earn half of the vote, they will win - and they will win 100% of their state's electoral votes if they simply win 50% of the vote. Thus, a candidate who competes *only in a single state* could easily win 2% of the electoral votes with 1% of the total popular vote.

This has several consequences. First and most obviously, sectional candidates can use their superior leverage in the Electoral College to try to strategically force a House contingent election. Segregationists' attempts to do so failed by narrow margins in 1948, 1960, and 1968. Second, in a three-candidate race, a candidate with a strong sectional base of support has a strong advantage over two national candidates who are spread similarly thinly - for example, Woodrow Wilson and the South in 1912.

Third, when the Electoral College itself fails to select a winner in an election with four or more candidates receiving electoral votes, the top three finishers are *unlikely* to include the most natural compromise candidates (e.g., Henry Clay in 1824) or the candidate with the broadest base of visible support from the electorate (e.g., Stephen Douglas in 1860). If the House contingent election process is invoked again, it is entirely possible that *none* of the top three finishers will be acceptable to more than half of the country, leading to a serious crisis.

Partisan advantage in the Electoral College

Currently, it is fashionable to suggest that Republicans have a significant and lasting structural advantage in the Electoral College. If we look at the 2000 and 2004 elections back to back, however, we can see that very minor shifts in political terrain can create a relative advantage or disadvantage. Speaking as a mathematician, I can say that it's very easy to see - and quantitatively describe - patterns in noise based on a small number of cases, and this is unfortunately what has happened with some recent analyses of the Electoral College.

If you look back through past political commentary, you can find countless dated analyses based on the previous several elections that announced that one or the other major party had a large and unfair advantage in the Electoral College. George W. Bush was the third, or possibly sixth,[11] president to win an election having earned fewer votes than his opponent. He also almost became the second incumbent president to be unseated by a challenger who earned fewer votes.

Instead of having any lasting bias towards either major party, the Electoral College system favors those who are in a position to control how votes are counted and recounted in key jurisdictions. This was true when the Tammany Hall machine controlled New York City more than a century ago; it was true in 2000 with Florida and in 2004 with Ohio.

---

[11] Recall that popular vote totals of several elections can be contested: The 1880 election featured a national popular vote within the margin of counting error, 1960's popular vote can be counted differently depending on how we think of Alabama's split electoral slate, and fraud was widespread enough in 1876 to render the national popular vote margin murky.

THE MODERN SYSTEM (1972-2020)

The 2000 election in brief

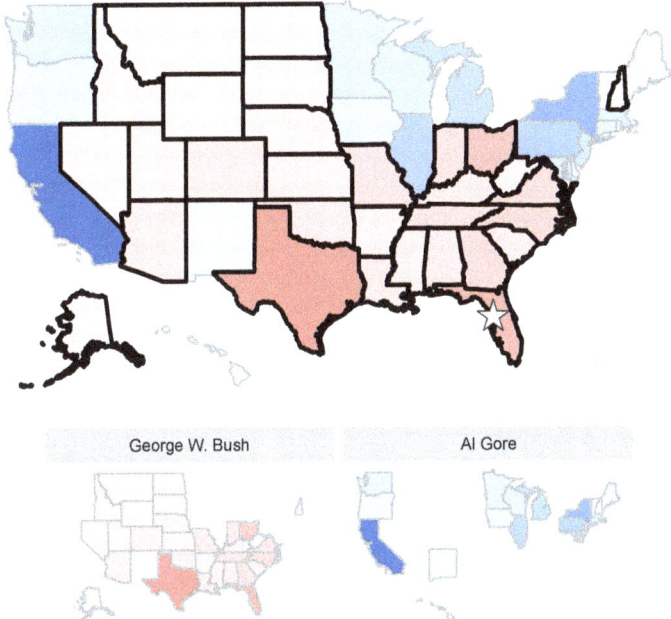

Figure 68: The 2000 presidential election.

Popular vote: 48%-48%
Electoral vote: 271-266
Pivotal state: Florida
Critical states: Every state won by Bush
Crucial state: Florida

Democrats nominated incumbent vice president Al Gore. Republicans nominated Texas governor George W. Bush, the son of the former president George H. W. Bush. Al Gore earned more votes nationally, by a margin of 0.5%. Ralph Nader, running on the Green Party ticket, took close to 5% of the vote nationally. However, while it was clear that Al Gore had earned more votes nationally, it was not clear which candidate had earned more votes in two states, Florida and New Mexico. New Mexico promptly completed a recount without fanfare, awarding its electoral slate to Al Gore without controversy.

Ralph Nader, running on the Green Party ticket, took close to 5% of the vote nationally. It is generally likely that most Green voters preferred Al Gore to George W. Bush.[12] While Ralph Nader was unable to spoil

---

[12] Al Gore was known as an environmentalist; George W. Bush had close ties to the oil industry.

Gore's margin of popular victory, he most likely functioned as a spoiler candidate on the state level in both Florida and New Hampshire.

In addition to the likely spoiler effect from Ralph Nader, the case of Florida was complicated by numerous irregularities and was ultimately decided by litigation, rather than by an effort to determine which candidate truly had more votes cast for them in Florida. One key point is that the state of Florida was governed by a Republican - in particular, Jeb Bush, the brother of the Republican presidential candidate. The Republican administration of Florida successfully blocked efforts to recount the state, fighting the matter all the way up to a controversial 5-4 decision by the Supreme Court.[13]

Amidst all other controversies, one presidential elector chose to symbolically abstain.[14]

Despite the irregularities involved with Florida's election and clear uncertainty over which candidate had earned more votes, Congress did not either throw out the votes (as happened in 1872 with electors of dubious legitimacy in Arkansas and Louisiana) or convene a special electoral commission to resolve the issue (as happened in 1876). No senator was willing to endorse a challenge to Florida's electoral vote.

This election also marked the third time in American history that the bonus "Senator" electors were decisive; without them, uncertainty surrounding Florida's actual vote count would not have been enough to prevent Al Gore from receiving a majority of electors. The previous two times were in 1796 and 1876. In the wake of the 2000 election, many voters presumed that the Electoral College had a significant Republican bias - pointing in particular to the fact that Bush had won more states.

---

[13]*Bush v. Gore*, 2000.

[14]Barbara Lett-Simmons of Washington, D.C.; she said it was a protest against the district's lack of representation in Congress.

THE MODERN SYSTEM (1972-2020)

The 2004 election in brief

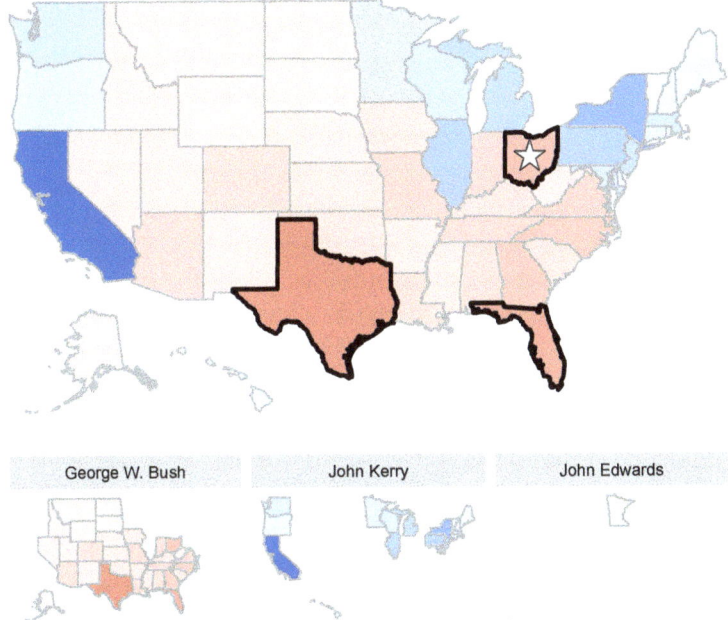

Figure 69: The 2004 presidential election.

Electoral vote: 286-251-1
Popular vote: 51%-48%
Pivotal state: Ohio (20 electoral votes)
Critical states: Florida, Ohio, Texas
Crucial state: Ohio

Democrats nominated Massachusetts Senator John Kerry. Republicans nominated the incumbent president, George W. Bush. President Bush won the national popular vote by a margin of about 3%. However, the margin was close in Ohio amid concerns about inappropriate voter roll scrubs, unverifiable and suddenly fluctuating counts from electronic voting machines, long lines in Democratic precincts, and discrepancies between results and exit polls. Similar disputes emerged in the critical battleground state of Florida, but Ohio took center stage as the pivotal battleground state.

One Minnesota elector cast a ballot for John Edwards instead of John Kerry.[15] This was apparently an accident rather than an intentional political act, and it is not known which Minnesota elector cast the errant ballot.

---

[15] Mis-spelled "John Ewards," but recorded and counted as for John Edwards.

While not as close as the margin in Florida in 2000, the margin of the election in key battleground states was close enough to be decided by voter access issues alone. However, even combining all of the irregularities identified related to statistically unusual results from suspect electronic voting machines and voter suppression in key battleground states, Bush's national popular vote margin was not subject to these concerns.

If Ohio had a Democratic governor and secretary of state, it's quite likely that Kerry would have carried Ohio even if he did not earn a single additional vote in other states; similarly, stronger get-out-the-vote efforts by the Kerry campaign on the ground in Ohio could have made the difference.[16] If this had happened, George W. Bush would have become the only president to have both won the Electoral College while losing the popular vote and lost the Electoral College while winning the popular vote.

Kerry did not attempt to contest the results of the vote in Ohio. Green Party candidate David Cobb, however, challenged the results and succeeded in obtaining a recount. This recount was marred by an inability to independently verify votes cast through touchscreen electronic voting machines without a paper trail, and also by criminal misbehavior by election officials. Two Cuyahoga County election officials were convicted of election malfeasance.[17] A lawsuit against Kenneth Blackwell alleging electronic tampering with the results[18] was significantly impaired by the fact that a key consultant who represented the link between Blackwell and Smartech died in a plane crash in 2008. There were also complaints that Blackwell had disproportionately "scrubbed" (de-registered) African-American voters from Ohio's voter rolls, and that resources had been selectively misallocated to make voting more difficult in Democratic precincts.

The legitimacy of Ohio's electoral slate went to a vote in Congress, marking the first time since the 1876 election that Congress had taken up a challenge. Congress voted to affirm the legitimacy of Ohio's electoral vote, however, and Bush was elected.

Republicans do not have a structural advantage in the Electoral College

The symmetry of Bush's popular vote loss in 2000 and popular vote win in 2004, with both victories depending on electoral votes from a single

---

[16] C.f. the 2008 presidential election results in Ohio.
[17] See "Election Staff Convicted in Recount Rig" (2007) by M. R. Kropko.
[18] "King Lincoln Bronzeville Neighborhood Association v. Blackwell" (2006)

contested state, underlines a key point: The Electoral College does *not* favor either major party in any significant and lasting way. Within the structure of a single election, it can appear as though Republicans or Democrats have an advantage; however, these structures are transient as well as potentially deceptive. If Democrats had done slightly better at campaigning in Ohio,[19] Bush might have lost the Electoral College while winning the popular vote, a mere four years after winning the Electoral College while losing the popular vote.

While it is true that the Republican Party has coincidentally been on the winning side of four cases in which the Electoral College granted more votes to a candidate who had earned fewer votes nationally, there are a couple of key points to consider. The first is that four is not a very large number. A second important factor is that the political geography has completely changed from 1876 to 2016. When the Republicans won the Electoral College without the popular vote in 1876 and 1888, it was a victory for New England over the South; in 2000 and 2016, it was a victory for the South over New England.

A third and crucial point to consider is that in the recent era, we *have* seen several "near miss" elections - 1960, 1980, and 2004 - where a Republican candidate came close to scenarios where they would have won the popular vote while losing the Electoral College. Arguably, Richard Nixon *did* win the national popular vote in 1960.[20]

The only thing in common between Bush's narrow victories in 2000 and 2004 is that Republicans controlled the state governments in the key battleground states of those two cycles. Controlling state governments gives some influence over how votes are cast and counted.[21] Similarly, the Republican victory in 1876 depended on Republican governors certifying the Republican slate of electors in key battleground states. Whoever controls the governor's mansion[22] in key battleground states has an advantage. Control of state and local government determines how votes are counted - and whether or not the state government cooperates with attempts to secure a recount in a close contest.

---

[19] Or possibly simply controlled the office of Ohio Secretary of State; it's possible that voter roll purges, voting machine irregularities, and distribution of election administration resources were enough to tip the balance in Ohio.

[20] The two main arguments are that either that fraud was widespread in Chicago and the Texas borderlands, or that votes for Alabama's divided electoral slate should only be counted as five-elevenths of a vote for Kennedy.

[21] The 14th, 15th, 19th, 24th, and 26th Amendments to the Constitution have limited this influence significantly, but not completely eliminated it. States still have the latitude to disenfranchise felons, maintain voter registration rolls, and can make it more or less convenient to vote.

[22] And/or the position of Secretary of State; the position of Secretary of State is typically important in administrating elections.

The Obama elections

During the 2008 and 2012 elections, there were quiet behind-the-scenes campaigns aimed at trying to get electors to break from their pledges and vote against Obama.[23] Opponents known as "birthers" contended that the popular politician was not a "born citizen" of the United States and therefore not eligible to be president. However, in contrast to the 2000 and 2004 elections, there was very little public controversy over the electoral results of the 2008 and 2012 elections, as they were not close elections.

The 2008 election in brief

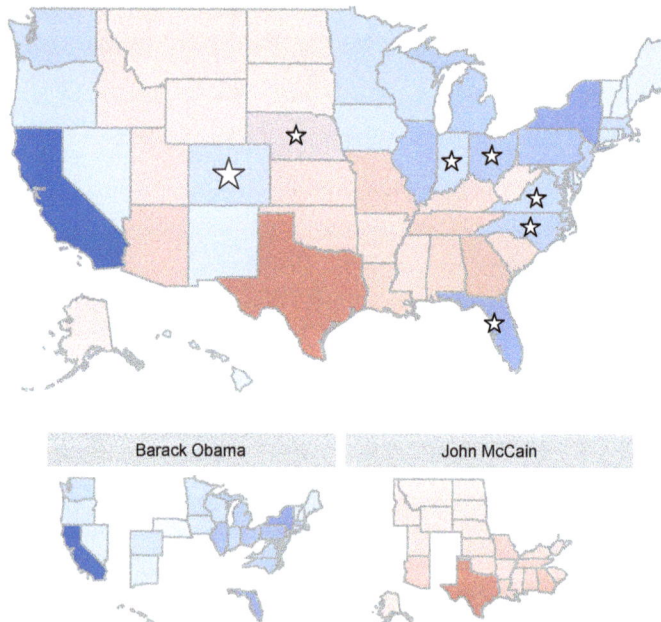

Figure 70: The 2008 presidential election.

Electoral vote: 365-173
Popular vote: 53%-46%
Pivotal state: Colorado
Critical states: None
Crucial states: Colorado, Virginia, Ohio, Florida, Indiana, North Carolina

---

[23]These are discussed at length in *Presidential Electors and the Electoral College: An Examination of Lobbying, Wavering Electors, and Campaigns for Faithless Votes* (2012) by Robert Alexander.

THE MODERN SYSTEM (1972-2020)

George W. Bush's popularity flagged following a financial crisis, the second Iraq war, mounting deficits, and an economic recession. Republicans nominated Senator John McCain of Arizona; Democrats nominated Senator Barack Obama of Illinois, creating a rare senator versus senator contest.[24]

Obama won a clear majority of the popular vote, the first candidate since 1992 to do so, but earned a similar Electoral College margin to Clinton's margin in 1992 and 1996. The pivotal state in this election was Colorado. This was the first occasion in which Colorado had a prominent electoral role since 1876, when Colorado was the last state to appoint electors without an election. Since Colorado only had nine electoral votes, this was one of the rare elections in which a merely medium-sized state was pivotal.

This election was also noteworthy as the first election since 1892 in which a state split its electoral slate based on district-level results. However, as with every election from 1828 to the present, the result would have been the same as if each state used a winner-take-all-rule.

The 2012 election in brief

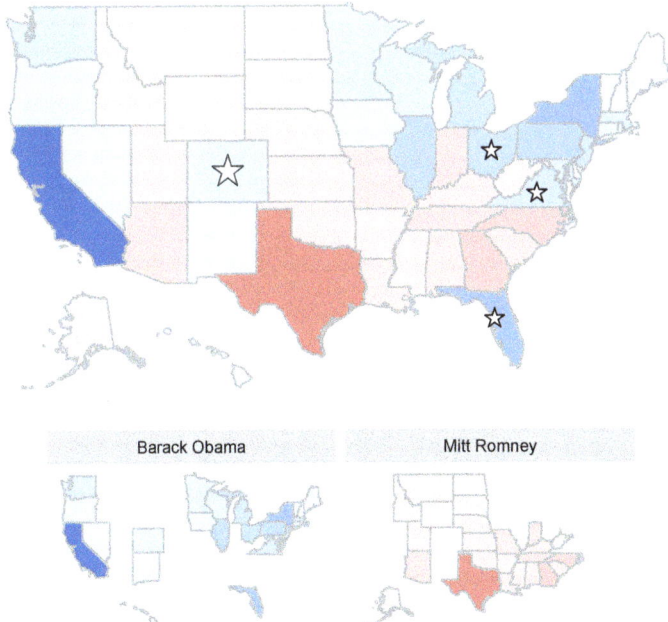

Figure 71: The 2012 presidential election.

---

[24]Senators are common presidential candidates, but they rarely face each other.

Electoral vote: 332-206
Popular vote: 51%-47%
Pivotal state: Colorado
Critical states: None
Crucial states: Colorado, Virginia, Ohio, Florida

Republicans nominated former Massachusetts governor Mitt Romney to challenge the incumbent president, Barack Obama. The election was slightly closer than the 2008 election, but the geographic structure of support was quite similar for the two candidates - making Colorado the pivotal state for the second election in a row, and marking the third time Colorado had a prominent role in a presidential election.

The Trump elections

During the Obama era, popular wisdom slowly came around to the idea that Democrats had a large current advantage in the Electoral College. After all, there had been four resounding Democratic victories in the Electoral College, two narrow Republican victories in the Electoral College, and in those six elections, a "blue wall" consisting of consistently Democratic states supposedly made it difficult for any Republican to win.

2016: The electors who would not concede

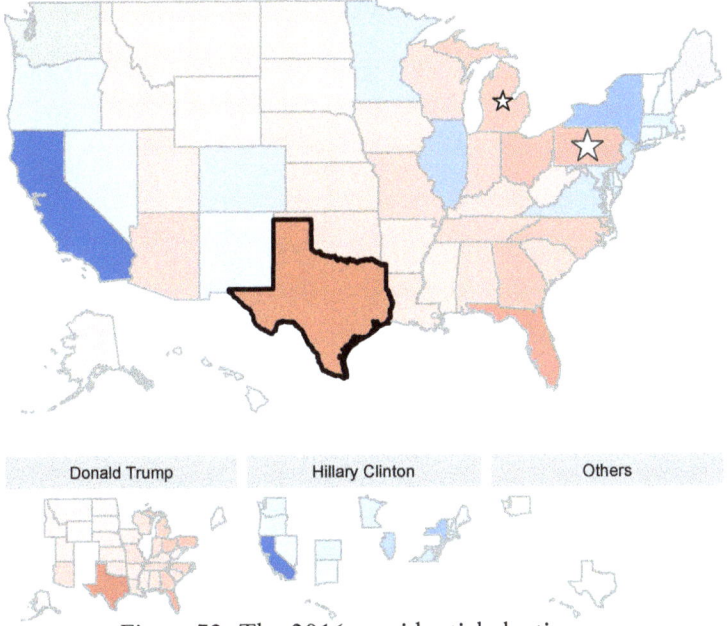

Figure 72: The 2016 presidential election.

Electoral vote: 304-227-3-1-1-1-1
Popular vote: 48%-46%
Pivotal state: Pennsylvania
Critical states: Texas
Crucial states: Pennsylvania, Michigan; arguably also Wisconsin

Leading into the 2016 election, many political analysts confidently affirmed the existence of a "blue wall" of states adding up to a total of 254 electoral votes. These states, from New York to California, had voted Democratic in each election since 1992. With the narrow victories of George W. Bush surrounded by much larger electoral victories by Bill Clinton and Barack Obama, it sounded reasonable to conclude Democrats had an advantage.

The proposition that Democrats had a real and significant advantage in the Electoral College due to current political geography was coupled with assurances that a Democratic victory in 2016 was inevitable. After the 2016 election, the idea of a "blue wall" had lost all credibility, and public opinion re-oriented in the opposite direction. It became widely presumed, both by Democrats and Republicans, that the Republicans had a real and lasting advantage in the Electoral College.

In a particularly contentious nominating process, Republicans nominated businessman Donald Trump. Democrats nominated Hillary Clinton, the wife of former president Bill Clinton, who had been Senator and then Secretary of State after her term as First Lady. While wives succeeding or attempting to succeed their husbands in office had happened before in American history, this was the first time that wife of a former president earned a major party nomination. The other 6% of the vote was scattered between a variety of third-party candidates. Among those third-party candidates, the one who earned the most votes was Gary Johnson, at 3% of the national vote; Evan McMullin, however, came closer to having an impact, as his 0.5% of the national vote included 21% of the vote in his home state of Utah - recall that sectional candidates do better in the Electoral College system than national candidates.

Hillary Clinton won significantly more votes nationally, but thanks to narrow margins in key battleground states, Donald Trump emerged with an apparent electoral majority. On election night, it appeared that there were three crucial states (Pennsylvania, Michigan, and Wisconsin), decided by a narrow combined margin of just under 80,000 votes. However, the Electoral College itself was unusually fractious and contained surprises. Seven different candidates received votes in the Electoral College, the largest number since 1796.

The precise identity of the pivotal and crucial states in this election is complicated by the presence of electors who chose to exercise their free will. If we account for the defection of two Texas electors expected to vote for Trump, Trump's Electoral College majority would not have been secure if he had won Wisconsin while losing Pennsylvania and Michigan – and what the outcome of a House contingent election would have been is unclear. Arguably, therefore, the election hinged on a margin of only 55,000 votes in Pennsylvania and Michigan.

In those states, both Gary Johnson and Jill Stein earned enough votes to account for this margin via the spoiler effect; this was a close election in many ways.

The Hamilton electors

There were public calls for electors to repair the outcome of the Electoral College. A group of electors calling themselves the "Hamilton electors" rose to meet the call; according to my conversations with several of the electors involved in the effort, upwards of fifty electors considered switching their vote.[25] The plan was for enough electors to throw their

---

[25]This is roughly in line with the survey results reported by Robert Alexander in *Representation and the Electoral College* (2019).

support behind a more conventional moderate Republican candidate - such as John Kasich or Colin Powell - to force a House contingent election, in the hopes that Republicans in the House would be willing to support an alternative to Trump.

However, the group had difficulty securing cooperation from Republican electors; reportedly, many were concerned that Hillary Clinton would be able to win a House contingent election. Under a combination of pressure and coercion, only seven electoral votes were cast for other candidates. This was arguably the largest number of "faithless" presidential electors since 1796; larger exercises of free will by electors have occurred in vice presidential votes and when Horace Greeley died prior to the electors voting.

The figures would have been larger without the pressure of laws designed to coerce electors into fulfilling their pledges. The Supreme Court would later hear cases linked to the removal and replacement of a Colorado elector, Michael Baca, as well as fines issued to four electors from Washington State. The decision in *Chiafalo v. Washington* (2020) affirmed that the states' power of appointment of electors extended to the right to compel electors to vote in a particular way.

The case of the Hamilton electors underlines one of the key problems with saying that most presidential electors vote "faithfully;" on the occasions that electors decide to take action, they can - and will - do so in groups. This happened in 1796, 1836, and 2016. If states do not compel electors to vote as directed, then a highly unpopular reversal of a future presidential election will eventually occur because of electors choosing to act at their own discretion.

Conversely, if states compel electors, this practice makes a mockery out of the Framers' design. Pledged electors are an unanticipated evolution of the system rather than an intentional design feature. For the same reason, eliminating the discretion of electors also undercuts one of the most popular arguments routinely offered in favor of the Electoral College: That wise electors deliberating carefully prevents the election of a simple demagogue.[26]

---

[26] See, once again, the oft-cited Federalist #68.

2020: The candidate who would not concede

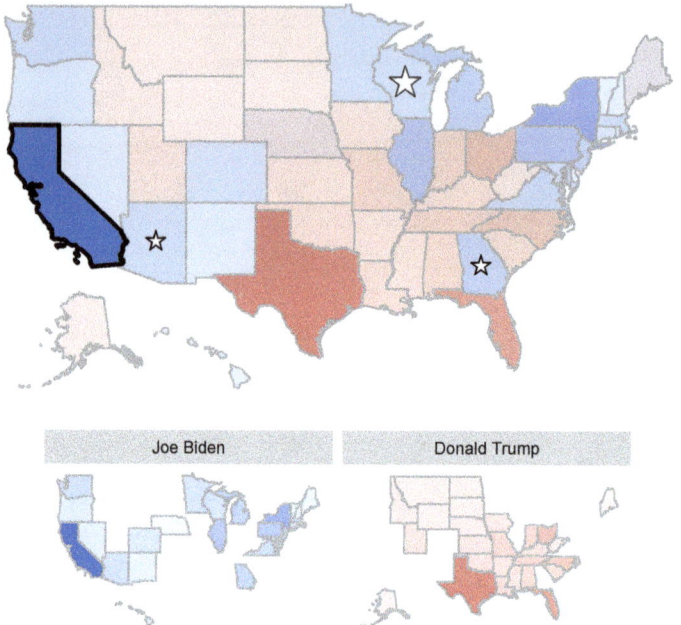

Figure 73: The 2020 presidential election.

Electoral vote: 306-232
Popular vote: 51%-47%
Pivotal state: Wisconsin
Critical states: California
Crucial states: Wisconsin, Georgia, Arizona

Republicans renominated incumbent president Donald Trump; Democrats nominated former vice president Joe Biden. Due to a major pandemic, a large number of ballots were cast by mail. Turnout was historically and exceptionally high. Joe Biden won an outright majority of the popular vote as well as a majority of the Electoral College.

Biden's victory in the Electoral College depended on a combined margin of 43,000 votes in three crucial states: Wisconsin, Georgia, and Arizona. Trump filed dozens of lawsuits trying to halt the counting of mail-in ballots, contesting the results in those three states, as well as other close battleground states that could potentially play a decisive role(e.g., Michigan and Pennsylvania). There were two statewide recounts in Georgia (one technically an audit, one an additional recount requested by the Trump campaign) and a partial recount in Wisconsin (requested by the Trump campaign).

THE MODERN SYSTEM (1972-2020)

While all electors were chosen on the basis of popular votes (as has happened in every election after 1876), Trump and some of his allies called on Republican state legislatures in those five key battleground states to retroactively take back the right to appoint electors directly. Trump attempted to pressure state legislators and state officials into backing the appointment of Trump electors in key battleground states. When cooperation from state officials and state legislatures was not forthcoming, Trump's partisans ceremoniously assembled alternate slates of self-appointed electors in a total of seven key states.

Trump publicly called on his vice president, Mike Pence, to discard or send back votes from states won by Joe Biden; the vice president declined. On January 6th, the day of the official counting process, some of Trump's supporters gathered in Washington and broke into the Capitol building, intending to disrupt the counting process. Congress was evacuated, and the counting was postponed until later that night. Allies of Trump in Congress filed objections to the counting of votes from both Pennsylvania and Arizona. The official count was completed at 3:24 am on the following Thursday morning.

The challenges to the system

Arguably, a modern era of constantly-litigated results started with the election of 2000, when George W. Bush's slate of electors were certified as the winners of the presidential election in Florida and counted by Congress even though more voters had cast ballots for Al Gore and the state government had obstructed efforts to recount votes in the state.[27] Attacks on the legitimacy of the presidential election process continued from the Democratic side in 2004 and mounted on the Republican side with the "birther" movement in 2008 and 2012.

In 2016 and 2020, people on both sides of the aisle became more aware of the vulnerabilities of the Electoral College system and more willing to attempt to exploit them. In some ways, the 2000-2020 era has significant parallels to the 1868-1888 era, representing a series of substantial tests of the vulnerabilities of the Electoral College system. The Bush elections were tainted by concerns about whether he had legitimately won a key pivotal state, or whether it was stolen on his behalf by partisan state officials. The legitimacy of the Obama elections was questioned by "birthers." The first Trump election featured coordinated action from presidential electors on a level not seen since 1796; the second featured pleas for state legislatures to retake the power of selection of electors and a failed counting day putsch.

---

[27] Congress last refused to count electoral votes from a state in 1872.

With these vulnerabilities clearly highlighted, the question that awaits us is a simple one: Does the Electoral College have redeeming characteristics? It is not a body ruled by wise deliberation and careful discernment. The results are vulnerable to fraud, chicanery, manipulation, and simple counting errors. Does it protect those living in small states from being overwhelmed by the votes of those living in large states? The answer to this question is a resounding *no*, as we shall see in the next chapter.

CHAPTER 11

A Primer on Power in the Electoral College

The Electoral College does not empower small states or the residents of those states. The Electoral College itself wasn't *intended* to help small states. The Framers of the Constitution expected the Electoral College system to be dominated by large states, and it has. Delegates who favored small-state interests agreed to the system based on a mistaken understanding that the House contingent election system would play a prominent role.

Small states indeed have a higher ratio of electoral votes to popular votes, but the mathematics of power is more complex than simply looking at the ratio of electoral votes to voters. Looking at the history and the math, it's clear the balance of power has usually been held by key large states. This was true early in the history of the country; it is also true today.

Despite the fact that key large battleground states have held the balance of power, the opposite contention is a very persistent myth. Many scholars know better, including those who have defended the Electoral College as well as those criticizing it.[1] The fact that large states have held the balance of power is not a matter of subjective opinion; this is a point of historical record that is obvious after mathematical analysis.

---

[1] See, for example, Judith Best in *The Case Against Direct Election of the President: A Defense of the Electoral College* (1975) and Robert Alexander in *Representation and the Electoral College* (2019).

A PRIMER ON POWER IN THE ELECTORAL COLLEGE

To better understand this type of analysis, we will first go over a few basic facts about how we can mathematically measure power in the Electoral College.

The mathematics of power in the Electoral College

The evolved Electoral College generally works as what experts like to refer to as a *weighted voting system*. Each state controls[2] a slate of electors, and can therefore effectively control a bloc, or group, of votes. The size of the bloc is referred to as its weight. There are other weighted voting systems; for example, shareholders of companies typically vote by share.

The mathematically tricky thing about this is that power and weight, while related, aren't the same. For example, a shareholder who controls 51% of voting shares does not have 51% of the power. We'll start with three examples that show off the interesting quirks of weighted voting systems.

Example 1: There are four voters. Cal controls a bloc of 55 votes. The other three voters, Tex, Ari, and Nem, have blocs of 38 votes, 11 votes, and 5 votes, respectively. There are a total of 109 votes divided between the four voters, and a majority of 55 votes is required to make any decision.

How is power distributed between the four voters? Cal has 55 votes, and the other three voters have a total of 54 votes combined, so Cal has 100% of the power (even though Cal only has about 51% of the vote). Tex may have over a third of the vote, but has 0% of the power, just like Ari and Nem do. Large blocs are much more powerful than small blocs!

Example 2: There are four voters. Penn controls a bloc of 20 votes. The other three voters, Hi, Mitch, and Indy, control blocs of 18, 16, and 11 votes, respectively. There are a total of 65 votes, and a majority of 33 votes is required to make any decision.

How is power distributed between the four voters? To get a majority, you need 33 votes. There are three different ways to get to that majority using only two voters: Penn and Hi (38 votes), Penn and Mitch (36 votes), or Mitch and Hi (34 votes). It doesn't matter how Indy votes at all; despite having 17% of the total vote, Indy has 0% of the power. Mitch, Hi, and Penn each have an equal 33% of the power; any two of them can combine

---

[2] Not completely, but almost completely. Independent decisions by electors have not altered an election result since 1796. They are unlikely to do so in the future given the Supreme Court's recent decision in *Chiafalo v. Washington*.

A PRIMER ON POWER IN THE ELECTORAL COLLEGE 191

their votes to make a decision, and it doesn't matter which. Mitch has a whopping 33% of the power in spite of only controlling 25% of the votes.

Example 3: There are four voters. Massy controls a bloc of 11 votes. The other three voters, Connie, Rhody, and Ham, control blocs of 7, 4, and 4 votes, respectively. There are a total of 26 votes, and a majority is required to make any decision.

There are two basic ways to get to a working majority of 15 votes: Massy plus one other voter, or all three of Connie, Rhody, and Ham. It's clear that Massy has more leverage than the other three voters, but the other three voters (Connie, Rhody, and Ham) all have equal power, even though they don't have the same number of votes. How can we quantify this?

It turns out that depending on your perspective, there are many different ways to try to calculate the exact quantity of power that Massy has. A method of quantifying power in a weighted voting system is called a *power index*, and most of the power indices used in mathematical voting theory are based on the same key concepts.[3] We will step through these key concepts briefly; they are not complex, but they are distinct.

A *coalition* is simply a collection of voters. A *winning coalition* of voters is one that has enough votes to win; a *losing coalition* of voters is one that doesn't. In Example 1, Cal plus Tex would be a winning coalition. Cal alone would also be a winning coalition. In Example 2, Penn alone would be a losing coalition, but Penn plus Mitch would be a winning coalition. In the current Electoral College system, any combination of states adding up to 270 electoral votes can be considered a winning coalition of states.

A *pivotal voter* is the voter that changes a losing coalition to a winning one. If voters are acting in sequence, we can identify the pivotal voter easily; however, in scenarios where all votes are cast at the same time, we usually infer an order based on how strongly each voter is attached to the winning position. For states in the Electoral College, it's natural to infer an order based on the margins; states are ordered from largest margin to smallest margin. For example, in the 2000 presidential election, Florida is usually identified as pivotal, because it was decided by a margin of

---

[3] Two of the most common are the Banzhaf or Penrose and Shapley-Shubik power indices, which rely on critical and pivotal power. See "Mathematical Properties of the Banzhaf Power Index" (1979) by Pradeep Dubey and Lloyd Shapley for a more technical discussion of both indices, "One Man, 3.312 Votes: A Mathematical Analysis of the Electoral College" (1968) by John Banzhaf for an early look at the Electoral College using the Banzhaf index, and "Values of Large Games. 6: Evaluating the Electoral College Exactly" (1962) by Lloyd Shapley and Erwin Mann for an early look at the Electoral College using the Shapley-Shubik index. Another index worth noting is the Johnston index from "On the Measurement of Power: Some Reactions to Laver" (1978) by Ronald Johnston, which is based on critical power and more closely related to the retroactive measure of critical power used in this chapter.

less than 0.01% and its 25 electoral votes were enough to take Bush's total from a losing coalition of 245 electors to a winning coalition of 270 electors. Pivotal states are commonly referred to as *tipping point states* - "pivot" and "tipping point" mean the same thing.

It's easy to identify a tipping point state after the fact, but difficult to do so ahead of time - we don't actually know which states will have smaller or larger margins until the election happens. The likely pivotal states are what we refer to as *battleground states* in pre-election coverage because candidates tend to concentrate their efforts in states that are likely to be decisive. When talking about elections that have already happened, battleground states are usually identified as those that had a margin close to the margin in the pivotal state.

A *critical voter* is a voter who could change a winning coalition into a losing coalition by changing their vote. For example, in the 2004 presidential election, Bush earned 286 electoral votes by winning a collection of states including Texas (with 34 electoral votes), Ohio (with 20 electoral votes), and Florida (with 27 electoral votes). Texas, Ohio, and Florida were all critical states in the 2004 election.

It's worth noting that the pivotal voter is unique in any given election. We can, in principle, identify a pivotal state in every presidential election.[4] Critical voters are not unique, and in some cases might not even exist. In most presidential elections, in fact, the margin was large enough that there were no critical states, but in close elections, there are multiple critical states. In 2000, all 30 states won by Bush were critical to his winning coalition; in 2008, Obama's margin of victory was large enough that not even California was critical to his victory.

A voter is clearly *decisive* if the voter was both pivotal and critical. In some elections, we have clearly decisive states, such as Florida in 2000 or Ohio in 2004. Few people have claimed that Texan voters were responsible for the election of George W. Bush in 2000 and his re-election in 2004, even though Texas was a critical state in both elections. Similarly, while Colorado was seen as an important battleground state leading into the 2008 election and can be identified as a pivotal state after the fact, very few people would claim that Coloradans were responsible for electing Barack Obama to the presidency. After all, while the state was pivotal, its 9 electoral votes were not critical in Obama's 365-173 victory.

How likely a voter is to be critical and how likely a voter is to be pivotal are closely related. In Example 1, Cal is both critical and pivotal in every

---

[4] In some cases, which state was pivotal is up for debate. In 1876, for example, there were disputes over the vote totals in three different states, and the true margins are a matter of historical uncertainty. In 1824, with four different candidates and a significant number of electors appointed by state legislature, the task of identifying a pivotal state is difficult.

winning coalition, with the other three voters never being pivotal or critical. In Example 2, Indy is never critical and never pivotal, while the other three voters are pivotal or critical in an equal number of different circumstances. Every method of measuring power agrees in cases like those two examples - and every method of measuring power will agree on which voters are more or less powerful. The question of *how* much more or less power, however, is where the differences emerge.

In Example 3, Massy is pivotal in twelve out of twenty-four different situations, while the other three voters are pivotal four times each. There are seven different winning coalitions, with Massy critical to seven of them; each other voter is critical in two winning coalitions. Depending on the choice of power index used to calculate power, Massy can easily be seen as having anywhere from 50% to 64% of the power – definitely more than Massy's 42% share of the vote, but how much more is unclear.

Got it? Good.

The first thing to note is that larger blocs of votes are typically disproportionately more powerful. Having ten votes is usually *more than* ten times as powerful as having one vote. The size of this distortion depends on how votes will be distributed over time and whether we look at critical status, pivotal status, or both.

Historical distribution of power in the Electoral College

In addition to the very real complexities of trying to measure power within a weighted voting system, there are two important factors to consider when studying power within the Electoral College. The first is that the Electoral College is a body of individual voters who may vote differently although they are customarily pressured to vote as a bloc. This is an important caveat because in some cases, those individual voters might vote in unexpected ways - remember Samuel Miles in 1796? The second important factor is that we have the historical record of past election results to consider.

The evolved Electoral College system has been in place for forty-nine elections, from 1828 to 2020. The first ten elections, from 1788 to 1824, were conducted under significantly different rules. Note that due to its consistently large size over time, New York's delegates have cast the largest number of electoral votes; on average, New York has controlled 9% of the electoral votes in any given election from 1828 to 2020.

We can identify a pivotal state in all of these elections. Half of the time,

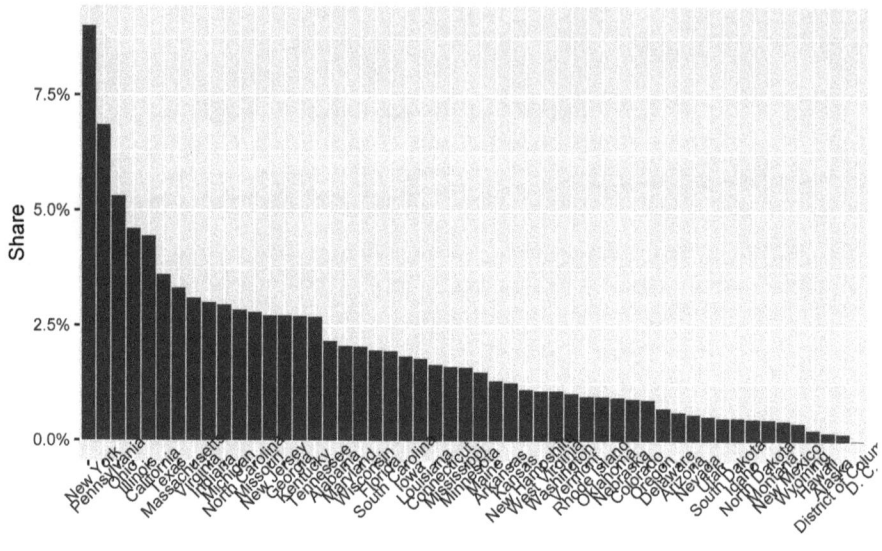

Figure 74: Average share of electoral votes by state in elections 1828-2020.

the pivotal state has been New York, Ohio, Illinois, or Pennsylvania. Not coincidentally, these are the four states with the largest cumulative share of electoral votes. No other states have been pivotal more than twice in that time, and many states have never been pivotal. States in the South and New England have rarely been pivotal.

Out of those forty-nine elections, seventeen have been close enough to have at least one critical state. Dividing the critical power between all critical states, it's clear that critical power has been even more narrowly concentrated than pivotal power. New York alone accounts for nearly half of all critical power exercised by the various states, with Pennsylvania, Texas, and California making up a majority of the remainder. While forty-three states have been critical at least once, most of those have only been critical once or twice, in 1876 or 2000; and in those cases, they shared that critical status with many other states. So, for example, Wyoming was one of thirty critical states in 2000, meaning that Wyoming had about 0.03 elections' worth of critical power out of those seventeen close elections.

In eleven of those elections, including the disputed election of 1876, one of the critical states has been pivotal, giving us the ability to clearly identify a unique key state in ten elections. Eleven times, a state has been both pivotal and critical. Five out of eleven times, the critical and pivotal state was New York. It has been Pennsylvania twice, California once, and

A PRIMER ON POWER IN THE ELECTORAL COLLEGE

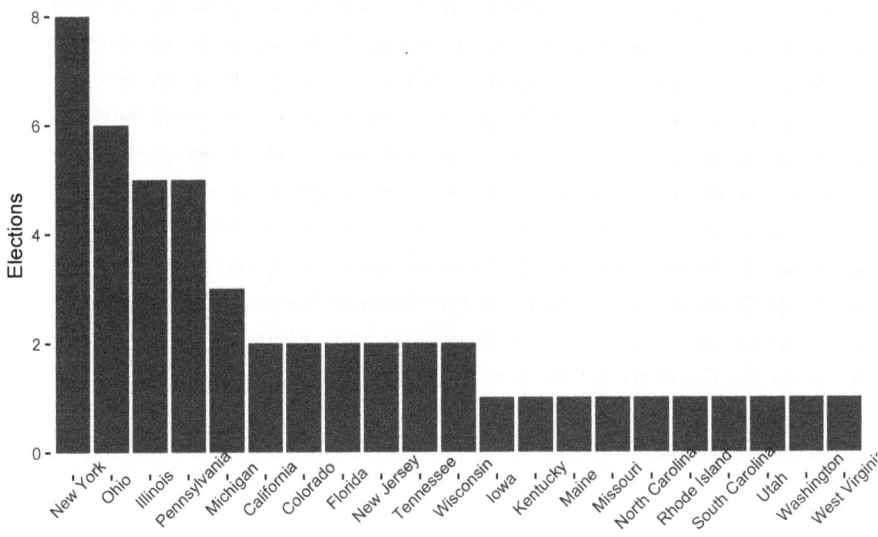

Figure 75: Pivotal status by state in elections 1828-2020.

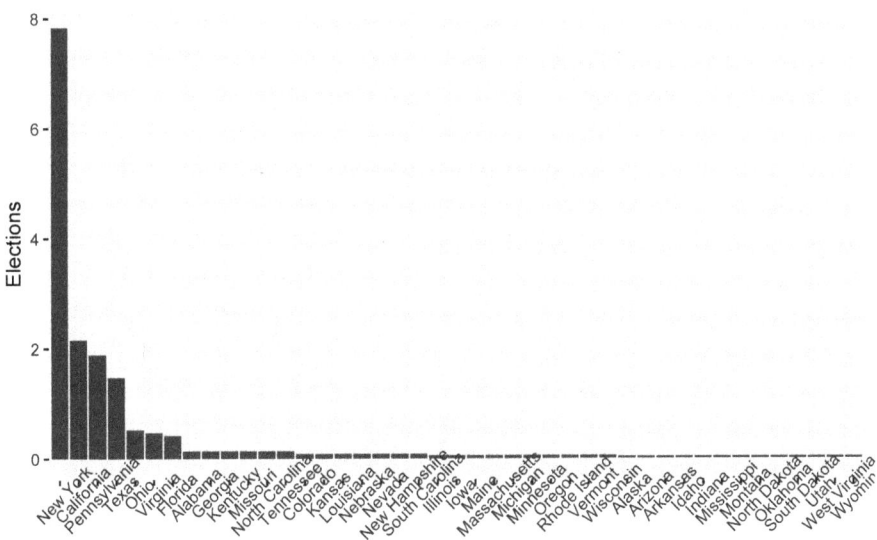

Figure 76: Critical power by state in elections 1828-2020.

Ohio once; eight out of eleven times, the single key state of the election had at least twenty electoral votes. The only time a state with fewer than ten electoral votes was clearly decisive was in 1876, when either South Carolina, Florida, or Louisiana could be identified as pivotal.[5]

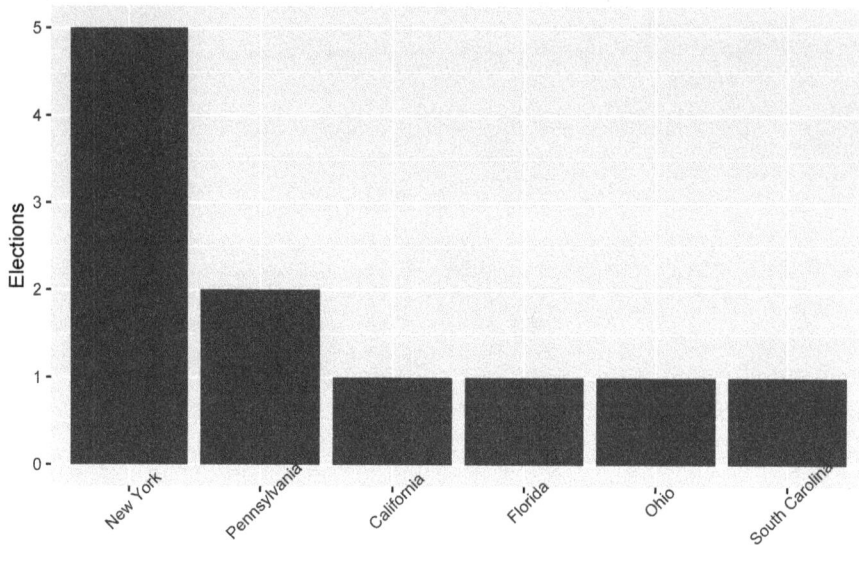

Figure 77: Joint pivotal and critical status by state in elections 1828-2020.

Whether we measure by share of critical power or share of pivotal power, small states have had less power than expected based on their share of electoral votes. For example, small states with six or fewer votes have had about 15% of the votes in the Electoral College, but only 4-6% of the power. The very largest states, with twenty or more electoral votes, only control about a third of the votes in the Electoral College - but have been pivotal twenty-eight times (57% of the time) from 1828-2020. They've had about 84% of the total critical power in the seventeen closest elections.

Overall, pivotal power is the easiest to measure; arguably, it also best reflects the distribution of political leverage. Presidential campaigns target potential tipping point states. However, while the distribution of pivotal power by state size comes closest to the distribution of electoral votes, it is strongly skewed toward larger states. The typical state has 8 electoral votes; states with 8 or fewer electoral votes have been pivotal in only five of the last forty-nine elections (just over 10%), in spite of

---

[5]For quantitative calculations, we have gone with South Carolina on the basis of official returns, but as you may recall from Chapter 7, the returns of the 1876 election were contested in all three states, making it difficult to identify a singular pivotal state.

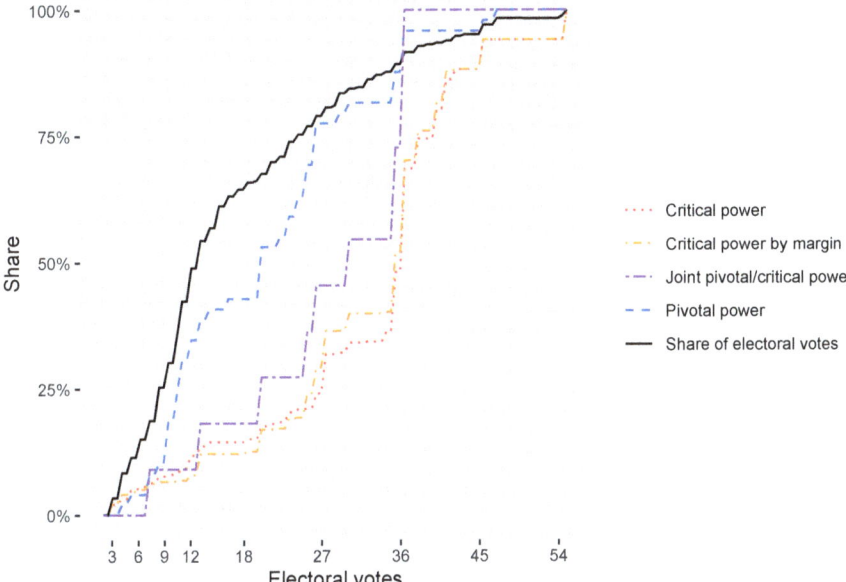

Figure 78: Cumulative distribution of electoral votes and power in the Electoral College by number of electoral votes.

averaging a quarter of the votes in the Electoral College.

States with twenty or more electors are rare - and only hold about a third of electoral votes in a typical election. However, they've been pivotal in twenty-eight out of the last forty-nine elections - about 57% of the time, in other words. Battleground states are large. They're also not distributed evenly across the country.

There are twenty-nine states that have never been pivotal. This isn't simply a matter of some states being new - this includes seven of the original thirteen colonies! In half of all elections from 1828-2020, the pivotal state has been one of only four states: New York, Ohio, Illinois, or Pennsylvania.[6] Colorado is the only state to have been pivotal twice with fewer than ten electoral votes.[7] Although the political geography of the country has varied significantly over time, it's rare to find pivotal states in either New England or the South.

Looking at all three measures at once, it's clear that New York has exercised more power over presidential elections than any other state.

---

[6]In most elections 1796-1824, the pivotal state was likely either Pennsylvania or New York, but it's hard to be certain when different states used different methods for selecting electors.

[7]And that only barely! Colorado had nine electoral votes in 2008 and 2012, qualifying it as a medium-sized state.

Ohio and Pennsylvania have also clearly had a powerful influence over presidential elections, and a clear majority of states have exercised almost no power. There are clear patterns of size. Overall, larger states are disproportionately likely to be near the center of the political geography of the United States. They've exercised more critical power and more pivotal power. Overall, smaller states, with their more homogeneous populations, tend to be disproportionately safe states.

Power in systems other than the Electoral College

For the Framers, the major alternative to the Electoral College system was election by Congress. Since members of Congress would vote individually and small states have a disproportionately large share of senators, election by Congress would favor small states over large states. If the House contingent election process was actually used as often as George Mason expected,[8] that process would favor small states even more strongly.

In a national popular vote, states' power is exactly proportionate to the number of voters residing in the state. Since power in the Electoral College is strongly concentrated in larger states, this means that small and medium-sized states have more power in a national popular vote.

It's possible to adapt the concept of *critical* power to ask when the national popular margin is close enough to be decided by a single state; this has been one of the recent talking points used in rhetoric used to defend the Electoral College system. From 1828-2020, there have been seven elections - 1836, 1880, 1884, 1888, 1960, 2000, and 2016 - when the national popular margin was smaller than the popular margin in at least one state.

In another four elections, the margin in at least one state was over half the national margin - meaning that if the margin had been reversed in that state, the other candidate would have won the popular vote. This includes 1848, 1968, 2004, and 2012.

Of those eleven elections where the national popular vote margin was no more than twice the margin in individual states, only one - 2012 - was secure in the Electoral College. If Barack Obama had lost California to Mitt Romney by a margin of 60% to 37% instead of vice versa, he would have won in the Electoral College while narrowly losing the popular vote.

However, in six other elections (1844, 1856, 1860, 1876, 1916, and 1976) there was a critical state in the Electoral College without any one

---

[8] I.e., 95% of the time.

A PRIMER ON POWER IN THE ELECTORAL COLLEGE 199

state having a popular margin equal to half or more of the national margin. This underlines what we would expect from probability: The result in a single state is *fundamentally more likely to be decisive in the Electoral College than in a popular vote.* From 1828 to 2020, the effective popular margin in the Electoral College has been closer than the national popular margin only once. This happened in the election of 1880; both the national popular margin and the effective popular margin in the Electoral College were quite small in 1880.

The difference between small and large states' power

Different researchers have come to different conclusions about the power of larger and smaller states in the Electoral College system based on the current distribution of electoral votes and statistical theories about how results are likely to be distributed. It is difficult to model the distribution of voting patterns *a priori*, or to anticipate future shifts in political geography. The only real constant of the Electoral College system is that there will be unequal treatment of voters based on political geography. Mathematical analysis of the historical record tells us that the balance of power has favored large states over small states.

Not all large states are equally favored, and geography shifts over time; but ultimately, once we try to measure power carefully, it quickly becomes clear that there are only a handful of states, most of them large, that have held disproportionate electoral power.

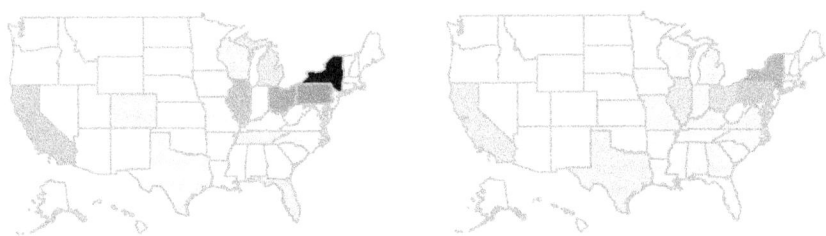

Figure 79: Comparison of share of electoral votes and electoral power by state, 1828-2020. Critical and pivotal power is combined.

The fact that small states have more electors per voter is interesting, but these minor variations are most important in comparing the relative power *between different small states*.[9] The fact of the matter is that two

---

[9]For example, in 2020, Montanans cast over 200,000 votes per presidential elector,

bonus electors per state don't make much of a difference when small states aren't aligned together as a single voting bloc. If we subtract the bonus electors' votes from every presidential election from 1788 to 2020, it only makes a difference in at most four cases: 1796, 1876, 1916, and 2000.[10] The "senator" electors, as a diffuse group of up to 102 electors, have been critical about as often as Hampshire's small bloc of 4 to 8 electors.[11]

Three of those four elections also featured important and potentially decisive irregularities - fraud, error, litigation, and intrigue among electors. We can meaningfully say that those three elections were within the *margin of error* of the Electoral College system, featuring elections that could have been decided differently on the basis of a single key decision made by a few people after electors had been chosen.[12] These were not the only elections within the margin of error of the system - we can also add 1800 and 1824 as elections that were decided narrowly in the House. The presidential election system is full of quirks.

---

while Rhode Islanders cast about 130,000 votes per presidential elector.

[10] The uncertain election under this hypothetical subtraction is the 1796 election, due to the fact that four states' electoral slates were divided.

[11] New Hampshire was a critical state in the 1796, 1876, and 2000 elections.

[12] Note first that a few electors could have made these decisions, but also note the 5-4 decision of *Bush v. Gore* resolving the 2000 election, the 8-7 decisions of the Electoral Commission resolving the 1876 election, and the rumored Alexander Hamilton plot that backfired in 1796.

CHAPTER 12

Problems and solutions

We've explored the various properties of the Electoral College system. It has many flaws. There have also been numerous attempts to solve those flaws - literally hundreds of serious proposals. It was successfully altered in 1804 with the 12th Amendment. In 1968, the proposed Bayh-Celler Amendment was stopped narrowly by a filibuster by segregationists in the Senate. Due to space constraints, it is not possible to cover every reform proposal in detail; however, this chapter will categorize the possibilities for reform.

Because the Electoral College system is deeply flawed, almost every serious proposal to reform the Electoral College would improve it, with a small number of arguable exceptions such as a district-based version of the system.[1] Reforms can be divided up into two general categories: Reforms that adjust the existing system, and reforms that abolish the system in favor of a different form of election entirely.

---

[1] Conversely, almost any serious effort to reconsider the structure of American democracy includes reform or abolition of the Electoral College as part of a package of proposals. For an example, see "Electoral Structure Matters: Fixing the Creaks and Cracks in the Constitution by Its Quarter Millennium" (2020) by Rick LaRue.

The quirks of the Electoral College system

At the beginning of the book, we covered how the Electoral College was very much like a more chaotic version of a plurality vote - one type of direct popular vote, in other words. The Electoral College shares most of the quirks that a plurality vote has, along with some additional quirks that are peculiar to the Electoral College system.

The bonus "senator" electors

One of the frequent criticisms of the Electoral College is that all states receive two extra electors based on their Senate representation, meaning that out of 538 electors, 102 of them are allocated in a highly undemocratic fashion rather than based on population. This is a feature of the Electoral College system inherited from the Connecticut Compromise, and it can rightly be seen as a feature of the Electoral College that assists small states.

Although it is one of the most obvious flaws of the Electoral College system, the bonus "senator" electors have only been critical in at most four close elections: 1796, 1876, 1916, and 2000. With the exception of 1916, these elections were also close enough to be decided by a reversal of the margin of victory in any of the states in the winning coalition. On the balance, the Electoral College itself favors large states, as anticipated by the Framers. Given that fact, the "senator" electors are the single least troublesome quirk of the Electoral College as it currently exists.

Unreliable electors

There is a fundamental disconnect between how most voters think of the Electoral College (in terms of states being worth points) and the actual mechanisms of the Electoral College (involving specific voters who have free will, and may - as in the case of Samuel Miles in 1796 - vote in unexpected ways). For those who, like Alexander Hamilton, are fans of indirect elections, the fact that electors are chosen almost anonymously and pressured to vote a certain way by the party is an atrocious infringement on the ability to have a good indirect election.

For those who think that the unit rule works adequately, the fact that human electors are potentially unreliable is an atrocious vulnerability that has only recently been shored up by the *Chiafalo v. Washington* case. As matters currently stand, neither principle is fully satisfied. Until all states have passed strong "faithless elector" laws, the Electoral

PROBLEMS AND SOLUTIONS

College is not a reliable way to translate a set of multiple states' popular votes into electoral votes. Conversely, the presence of pledges and the enforcement of them by "faithless elector" laws prevent it from being a wise and deliberative process.

Contested outcomes

In the case of a close or contested outcome, disputes in the Electoral College system are not generally resolved by either recounting the ballots or by holding a second round of voting in states where the results are contested. The Framers intended for close election results to be resolved by the House contingent election process; this has generally failed to happen. Most experts, including those who favor the Electoral College system, believe that the House contingent election process is best avoided as much as possible.

The House contingent election process has been used twice (1800 and 1824) to contentious effect. There have been at least four elections (1876, 1960, 2000, and 2004) in which there were serious challenges to the legitimacy of the Electoral College outcome. In one of those cases (2000), an unofficial recount found that the wrong slate of electors had been appointed in a critical state via counting errors. In all four cases, various forms of electoral malpractice render the legitimate outcome unclear.

It is worth noting that in all four cases, the national popular margin was less contestable, and less likely to have been reversed in a national recount or revote than a complete recount or revote carried out to resolve the uncertainty over the legitimacy of the Electoral College results – and that out of the last forty-nine presidential elections, only the election of 1880 had a national popular margin smaller than the effective popular margin in the Electoral College. Because the winner-take-all rules artificially inflate the margin of a state to a 100%-0% margin, small irregularities in one or two battleground states can often cast doubt on the legitimacy of the entire national election.

The margin in a single state exceeds the margin of victory

In some cases, the margin of victory in a single large state can exceed the total margin of victory in the entire country. This is a quirk that the Electoral College shares with a simple popular vote; for example, in 2016, the popular margin in California exceeded the overall national popular margin, but the electoral vote margin in Texas exceeded the overall electoral vote margin. In these cases, the state was critical, in the very precise way that I've talked about states being critical throughout this whole book, and it could be argued that the state was decisive.

To some degree, this is a natural consequence of the fact that some elections are very close nationally; no matter what method of election is used, if an election is nearly tied nationally, it is natural that some large states on either side of the election would have a larger margin than the entire country. However, this is much more likely to happen under the Electoral College than in a popular vote.

From 1796 to 2020, there have been twenty-one cases where flipping the result in a single state would reverse the result of the Electoral College. It is difficult to talk meaningfully about a national popular margin until after 1824, as state legislatures were commonly used to select electors through the 1824 election. As a point of comparison, there have been only five cases after 1824 in which the national popular margin was smaller than the margin of victory by the popular winner in a single state. The modern Electoral College system is much more likely to be decided by a single state than a national popular vote of any kind.

The reason for this is that the unit rule increases the margin within each state to the maximum possible 100%-0% landslide. In every election except for the election of 1880, the national results are effectively closer within the Electoral College than in terms of a national popular vote. Even the election of 1880, with a virtually tied national popular vote, was nevertheless also close in the Electoral College system; a reversal of New York's electoral slate would have reversed the national election result.

Spoiler effects and third-party candidates

As we have seen, the relationship between support in the Electoral College and popular support becomes more complex when there are three or more candidates, including cases like 1844, where the third party candidate is a quixotic protest candidate who does not anticipate receiving many votes. The Electoral College is just as vulnerable to spoiler effects as a single-round plurality election - which is to say, worse than most other voting systems.

This is particularly disappointing when we consider the design intentions of the Framers. The Framers intended that only a rare clear electoral majority would be decisive in the Electoral College, with all other results being resolved by a deliberate and deliberative House contingent election process. The system was designed to be mainly a two-round process, and two-round processes are usually less vulnerable to spoiler effects.

PROBLEMS AND SOLUTIONS

Interestingly, the elections that may have been decided by a spoiler effect include some elections in which there were very large electoral margins, such as the elections of 1912 and 1980. Unfortunately, the ways in which the Electoral College sometimes *resists* a spoiler effect, such as in 1856 and 1860, might give even worse outcomes. The fact that an extremely polarized electorate can lead to a minority victory by more polarizing candidates over potential compromise candidates is troublesome.

Regional candidates and civil war

Internationally and historically, presidential systems tend to fail in two ways. First, a president becomes a dictator. Second, a controversial election result leads to a civil war. The United States experienced the latter in 1860, an election that was very strongly affected in numerous ways by the quirks of the Electoral College system.

More subtly, the quirks of the Electoral College also played a key role in the election of President Polk, leading to the annexation of large portions of Mexico and the subsequent dispute over the expansion of slavery westward; and also in the election of President Buchanan, whose administration helped set the stage for the Civil War in numerous ways both large and small.

It is entirely possible that there would have been a civil war in the United States over the issue of slavery regardless of the electoral system; however, it is also clear that the immediate and proximate trigger for secession was the Electoral College. Contrary to what Calhoun might have hoped - or the similar rhetoric we see from modern defenders of the Electoral College - Lincoln did not need to win concurrent majorities in both the slave states and free states to win the election of 1860.[2] Since the theory of concurrent majorities is poorly justified in the first place, and the Electoral College doesn't follow its principles anyway, defending the Electoral College using the logic of concurrent majorities is doubly wrong.

Lincoln's victory with less than 40% of the vote - secured by narrow majorities and undermined by deep losses - is alarming, not because it violates the logic of concurrent majorities, but because he could have won it against an opponent who enjoyed the broad support of 60% of the voting public. The fact that Stephen Douglas placed fourth in the Electoral College as the candidate with the second-largest number

---

[2]Calhoun describes his concept of concurrent majorities in *A Disquisition on Government* (1851). He does not mention presidential elections, but it's worth noting that candidates from the South had been doing quite well in presidential elections up to the time of Calhoun's death.

of votes and the broadest national appeal is even more alarming. If Lincoln had to face a contingent election in the House, his most qualified opponent would have been absent.

This is because, as we've seen, the winner-take-all system of the Electoral College provides a large advantage to regional candidates. Unproven theorizing that the Electoral College helps maintain a two-party system must be measured against the reality that regionally polarizing candidates can do very well in the Electoral College, even as the national standard-bearer for one of the two major parties struggles. Mathematically, fifty single-state candidates can handily defeat a pair of national candidates. Minor party candidates - such as Strom Thurmond in 1948 - can perform disproportionately well with a narrow regional base of support.

Minor reforms

Minor reforms retain something called an Electoral College, but one that operates by slightly different rules. All minor reforms of the Electoral College have two features in common: First, minor reforms are impacted by the allocation problem, just like the original Electoral College. As the decennial census figures become outdated, states with a declining share of the population have an advantage; states with an increasing share of the population are penalized. Second, voters in different states are always treated unequally.

An automatic electoral college

In *The Case Against Direct Election of the President: A Defense of the Electoral College* (1975), Judith Best, one of the most notable defenders of the Electoral College system, noted that there is a reform she would not mind: Amending the Constitution to awarding electoral votes automatically, forcing all states to use the unit rule - essentially, a regularization of the current system. While she noted that no faithless elector has altered the result of any recent presidential election,[3] Judith Best said that it would be preferable that states simply assigned electoral votes automatically to avoid subversion of the will of the people.

Many of the proposed reforms of the Electoral College have *started* by making electoral votes automatic; this is both a method of reform as well as a feature of many other reforms. An automatic Electoral

---

[3] The only arguable exception is the election of 1796.

College using the unit rule has almost all of the same problems that the Electoral College currently has, with the exception that there is no uncertainty surrounding electors acting freely. The Supreme Court decision in *Chiafalo v. Washington* (2020) affirms that states can effect this type of reform at the state level without any need for a constitutional amendment; it is likely that most states will eventually do so as a matter of course.

Proportional systems

The way to reduce the chaos of the Electoral College without changing its structure is to allocate electors proportionately to the votes earned by the ticket statewide. If combined with making electoral votes an exercise in truly automatic accounting, rather than having actual human electors, we can even allocate fractional electoral votes, which eliminates the chaotic effects completely. Eliminating the chaos caused by linking large blocs of votes to narrow margins in key battleground states also eliminates the extra power held by large states; under a proportional system that retained the bonus "senator" electors, small state voters really would have more power than large state voters.

Even with whole electoral votes, however, the level of potential chaos in a proportional allocation system is very small - essentially, cumulative rounding errors.[4] This does not rule out situations like the election of 1876, where every single elector is critical with disputes over results in multiple states; but it would limit the scope for potential disputes over vote totals to the margin of a single elector per state.

A notable concern in a proportional system is what minimum threshold a candidate must reach in order to earn *any* electors; for example, should a candidate who earns 2% of the vote in California earn a Californian elector? Internationally, legislatures with proportional representation typically have a threshold of around 5%. The Democratic presidential primary currently uses a standard of 15% for a minimum viability threshold. With a low threshold, minor parties can win presidential electors, and House contingent elections are more likely; with a higher threshold, however, distortions from the popular vote are larger.

District-based systems

The main method of choosing electors that Wilson, Morris, and Madison had in mind when they advanced it at the Constitutional Convention was

---

[4]Statistically, the average cumulative rounding error would be about 2 electoral votes, which is rarely decisive.

that each elector would represent a district within a state. Two states currently use a district-based system that - rather than having simply one elector per district - allocates two electors to the state at large and then one per Congressional district. Winner-take-all by district is less chaotic than winner-take-all by state because the stakes in each district are smaller; however, this reduces, rather than eliminates, the chaos.

The high-stakes battleground states are replaced by battleground districts, which in the modern environment can be targeted with surgical precision for rallies, get-out-the-vote efforts, et cetera. As with a proportional system, in a district-based system - *especially* one like the current systems in Maine and Nebraska, which keep two at-large electors - small states gain an advantage over large states. Bloc effects both generate chaos and empower large states; if we remove the bloc effects that benefit large states while retaining one three-vote 'bloc' for the smallest states, small states have a clear advantage due to the electors corresponding to senators.

There is one major new flaw introduced by a district-based system: Gerrymandering. State boundaries are fixed; district boundaries would need to be redrawn after every decennial census, and whichever party drew the lines could claim an advantage. Additionally, the allocation problem is compounded by the fact that due to population growth, age distribution, and citizenship, not all districts have the same number of voters. For example, in 2018, fewer than 114,000 voters cast ballots in a tightly-contested House race in California's 21st district; meanwhile, the House race in Colorado's 2nd district, including rapidly-growing Boulder, had over 430,000 votes cast.

Overall, from the perspective of fixing the flaws of the existing system, a district-based system is inferior to a proportional system; it does a worse job of mitigating the existing flaws, and *also* introduces a significant vulnerability to gerrymandering.

Changes to the contingent election system

The least democratic element within the Electoral College system is what happens when the Electoral College itself fails to select a victor. This is the House contingent election process, in which each state's delegation gets one vote. As seen in the 36 ballot deadlock of 1800, it is not difficult for individual states' delegations to tie, or the whole House. It's also quite possible, as in 1824, to secure a victory with the support of a minority of members of the House.

It is this element of the system that segregationists attempted to use in 1948, 1960, and 1968. Perhaps the clearest testimony to the flaws in the contingent election system, however, is that in the elections where it was clear that neither candidate had a certain claim to a legitimate majority in the Electoral College, both parties cooperated to avoid a House contingent election. The House contingent election process was designed to resolve cases where neither candidate could command a clear majority.

The most obvious way to reform the House contingent election process without totally replacing it involve removing the "one state, one vote" rule and changing it to a joint session of Congress - a type of election that more closely mirrors the structure of the Electoral Colleges and is less likely to deadlock. A more significant method of reforming it is to replace it with a runoff election.

Those who defend the Electoral College commonly attack runoff elections as expensive and troublesome, but they have been widely used both in the United States and internationally as an effective stopgap against unsuitable candidates. Runoffs serve the sort of role that the Electoral College is wrongly alleged to serve, preventing the election of radical demagogues who have the fervent support of a minority of voters.[5]

There are few outcomes more expensive than electing an unqualified president; the cost associated with running an entire second national election is trivial compared to war, famine, pestilence, or a banking crisis. A fairly minor mistake on the scale of presidential decisions can easily match the cost and inconvenience of an extra national election.

Major reforms

Minor reforms concentrate on the chaotic nature of the Electoral College by smoothing its operation. Major reforms concentrate on its potential for disproportionality. In theory, while the Electoral College generally tracks closely with popular support, major exceptions can occur when the party system fragments and a divisive figure wins an Electoral College majority with the support of a minority of the population. Most major reforms either involve directly replacing the Electoral College with a popular vote or cause the Electoral College to closely approximate a popular vote.

Reforms that call for the President to be selected by Congress are uncommon, possibly because Congress is usually unpopular.

---

[5]Radical demagogues with the fervent support of the majority of voters can take power in *any* democratic system; only a flawed electoral system allows a radical demagogue to take power with the support of a fervent minority.

Pragmatically, such a system would likely be viable once implemented.[6] Given the magnitude of the differences between the original vision and the historical record, and particularly the infrequency of House contingent elections, it seems unlikely that the Framers would have approved of the Electoral College over election by Congress if they had better foresight.

I will briefly discuss three notable recent reform proposals. Each one of these reforms would represent a major improvement from the existing Electoral College system; none is perfect. As I've noted before, there have been literally *hundreds* of proposals to reform the Electoral College.[7]

The Bayh-Celler amendment: Plurality vote with runoff

Following the third attempt by segregationists to force a House contingent election in 1968, the Electoral College was deeply unpopular and the time was ripe for reform. As mentioned earlier, this proposed amendment passed the House, but stalled in the Senate, falling short of the 2/3 supermajority needed to put a constitutional amendment to the states.

This amendment would have replaced the Electoral College with a national plurality vote. If no candidate earned more than 40% of the vote, a runoff election would determine the actual winner. This threshold is close to the smallest share of the vote earned by candidates who won a majority in the Electoral College,[8] making runoffs rare.

The purpose of making runoffs rare was to ensure partisan support for the bill; both Democrats and Republicans have reason to be concerned about any major structural change that might upset a two-party system, and simple "first past the post" systems are thought to encourage two-party systems.[9] A plurality vote with a majority runoff - that is, requiring the

---

[6] Quite a few versions of such systems exist elsewhere in the world.

[7] Again, for the most recent accounting of these, see *Why Do We Still Have the Electoral College?* (2020) by Alexander Keyssar.

[8] Namely, Abraham Lincoln at just under 40% in 1860, and Woodrow Wilson at just over 40% in 1912.

[9] The theoretical link between a two-party system is known as Duverger's Law; it is generally supported by a very simple game-theoretic argument involving "wasted" votes. A similar game-theoretic argument suggests that voters should ignore all but the top three candidates if there is to be a runoff between the top two. These types of argument tend to fall apart if the space of political issues is more complex or if voters have trouble evaluating which candidates are likely front-runners. See "Rethinking Duverger's Law: Predicting the Effective Number of Parties in Plurality and PR Systems–Parties Minus Issues Equals One" (1985) by Rein Taagepera for a sketch of what is expected to happen when politics is fundamentally multidimensional.

winner to have a majority of the vote in order to avoid a runoff election - is the current international gold standard for a simple direct election.

Personally, I doubt that *any* change in the mechanisms for electing presidents will, in and of itself, break the two-party system. Governors, senators, representatives, local officials, et cetera are all also elected, and most presidents come up through the ranks from lower-level elected positions. The existing political parties are institutions with significant resources, popularity, and expertise, and there is still only one president.[10]

The fact that the Electoral College system itself is not a simple plurality vote is also relevant. Candidates like George Wallace are irrelevant in a national popular vote; however, within the Electoral College system, they had a shot at influencing the outcome. The Bayh-Celler amendment was proposed in response to fragmentation *encouraged* by the Electoral College. Southern Democrats had remained politically distinct from northern Democrats for more than a century, running separate presidential candidates four times from 1860 to 1968.

The National Bonus Plan: Nearly a plurality vote

The National Bonus Plan is interesting in that it retains the formal structure of the Electoral College while more closely approximating a national popular vote. It was recommended by a task force formed to address reform of the presidential election system in the wake of the narrow 1976 election,[11] and is highly recommended by experts. The bonus plan consists of three separate revisions to the Electoral College system.

First, it makes the awarding of electoral votes automatic, which is by itself a minor reform. Second, it adds a pool of national bonus votes to match the states' bonus electors (i.e., the extra two "senator" electors per state not tied to population). These extra 102 electoral votes are awarded to the candidate with the most votes nationally. Third, if no candidate has a majority of the electoral votes, a runoff election between the top two candidates follows under the same rules.

As with the Bayh-Celler amendment or the actual Electoral College system, the threshold for a runoff is not very high. Abraham Lincoln would have triggered the Bayh-Celler runoff threshold in 1860; under the bonus plan, he would have had a secure majority of electoral votes.

---

[10]The natural corollary of Duverger's Law is that proportional representation goes hand-in-hand with multi-party systems.

[11]See *Winner Take All: Report of the Twentieth Century Fund Task Force on Reform of the Presidential Election Process* (1978) by William Keech.

The bonus attached to winning more votes nationally is large enough to swamp the chaotic effects of large states with small margins. While it is still theoretically possible for a candidate to win a majority of electoral votes without having the most votes, it is very difficult.

In other words, barring unprecedented shifts within the American political system, the National Bonus Plan is equivalent to a simple plurality vote.

The National Popular Vote Interstate Compact: A plurality vote without a constitutional amendment

A recent and new innovation in the perpetually active area of Electoral College reform is the National Popular Vote Interstate Compact (NPVIC). Unlike most proposed major reforms, the NPVIC does not require a constitutional amendment.[12] In fact, it does not even require the support of a majority of states. There are some potential complications, in that there are a lot of untested questions about interstate compacts[13] and because electors may not vote as instructed. The NPVIC makes full use of the latitude given to states in how they assign their electoral votes.

It's worth underlining just how broad that latitude is. If the state legislature of South Carolina decided that their presidential electors would solely consist of descendants of Charles Pinckney, selected by seniority according to the traditional feudal principles of primogeniture, *that would be allowed under the Constitution.* States do not have to hold presidential elections at all.[14] This is a large potential vulnerability in the Electoral College system, and closing this loophole would require a constitutional amendment.

The idea behind the NPVIC is very simple. Once enough states agree, all participating states will choose electors based on the results of the national popular vote, rather than the vote within their own borders. The compact is triggered by having enough states to make up a majority of the Electoral College, meaning that a majority outcome is guaranteed by the compact.

Interestingly and ironically, fear of coordination between different states on how to assign their electors is one of the reasons why each state's Electoral College meets separately. That said, the expectation that electors in different states would act largely independently was first violated in 1788 when Hamilton tried to make sure that not too

---

[12] Conversely, dissolving it would also not require a constitutional amendment.

[13] See "Every Vote Equal" (2013) for the case in favor of the NPVIC.

[14] If they do hold elections, then an assortment of laws apply about how they can hold elections.

many of them voted for John Adams. It turned out that coordinating electors in different states was not difficult, and both Federalists and Democratic-Republicans mastered this art by 1800 or so.

Recommendations

Using a mathematical perspective to view the many alternatives to plurality voting, runoff elections, ranked choice voting, and all variants of the Electoral College system, *almost any of the reforms proposed over the last couple of centuries would improve the Electoral College system.* The major exception is the district-based system, which is vulnerable to gerrymandering.

The fact is that we don't actually know what is the *best* way to elect a president. Some methods are theoretically promising but little tested empirically. We don't honestly know how American voters will behave either in the short term or the long term when faced with an entirely different voting system.[15] What we need is the ability to figure out what methods work well *without* making the system flexible enough that politicians can strategically rewrite the rules for their own upcoming elections.

My recommendation for long-term reform would be a constitutional amendment that covers the following five points:

- First, the president shall be elected by the citizens of the United States at large, by a direct popular vote.
- Second, the laws and amendments currently applicable to elections *for presidential electors* shall apply to *elections for president.*
- Third, Congress shall have the power to change, via legislation, the method by which this direct popular vote is carried out.
- Fourth, no such change enacted by Congress may take effect until five years after its passage.
- Fifth, the next presidential election after the amendment goes into effect shall be carried out as a national plurality vote with a majority runoff.

The first point is a core principle: A mandate that whatever method is used to elect the president should be democratic and proceed directly from the votes of the people. Second, existing protections for voters,

---

[15]Will voters Borda-bury if they use a Borda count? Will they bullet vote an approval ballot? Will they strategically betray their favorite on a ranked choice ballot? There is a great deal of theory and only small chunks of relevant behavioral data.

such as are provided by the 14th Amendment, need to be retained in any new system; this might be implied, but it doesn't hurt to make that explicit. Third, finding the right system will probably - as a general principle of trial and error - require many small changes. Fourth, we don't want Congress changing the rules for a current president or based on what the current majority party thinks will benefit it in the next cycle; a five-year waiting period mitigates that danger. Any adjustments will have to be made with a long view. Fifth, quite simply, we need to start somewhere. A plurality vote with a runoff required in any case that no candidate wins a majority is not complicated either for voters or for election officials. It is almost certainly not the *best* election method, but it is a practical one that works reasonably well.

A few final words

To keep this book short and to the point, I have included only a small selection of the quirky events and stories that show the oddities that fill the Electoral College. There have been cases where electors have died after being chosen or otherwise couldn't make it to the state capital. Replacement electors have in some cases been chosen at the very last minute, selected hastily from whoever is at hand. Concerted efforts to get electors to vote against their pledges have happened both recently and in the distant past,[16] though the Supreme Court has provided an answer to the issue of faithless electors with its decision in *Chiafalo v. Washington* (2020).

The flaws in the Electoral College system have been and remain numerous. The way that the evolved Electoral College operates today has very little to do with how it was intended to work. The strongest reasons for having an Electoral College (states having different rules about who is allowed to vote) lie in the past. Even when voting rights were very unequally distributed in different states, however, the Electoral College system did *not* ease the factional pressures that led to the bloodiest and most damaging war in American history.[17] The only function that any of the designers of the Electoral College had in mind that it serves today is as *a close approximation of a popular vote*, and those particular Framers would have preferred a popular vote in the first place.

The closest that the Electoral College system has come to working as

---

[16]See in particular *Presidential Electors and the Electoral College: An Examination of Lobbying, Wavering Electors, and Campaigns for Faithless Votes* (2012) by Robert Alexander.

[17]If anything, it ended up providing the triggering spark in the 1860 election.

originally expected was in the election of 1824, which was a bizarre and undemocratic event by modern standards. Other than in rare House contingent elections, the presidential election system doesn't protect small states - nor was the Electoral College itself intended to protect the interests of small states. It was neither designed to protect slavery nor did it have the effect of doing so. Any perceived partisan advantage of the Electoral College is at best transient and at worst the result of systematic fraud.[18] In most cases, as with the "blue wall" that political commentators imagined would ensure Hillary Clinton's election in 2016, perceiving a lasting partisan advantage is just imagining a pattern in chaotic noise.

The winner-take-all rule does provide a strong incentive for election fraud in key battleground states, and when the party system fragments, it gives an advantage to sectional candidates over unifying candidates with broad support. Population-based allocations give extra weight to states with large non-voting populations and favor states with declining shares of the population (like New York) over states with rapidly growing populations (like Texas).

There are also difficulties the Electoral College system shares with a simple direct plurality vote, such as vulnerability to spoiler effects. The famous "inverted" elections where the Electoral College has given a different result from the national popular vote simply cannot be justified with a consistent, coherent, and correct rationale. The Electoral College system is simply more chaotic than a direct vote. It is not more deliberative, it does not encourage candidates to appeal broadly to voters in every state, and it doesn't prevent the election of presidents who are either incompetent or unpopular.

The best time to fix the Electoral College and replace it with a better system was at the Constitutional Convention in 1787. The second-best time was in 1788 after the first presidential election had finished. The third-best time to start rolling out a replacement was in 1789 when the Bill of Rights was written up. When this book goes into press, it will be the 236th best year to move forward with abolishing the Electoral College. I hope it will soon be time for us to graduate from the Electoral College.

---

[18] E.g., as in New York City in the election of 1888.

Bibliography

Ackerman, B., and D. Fontana. 2004. "Thomas Jefferson Counts Himself into the Presidency." *Virginia Law Review* 90.

Alexander, Robert M. 2012. *Presidential Electors and the Electoral College: An Examination of Lobbying, Wavering Electors, and Campaigns for Faithless Votes*. Cambria Press.

———. 2019. *Representation and the Electoral College*. Oxford University Press.

Amar, Akhil Reed. 2016. *The Constitution Today: Timeless Lessons for the Issues of Our Era*. Basic Books.

Arrow, Kenneth J. 1950. "A Difficulty in the Concept of Social Welfare." *Journal of Political Economy* 58 (4): 328–46.

Banzhaf III, John F. 1968. "One Man, 3.312 Votes: A Mathematical Analysis of the Electoral College." *Vill. L. Rev.* 13: 304.

Basset, John. 1911. *The Life of Andrew Jackson*. Doubleday, Page & Doran.

Best, Judith. 1975. *The Case Against Direct Election of the President: A Defense of the Electoral College*. Cornell University Press Ithaca, NY.

Best, Judith, and Thomas E Cronin. 1996. *The Choice of the People?: Debating the Electoral College*. Rowman & Littlefield.

Bilder, Mary Sarah. 2015. *Madison's Hand*. Harvard University Press.

Birney, William. 1890. *James G. Birney and His Times: The Genesis of the Republican Party with Some Account of Abolition Movements in the South Before 1828*. D. Appleton & Company.

Boulard, G. 2015. *The Worst President–the Story of James Buchanan*. iUniverse.

Buchanan, James. 1866. *Mr. Buchanan's Administration on the Eve of the Rebellion*. New York.

Bugh, Gary. 2016. *Electoral College Reform: Challenges and Possibilities*. Routledge.

Burin, Eric. 2017. *Picking the President: Understanding the Electoral*

College. The Digital Press at the University of North Dakota.
Calhoun, John Caldwell. 1851. *A Disquisition on Government*. Vol. 1. Press of Walker & James.
Caritat, Marie Jean Antoine Nicolas de. 1785. *Essai Sur l'application de l'analyse à La Probabilité Des décisions Rendues à La Pluralité Des Voix*.
Chernow, Ron. 2004. *Alexander Hamilton*. The Penguin Press.
Congress, US. 1832. "Register of Debates in Congress." Gales & Seaton Washington, DC.
Dippre, Harold C. 1966. "Corruption and the Disputed Election Vote of Oregon in the 1876 Election." *Oregon Historical Quarterly* 67 (3): 257–72.
Dubey, Pradeep, and Lloyd S Shapley. 1979. "Mathematical Properties of the Banzhaf Power Index." *Mathematics of Operations Research* 4 (2): 99–131.
Edwards, George C. 2019. *Why the Electoral College Is Bad for America*. Yale University Press.
Farrand, Max. 1911. *The Records of the Federal Convention of 1787*. Yale University Press.
Finkelman, Paul. 2001. "The Proslavery Origins of the Electoral College." *Cardozo L. Rev.* 23: 1145.
Freeman, Jo. 1999. "Gender Gaps in Presidential Elections." *PS: Political Science & Politics* 32 (2): 191–92.
Government Commission, Continuity of et al. 2009. "Preserving Our Institutions: The Continuity of the Presidency (Second Report)."
Gresham, Matilda. 1919. *Life of Walter Quintin Gresham, 1832-1895*. v. 2. Rand, McNally.
Higginson, Stephen. 1796. "To Alexander Hamilton."
Hildreth, Richard. 1840. *The Contrast, or, William Henry Harrison Versus Martin van Buren*. Weeks, Jordan.
Jenkins, Jeffery A., and Brian R. Sala. 1998. "The Spatial Theory of Voting and the Presidential Election of 1824." *American Journal of Political Science* 42 (4): 1157–79.
Johnston, Ronald John. 1978. "On the Measurement of Power: Some Reactions to Laver." *Environment and Planning A* 10 (8): 907–14.
Kalk, Bruce. 2000. "Review of Truman Defeats Dewey by Gary A. Donaldson." *The South Carolina Historical Magazine* 101 (2): 156–58.
Kallina, Edmund F. 1978. "The State's Attorney and the President: The Inside Story of the 1960 Presidential Election in Illinois." *Journal of American Studies* 12 (2): 147–60.
———. 1985. "Was the 1960 Presidential Election Stolen? The Case of Illinois." *Presidential Studies Quarterly*, 113–18.
Keech, William R. 1978. *Winner Take All: Report of the Twentieth Century Fund Task Force on Reform of the Presidential Election*

Process. Holmes & Meier Pub.

Keyssar, Alexander. 2020. *Why Do We Still Have the Electoral College?* Harvard University Press.

"King Lincoln Bronzeville Neighborhood Association v. Blackwell." 2006.

King, Ronald F. 2001. "A Most Corrupt Election: Louisiana in 1876." *Studies in American Political Development* 15 (2): 123–37.

Kornblith, Gary J. 2003. "Rethinking the Coming of the Civil War: A Counterfactual Exercise." *The Journal of American History* 90 (1): 76–105.

Koza, John R, Barry Fadem, Mark Grueskin, Michael S Mandell, Robert Richie, Joseph F Zimmerman, John B Anderson, Birch Bayh, John Buchanan, and Tom Campbell. 2013. "Every Vote Equal." *A State-Based Plan for Electing the President by National Popular Vote* 3: 1–716.

Kropko, M. R. 2007. "Election Staff Convicted in Recount Rig." *Associated Press*, January.

Kurlansky, M. 2005. *1968: The Year That Rocked the World*. Random House Publishing Group.

Lampi, Philip J. 2007. "A New Nation Votes: American Election Returns 1787-1825." Tufts Digital Collections; Archives.

Larson, E. J. 2015. *The Return of George Washington: Uniting the States, 1783-1789*. HarperCollins.

LaRue, Rick. 2020. "Electoral Structure Matters: Fixing the Creaks and Cracks in the Constitution by Its Quarter Millennium." *Idaho L. Rev.* 56: 193.

Lee, Eugene C, and William Buchanan. 1961. "The 1960 Election in California." *Western Political Quarterly* 14 (1): 309–26.

Leip, Dave. 2017. "David Leip's Atlas of US Presidential Elections, Datasets." *Harvard Dataverse*.

Lonnstrom, Douglas A, and Thomas O Kelly. 2018. "America's Presidents: Greatest and Worst: Siena's 6th Presidential Expert Poll 1982-2018." Siena Research Institute.

Lossing, Benson J., ed. 1873. "Auto-Biographical Sketch of Samuel Miles." *The American Historical Record* 2 (13): 49–53, 114–18.

Mann, Irwin, and Lloyd S Shapley. 1962. "Values of Large Games. 6: Evaluating the Electoral College Exactly." RAND CORP Santa Monica, CA.

McClure, Alexander Kelly. 1905. *Old Time Notes of Pennsylvania: A Connected and Chronological Record of the Commercial, Industrial and Educational Advancement of Pennsylvania, and the Inner History of All Political Movements Since the Adoption of the Constitution of 1838*. Library of American Civilization, v. 2. John C. Winston.

McConnaughy, Corrine M. 2013. *The Woman Suffrage Movement in*

America: A Reassessment. Cambridge University Press.
McCormick, Richard P. 1984. "Was There a "Whig Strategy" in 1836?" *Journal of the Early Republic* 4 (1): 47–70.
Nagle, John Copeland. 2004. "How Not to Count Votes." *COLuM. L. REv*. 104: 1732.
Neale, Thomas H. 2014. "Electoral College Reform: Contemporary Issues for Congress." In. Congressional Research Service, the Library of Congress.
O'Donnell, Lilly. 2016. "Meet the 'Hamilton Electors' Hoping for an Electoral College Revolt." *The Atlantic*, November.
Peirce, Neal R, and Lawrence D Longley. 1968. *The People's President: The Electoral College in American History and the Direct-Vote Alternative*. Simon & Schuster New York.
Peskin, Allan. 1973. "Was There a Compromise of 1877." *The Journal of American History* 60 (1): 63–75.
Phillips, Ulrich B. 1909. "The South Carolina Federalists, II." *The American Historical Review* 14 (4): 731–43.
Rae, Nicol C. 2013. "The Reaffirmation of the Post–Cold War Electoral Order: The Meaning of the 2012 Election." In *The American Elections of 2012*, 227–48. Routledge.
Ratcliffe, Donald. 2013. "The Right to Vote and the Rise of Democracy, 1787—1828." *Journal of the Early Republic* 33 (2): 219–54.
Roberts, Derrell. 1962. "Joseph E. Brown and the Florida Election of 1876." *The Florida Historical Quarterly* 40 (3): 217–25.
Ross, Tara. 2017. "The Indispensable Electoral College." Washington: Regnery Gateway.
Rottinghaus, Brandon, and Justin S Vaughn. 2017. "Presidential Greatness and Political Science: Assessing the 2014 APSA Presidents and Executive Politics Section Presidential Greatness Survey." *PS: Political Science & Politics* 50 (3): 824–30.
Sarkees, Meredith Reid, and Frank Wayman. 2010. *Resort to War: 1816-2007*. Cq Press.
Scudder, H. E. 1901. *James Russell Lowell: A Biography*. James Russell Lowell: A Biography, v. 2. The Riverside Press.
Strauss, R. 2016. *Worst. President. Ever.: James Buchanan, the POTUS Rating Game, and the Legacy of the Least of the Lesser Presidents*. Lyons Press.
Streb, Matthew J. 2015. *Rethinking American Electoral Democracy*. Controversies in Electoral Democracy and Representation. Taylor & Francis.
Taagepera, Rein. 1972. "The Size of National Assemblies." *Social Science Research* 1 (4): 385–401.
Taagepera, Rein, and Bernard Grofman. 1985. "Rethinking Duverger's Law: Predicting the Effective Number of Parties in Plurality and PR Systems–Parties Minus Issues Equals One." *European Journal of*

Political Research 13 (4): 341–52.
Tabarrok, Alexander. 2001. "President Perot or Fundamentals of Voting Theory Illustrated with the 1992 Election." *Public Choice* 106 (3-4): 275–97.
Tabarrok, Alexander, and Lee Spector. 1999. "Would the Borda Count Have Avoided the Civil War?" *Journal of Theoretical Politics* 11 (2): 261–88.
Tuttle Jr, Daniel W. 1961. "The 1960 Election in Hawaii." *Western Political Quarterly* 14 (1): 331–38.
United States Senate Committee on the Judiciary. 1977. *The Electoral College and Direct Election: Hearings Before the Committee on the Judiciary, United States Senate, Ninety-Fifth Congress, First Session on ... S.j. Res. 1, 8, and 1*. v. 2. U.S. Government Printing Office.
Wegman, J. 2020. *Let the People Pick the President: The Case for Abolishing the Electoral College*. St. Martin's Publishing Group.
Wolgemuth, Kathleen L. 1959. "Woodrow Wilson and Federal Segregation." *The Journal of Negro History* 44 (2): 158–73.
Woodward, C. Vann. 1951. *Reconstruction and Reunion: The Compromise of 1877 and the End of Reconstruction*. Little, Brown, & Co.
———. 1973. "Yes, There Was a Compromise of 1877." *Journal of American History* 60: 215–23.

About the author

Tomas J. McIntee is a mathematician and social scientist with stray degrees in physics and philosophy. He is proud to have an Erdős number of 3 and a sweet dog of many breeds. He has an enduring interest in politics and the mathematical problems linked to voting systems, and wrote an award-winning dissertation, *Geometric Ways of Understanding Voting Problems*, while at the Institute of Mathematical Behavioral Sciences within the University of California at Irvine. His other alma mater is Appalachian State University, where he sang in an all-male a capella group and learned to contra dance.

Index

12th Amendment, 5, 6, 20, 35, 37, 44, 47, 50–54, 59, 61, 62, 65, 141, 169, 201
13th Amendment, 9, 98
14th Amendment, 8, 98, 179
15th Amendment, 8, 98, 179
19th Amendment, 8, 124, 126, 179
22nd Amendment, 133
23rd Amendment, 146, 160
24th Amendment, 8, 105, 160
26th Amendment, 8, 146, 159, 160, 179

Adams, John, 29, 37–40, 42–45, 47, 48, 50–52, 55, 94, 95, 213
Adams, John Quincy, 31, 59, 61, 63, 64, 69, 70, 94, 119
Adams, Samuel, 43, 44
Agnew, Spiro, 155
allocation problem, 206
allocation problems, 129, 130, 215
Anti-Masonic Party, 70
approval voting, 213
Arrow's Impossibility Theorem, 76
Arthur, Chester A., 108, 114
automatic electoral college, 206

Bailey, Lloyd, 155
Banzhaf index, 191
Barkley, Alben, 141
Bayh-Celler amendment, 156
Bayh-Celler amondment, 211
Bell, John, 86, 91, 92, 120, 123
Bentsen, Lloyd, 167
Biden, Joe, 186, 187

Birney, James G., 78–81
Blaine, James, 108
blocks of five, 110
blue wall, 4, 182, 183
Borda count, 213
Bradley, Joseph P., 104
Breckinridge, John, 86, 87, 91, 92, 96, 120, 121, 123, 171
broad versus narrow coalitions, 5, 89, 120, 121, 140, 167, 169–171, 173, 184
Bryan, William Jennings, 106, 113–115, 121
Buchanan, James, 53, 85, 88, 89, 96, 109
Burr, Aaron, 6, 40, 44, 47, 48
Bush, George H. W., 167, 168, 170, 175
Bush, George W., 174, 175, 177, 178, 181, 183, 187, 192
Butler, Nicholas, 117
Byrd, Harry, 147

Carroll, Daniel, 27–29
Carter, Jimmy, 123, 163, 164, 167
Cass, Lewis, 80, 81, 90, 94, 96
census controversy, 129
Chafin, Eugene, 122
checks and balances, 7
Chiafalo v. Washington, 2, 24, 45, 101, 185, 202, 207, 214
Civil War, 84, 107
Clay, Henry, 61–64, 70, 77, 78, 94, 96, 97, 173
Cleveland, Grover, 105, 106, 108–112
Clinton, Bill, 168–170, 183, 184

INDEX

Clinton, DeWitt, 55, 57
Clinton, George, 38, 56
Clinton, Hillary, 2, 4, 31, 184, 185, 215
Cobb, David, 178
Coleman, Robert, 40
Compromise of 1877, 105
Condorcet loser, 121, 122
Condorcet paradox, 122
Condorcet problem, 116, 121
Condorcet winner, 122
Connecticut Compromise, 202
Constitutional Convention, 4, 15, 16, 18, 20–22, 24, 29, 36
Constitutional Union Party, 86
contingent election, 4, 14, 19, 20, 28–30, 33, 37, 44, 48, 49, 51–53, 60, 62–65, 72, 73, 81, 87, 89, 94, 104, 140–143, 150, 151, 155, 157, 169, 173, 184, 185, 189, 198, 203, 204, 206–210, 215
Coolidge, Calvin, 127
Cox, James M., 125
Crawford, William, 61, 94
critical power, 191
critical states, 32, 103, 192
critical voter, 192
crucial states, 33
cube root law, 132

Davis, David, 104
Davis, John W., 127
Debs, Eugene, 117, 122
Democratic-Republicans in disarray, 39, 40, 43, 44, 46, 61, 64
Democrats in disarray, 72, 74, 138, 158, 162, 211
Dewey, Thomas E., 137, 138, 140–142, 151
direct vote, 6, 11, 13, 27, 29, 92–96, 103, 105, 108, 173, 174, 177–179, 198, 204, 211, 212, 215
district rule, 208
Dixiecrats, 138–142, 144, 147, 155, 157, 211
Douglas, Stephen, 80, 86, 92, 120, 123, 170, 173, 205
Dukakis, Michael, 167
Duverger's Law, 210

Eagleton, Thomas, 161
Edmund Randolph, 17, 24
Edwards, John, 177
Eisenhower, Dwight D., 144, 145
election fraud, 148
Electoral Count Act, 105

electoral power, 4, 33, 189–194, 196–200

faithless electors, 5, 39, 40, 42–45, 145, 147, 163, 184, 202, 203, 214
Federalist #68, 2, 13
Federalist Papers, 2, 13, 15, 26, 35, 185
Federalists in disarray, 39, 40, 43, 44, 46, 57
felon disenfranchisement, 8, 132
filibuster, 156
Floyd, John, 70
Ford, Gerald, 163
Franklin, Benjamin, 16, 26
Fraser, Donald M., 159, 161
Free Soil party, 80, 90
Fremont, John, 81, 85, 87, 90
fusion voting, 86, 123

Garfield, James, 107, 108
Gerry, Elbridge, 16, 17, 23
Goldwater, Barry, 152
Gore, Al, 168, 175, 176, 187
Granger, Francis, 72
Grant, Ulysses S., 99, 100
Greeley, Horace, 100, 101, 185

Hamilton electors, 1, 5, 24, 42, 183–185
Hamilton Plan, 24
Hamilton, Alexander, 5, 6, 13, 24, 25, 29, 35, 37, 43, 48–51, 54, 202
Harding, Warren G., 125, 127, 139
Harrison, Benjamin, 110, 111
Harrison, William Henry, 70–78, 110
Hartzell, Jonas, 40
Hayes, Rutherford B., 102, 103, 105–107, 119
Hayes-Tilden Electoral Commission, 104
Herter, Christian A., 151
Hobart, Garret, 113
Holy Roman Empire, 22
home state advantage, 73, 103
Hoover, Herbert, 124, 125, 128, 131, 134
Hospers, John, 162
Hughes, Charles Evans, 118
Humphrey, Hubert, 33, 154, 158

indirect election, 13, 202
invalidated electoral votes, 101, 187

Jackson, Andrew, 61, 64, 66, 68–71, 83, 93–95
January 6th attack on the Capitol, 187
Jefferson, Thomas, 6, 29, 39, 40, 43, 44, 47–49, 51, 55, 56, 58, 94, 95

Jennedy, John F., 158
Jim Crow, 106, 110
Johnson, Andrew, 87, 99, 114
Johnson, Gary, 184
Johnson, Lyndon B., 123, 151–154, 158
Johnson, Richard M., 37, 72
Jones, Walter, 145

Kasich, John, 185
Kennedy, John F., 147, 152, 158
Kennedy, Robert F., 154, 158
Kerry, John, 177
King, Rufus, 17, 58
Know-Nothing Party, 85, 170

LaFollette, Robert, 127
Landon, Alf, 135
large and small states, 4, 65, 189–194, 196–200
Libertarian Party, 162
Liberty party, 78
Lincoln, Abraham, 5, 31, 84, 86–90, 92, 94, 96, 98, 109, 119–123, 139, 171, 205, 206, 210, 211
literacy tests, 139
losing coalition, 191

MacKean, Thomas, 40
Madison, James, 6, 15, 17–19, 21–24, 28, 29, 35, 56–58, 93, 94
majority runoff, 7, 76, 77, 93, 96, 97, 122, 150, 209, 210, 213
Mangum, Willie, 72, 73, 75
Marshall, George C., 141
Mason, George, 19
McCain, John, 181
McClellan, George, 88
McCormack, John, 155
McGovern, George, 159, 161
McGovern-Fraser Commission, 159–161
McKinley, William, 113
McMullin, Evan, 184
Mexican-American War, 80, 96, 107
Miles, Samuel, 40, 42, 43, 193, 202
Millard Fillmore, 82, 85, 91, 94, 114, 170
misfire elections, 149
Mondale, Walter, 166
Monroe, James, 58, 59, 119, 125, 134, 135, 153
Morris, Gouveneur, 19, 26–29, 35, 94, 207
Muskie, Edmund, 155

Nader, Ralph, 175, 176
National Bonus Plan, 211

national popular vote, 6, 11, 13, 27, 29, 92–96, 103, 105, 108, 173, 174, 177–179, 198, 204, 211, 212, 215
National Popular Vote Interstate Compact, 212
National Republican Party, 60, 70
National Union Party, 87
New Jersey Plan, 24
Nixon, Richard, 33, 147, 154, 156, 162, 179

Obama, Barack, 4, 180–183, 187, 192, 198

Parker, Alton B., 114
parliamentary system, 6, 7, 18, 27, 28, 93, 94, 198, 210
Pence, Mike, 187
Penrose index, 191
People's Party, 111
Perot, Ross, 168–173
Pierce, Franklin, 82, 85, 168
Pinckney Plan, 24
Pinckney, Charles, 17, 43, 55, 56, 212
Pinckney, Thomas, 40, 43, 44, 50
pivotal power, 191
pivotal state, 31, 103, 192
pivotal voter, 192
Polish-Lithuanian Commonwealth, 23
Polk, James, 77–80, 123, 140
poll taxes, 99, 139, 146
popular sovereignty, 90
Powell, Colin, 185
Powell, Leven, 43
power index, 191
presidential election of 1788, 36
presidential election of 1792, 38
presidential election of 1796, 6, 39, 40, 43, 44, 169, 184
presidential election of 1800, 6, 46
presidential election of 1804, 55
presidential election of 1808, 56
presidential election of 1812, 57
presidential election of 1816, 58
presidential election of 1820, 59
presidential election of 1824, 61
presidential election of 1828, 68
presidential election of 1832, 69
presidential election of 1836, 70, 71
presidential election of 1840, 70, 74
presidential election of 1844, 77, 140
presidential election of 1848, 79
presidential election of 1852, 82
presidential election of 1856, 85
presidential election of 1860, 86, 173
presidential election of 1864, 87

INDEX 225

presidential election of 1868, 99
presidential election of 1872, 100
presidential election of 1876, 101, 102, 178, 179, 181
presidential election of 1880, 107
presidential election of 1884, 108
presidential election of 1888, 4, 109, 179
presidential election of 1892, 111
presidential election of 1896, 112
presidential election of 1900, 113
presidential election of 1904, 114
presidential election of 1908, 115
presidential election of 1912, 116
presidential election of 1916, 118
presidential election of 1920, 125
presidential election of 1924, 126
presidential election of 1928, 128
presidential election of 1932, 134
presidential election of 1936, 135
presidential election of 1940, 136
presidential election of 1944, 137
presidential election of 1948, 138
presidential election of 1952, 143
presidential election of 1956, 144
presidential election of 1960, 4, 147, 179
presidential election of 1964, 152
presidential election of 1968, 154, 160
presidential election of 1972, 161
presidential election of 1976, 162
presidential election of 1980, 164, 179
presidential election of 1984, 165
presidential election of 1988, 166
presidential election of 1992, 121, 167, 181
presidential election of 1996, 169
presidential election of 2000, 175, 178, 179, 187
presidential election of 2004, 177–179, 187
presidential election of 2008, 180, 187
presidential election of 2012, 182, 187
presidential election of 2016, 1, 3–5, 31, 179, 183
presidential election of 2020, 166, 186
Presidential Succession Act, 141, 155
Prince-Elector of Hanover, 22
Progressive Party, 117, 124, 127, 170
property requirements for voting, 7, 9, 17, 26, 27
proportional rule, 207
public support for eliminating the Electoral College., 2

Quay, Matthew, 110

ranked choice voting, 7, 213
Ray v. Blair, 45

Rayburn, Sam, 141, 151
Reagan, Ronald, 163, 164, 166, 167
Reform party, 168, 169
regional candidates, 73, 89, 120, 121, 157, 184
Republicans in disarray, 117
Rockefeller, Nelson, 163
Romney, Mitt, 182, 198
Roosevelt, Franklin D., 126, 133–138
Roosevelt, Theodore, 113–115, 117, 120–122, 124
rural and urban voters, 4, 10
Rusk, Dean, 155

segregation, 123, 139, 142, 149, 150, 154, 155, 157, 201, 208, 210
Shapley-Shubik index, 191
Sherman, James, 117
Sherman, Roger, 4, 17, 28, 29, 52
Shriver, Sargent, 161
slavery, 5, 6, 8, 9, 11, 24, 27, 29, 62, 65, 70, 72, 78–81, 84, 88, 90–94, 96–98, 120, 129, 139, 173, 205, 215
Smith, Al, 128, 131, 132
Smith, William, 72
Solid South, 98, 137, 139, 153
spoiler effect, 76, 80, 81, 84, 88, 92, 112, 116, 119, 121–123, 171, 172, 176, 184, 204, 205, 215
Stein, Jill, 184
Stevenson, Adlai E., 144, 145
Stokley, Thomas, 40

Taft, William, 115, 117, 120–122, 170
Tammany Hall, 106
Taylor, Zachary, 80, 82, 90, 94
Three Fifths Compromise, 8, 9
Thurmond, Strom, 138–140, 142, 153, 156, 169, 173, 206
Tilden, Samuel, 102–106, 109
Tilden-Hayes Electoral Commission, 104
tipping point state, 31, 192
Truman, Harry, 123, 138–142, 144, 151
Trump, Donald, 1, 2, 24, 31, 33, 184, 186
Turner, William, 145
two-party system, 6, 30, 50, 52, 82, 116, 127, 142, 156, 170, 206, 210, 211
Tyler, John, 72, 74, 76, 77, 82, 114

unit rule, 62, 65, 66, 159, 181, 202–204, 208, 215

Van Buren, Martin, 63, 70, 71, 73, 74, 78, 80, 90, 170
Ventura, Jesse, 169
Vietnam War, 151
Virginia Plan, 18
voting by minors, 9, 10, 132
voting by non-citizens, 9, 10, 132
voting franchise, 7–11, 17, 26, 27, 98, 124, 132, 179
Voting Rights Act, 105, 152, 153, 159, 160

Wallace, George, 155, 211
Wallace, Henry, 140
Warren, Earl, 141
Washington, George, 22, 29, 36–38, 42, 43, 135
Watergate, 162
Watts, John, 103
Weaver, Benjamin, 111
Webster, Daniel, 63, 72, 73, 75
Whig Party, 70, 170
Whigs in disarray, 78, 82
White, Hugh L., 71, 75
Wilkie, Wendell, 136
Wilson, James, 6, 17, 18, 23, 24, 26, 29, 35, 94
Wilson, Woodrow, 116–123, 173, 210
Winfield Scott, 81, 82
winner-take-all, 62, 65, 66, 159, 181, 203, 204, 208, 215
winning coalition, 191
Wirt, William, 70